The Guga Hunters

The Guga Hunters

Donald S. Murray

BIRLINN

First published in 2008 by
Birlinn Limited
West Newington House
10 Newington Road
Edinburgh
EH9 1QS

www.birlinn.co.uk

ISBN13: 978 1 84158 684 7
ISBN10: 1 84158 684 6

British Library Cataloguing-in-Publication Data
A catalogue record for this book is available from the British Library

Typeset by Iolaire Typesetting, Newtonmore
Printed and bound by Creative Print and Design Wales, Blaina

To the people of Ness
'Far an d' fhuair mi m' àrach òg'

and in memory of
Murdo 'Deedo' Macdonald (1965–2008)
a very special Guga hunter
to whom this work owes so much

'report us fairly,
how we slaughter
for the common good'

– Seamus Heaney, from 'Kinship'

Contents

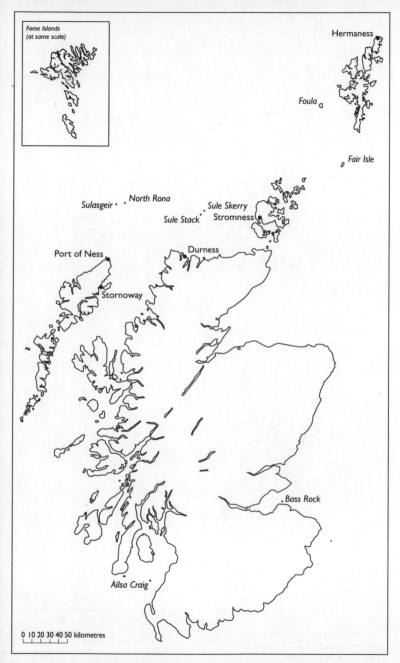

Faroe Islands
(at same scale)

Hermaness

Foula

Fair Isle

North Rona

Sulasgeir

Sule Skerry

Sule Stack

Stromness

Port of Ness

Durness

Stornoway

Bass Rock

Ailsa Craig

0 10 20 30 40 50 kilometres

An incomplete map of Scotland from the gannet's point of view

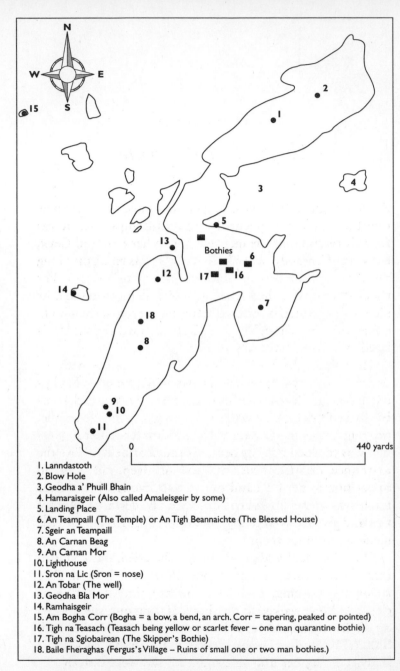

1. Lanndastoth
2. Blow Hole
3. Geodha a' Phuill Bhain
4. Hamaraisgeir (Also called Amaleisgeir by some)
5. Landing Place
6. An Teampaill (The Temple) or An Tigh Beannaichte (The Blessed House)
7. Sgeir an Teampaill
8. An Carnan Beag
9. An Carnan Mor
10. Lighthouse
11. Sron na Lic (Sron = nose)
12. An Tobar (The well)
13. Geodha Bla Mor
14. Ramhaisgeir
15. Am Bogha Corr (Bogha = a bow, a bend, an arch. Corr = tapering, peaked or pointed)
16. Tigh na Teasach (Teasach being yellow or scarlet fever – one man quarantine bothie)
17. Tigh na Sgiobairean (The Skipper's Bothie)
18. Baile Fheraghas (Fergus's Village – Ruins of small one or two man bothies.)

A map of Sulasgeir from a guga hunter's point of view

Frontpiece

Ceyx and Alcyone

As the daughter of Aeolus, king of the winds, Alcyone knew only too well what happened sometimes to ships at sea. It was for this reason that she quarrelled with her husband Ceyx, the king of Thessaly, when he told her he was going on a long voyage to consult with an oracle about a matter of state. For the first time ever, she argued with him, demanding that he should not go or, if he insisted on his journey, that she should come with him. Though he loved her very much, he shook his head. He would have to go alone.

That night, there was a great storm. Together with his entire crew, Ceyx drowned, the word 'Alcyone' on his lips as the waters closed over his dying body. Unaware that his life had ended, his wife walked every night to Hera's temple, praying for her man's return. The goddess heard her prayers and was touched both by her faith and her fidelity. With the assistance of Morpheus, the god of sleep, she sent an apparition in her husband's form to Alcyone's bed. 'Your name was on my lips when I drowned,' he declared. 'Accept this and give me your tears. Do not force me to step into the shadows without them.'

'Wait for me. I will go with you,' she cried, but he faded into the darkness, escaping her outstretched hand. The following morning, aware for the first time that he was dead, Alcyone walked to the shore. Staring out, she noticed an object floating towards her, coming to rest on the sand. She ran towards it, aware suddenly it was her husband's body. Curling her arms around him, she wept bitterly.

It was a sight that prompted the gods to pity. Ceyx and Alcyone were given new lives, transformed into birds. Ceyx was granted the white wings and yellow head of a gannet; Alcyone the magnificent shades of a kingfisher. One was given the width of the ocean to command; the other the banks and shallow water of a riverbank. Yet on occasional days of stillness and calm – the halcyon days of summer – the two birds still meet above the ocean.

The gannet greets his former lover with her name. 'Alcyone . . .' he says.

Introduction

Fifty-Nine Degrees North; Six Degrees West . . .

Men have been killing and eating seabirds since long before the Classical Age began.

It is a practice that has been going on since our early ancestors lived in caves that even today tunnel some of our shorelines. They would emerge from these, perhaps with club in hand, seeking to appease the hunger that so often must have drummed and boomed within their empty stomachs, seeing an opportunity to do this in some of the wings that flashed and trembled before them among rocks and crags. The jet-black plumage of the cormorant. The grey feathers of a gull. The awkward, almost comic flight of the puffin. And, of course, the magnificence of the great bird that is most often seen plunging like a white blade into the dark waters off our coast – the gannet, also called the solan goose.

It is a tradition, too, that has occurred throughout the globe. In Tierra del Fuego at the southern tip of South America, seabirds were hunted and eaten by the native Fuegan people; their catch drawn down by a long slender rod with a noose attached. At the other end of that great continent, the indigenous population of Alaska performed the same task with similar methods, trapping sea-fowl sometimes, perhaps, with the use of bait or stones or even fingers. The custom, too, has been followed in places as far apart as Hokkaido, the most northerly island of Japan,

Novaya Zemyla, the former gulag of the Soviet Union in the Arctic Ocean, Newfoundland and the Cape of Good Hope in South Africa.

Yet it was probably most common on the edges of the Atlantic in northern Europe, in the places occupied by both 'Norseman' and Celt. Their locations ranged from Greenland in the far north to the Blasket islands off the southwestern edge of Ireland – and many other coastal settings scattered east, west and in between. Much of this has to do with the waters of the North Atlantic, especially from 50 degrees, or Land's End, at the southern tip of England, northwards. The ocean in this area is comparatively shallow, with large areas, such as the majority of the North Sea and the entire Baltic Sea, lying on the Continental shelf. The fact that cold and warm ocean currents meet there also makes it ideal for the close partnership of plankton and fish that provide necessary links in the food-chain for seabirds to live and thrive.

Geologically speaking, there are other factors that make these areas ideal residences. Not only is food readily on hand (or foot or wing), there are also ready-made dwelling-places for the birds. These come in the shape of certain cliffs. Perfect for a number of reasons, many jut out over the oceans and offer horizontal ledges and small alcoves within the rock on which the birds can nest. In addition, they offer vantage points from which they can survey the oceans, spotting any likely shoals swimming in their direction. They provide a little shelter from the full force of the wind, allowing creatures that are more graceful in flight than take-off to leave their nests with a certain degree of grace and security. They grant safety, too, from predators that are all around them. These include mammals like seals, otters and polecats, and also feathered visitors, such as the skua or gulls, that tend to settle on flatter, less wave-buffeted land elsewhere.

And, of course, man. Throughout history, he has probably been the seabirds' most resourceful predator, developing one means after another to trap and catch these creatures for the pan or pot. It is a task that men still undertake today. It occurs in New Zealand, where a close relative of mine recently discovered gannet (or a form of it) on sale on a supermarket shelf in a small town called Napier in that country's South Island. It goes on, too, in places like Iceland and the Faroes where – as we will discover – hunters still head out to crag and cliff in order to obtain large quantities of seabirds, like the puffin or the guillemot, for their plates. They are sold in the shops of market-places of their national capitals, Reykjavik and Torshavn, tempting the taste-buds of even the urban consumer. Recipe books printed in the languages of these countries still feature ways of obtaining each last tingle of flavour from these birds with a range of different sauces to add relish to their meat.

There was a time when people throughout the British Isles also savoured similar meals. This was especially the case in Scotland and Ireland, where it was a taste that was largely determined by much of the geography of these nations. Both countries have a predominance of the type of coastal landscape favoured by seabirds. High cliffs and crags abound in locations as far apart as south-west Kerry and the north of Shetland. Much of Scotland, in particular, is ringed by these. Possessing 65 per cent of the coastline of the island of Britain, Scotland is home, too, to over 5 million birds, with 24 out of the 25 species either residing in or visiting these shores being found within its borders. In contrast, England – with the mud-flats and saltings of its large river-mouths and estuaries – seems to attract largely a different kind of bird. Mainly geese, ducks and wading birds cluster there, found in large quantities all the way from the Solway Firth to the Thames. Despite their smaller number, there is evidence that suggests the people living there shared similar tastes to their northern neighbours when the opportunity arose. In places like the Farne Islands and St Bees Head in Cumbria, seabirds clearly appealed to the palate. They also provided a valuable supplement to their daily fare in other areas.

Yet, whatever advantages various locations in both Scotland and Ireland might have in terms of providing the perfect residence for such birds, there is little doubt that the last few centuries have seen a marked decline in the taste for them among the humans living both nearby and far away from their nesting grounds. The population of the centre no longer dines on such delicacies and has not really done so to any great extent since around 1880–85.* This was partly a result of the Bird Preservation Acts which came into force during that period, but also because those in the south of Scotland, living in the vicinity, for instance, of Ailsa Craig or the Bass Rock, lost the taste for seabirds' oily meat. (In the case of the former, the taste for gannet continued till 1875, while those residing near Bass Rock stopped relishing its flavour some ten years later.) Since then the gannet has rarely appeared on the tables of citizens or kings – as they had done for many centuries in places such as Ayrshire or Edinburgh. Gannet grease is no longer spread upon a slice of bread. Neither is fulmar oil employed to grease machinery, nor bird-stomachs used to make a pouch

---

* It is tempting to suggest that the decline in the eating of seabirds may have been due to the fact that the Stewarts and, perhaps, even Scotland as a whole became increasingly influenced by both France (to a small extent) and England from the middle of the sixteenth century. There is little doubt that the larders of King James V (1511–42) were stuffed full of gannet. There are records of Bass Rock being raided on his behalf in, for instance, September 1511. One cannot imagine, however, Mary Queen of Scots (1542–67) having much taste for such cuisine, due to her years in France, while James VI and I probably ate it less and less after his court shifted south in 1603 – especially as such birds were less available in the south of England than at home. No doubt the North British of Scotland's Central Belt, influenced by the mores of high society, aped their betters in these matters, discarding the delights of the guga over the course of the next few centuries in favour of a more 'civilised' diet.

for tobacco or, even less imaginably, shoes for people's feet. We no longer have great need of their bones, once used to make pins and pipe-stems, and pegs for thatching.

In the early twentieth century, most of the last remnants of this trade began to fade away. One of the final aspects to disappear was the feather industry. Its products used to stuff pillows and mattresses, and to provide tippets to adorn ladies' hats, yet the business that had helped isolated places like St Kilda towards a little prosperity had almost disappeared by the outbreak of the First World War in 1914. (Much of its decline was due to the foul, oily smell that clung to seabird-feathers – almost impossible to remove.) The trade in bird-oil also came to a close at roughly the same time, as other substances were discovered and employed to grease both agricultural machinery and leather boots. To all intents and purposes, especially when seen from the viewpoint of those who live in the nation's urban heartland, one of Scotland's oldest and most timeless traditions seemed to have much in common with the bird that once clung to a perch in a pet-shop immortalised in a 'Monty Python' sketch. It was extinct. It had departed. It was no more . . .

This, however, is not entirely true. The trade continues on the edge of both law and nation in some corners of Scotland. In the old bird-killing parishes, men still head out some evenings with a rifle in their arms to shoot, say, a cormorant or shag. With the feathers being of no commercial value, they mark some special occasion, such as the old New Year's Day, 13 January for those who still keep to the Julian calendar, by skinning and cooking the seabird they have killed. Afterwards, they whisper about their meal, making sure they are out of earshot of either policeman or visitor while praising its richness and goodness out of the sides of their mouths.

And then there were those who could talk about their

deeds a little more openly – operating, perhaps, on the periphery of their country but well within the boundaries of the law. By and large, these are the men from Ness, a mainly Gaelic-speaking crofting community near the Butt of Lewis at the most northerly tip of the Western Isles or Outer Hebrides at Scotland's most north-westerly edge. For many centuries, since at least the sixteenth, they have voyaged to Sulasgeir, an outcrop of rock which, with adjustments for wind and tide, lies some 40 miles north-north-east by a half east off the Butt in search of the 'guga', a term used to describe the young gannet chick they hunt there in the last days of August. Home to 11 different types of seabird, from 9,000 pairs of gannets to nearly 8,000 pairs of fulmars plus a varied collection of guillemots, puffins, shags and even – perhaps – a lonely albatross jetting in from Hermaness in Shetland in extraordinary recent times, it is a place some who have visited it speak of in almost religious tones. Their hours hunting the 'guga' are almost an annual act of pilgrimage. They describe in hushed voices how the dark brown of that rock's surface glitters white, how wings circle around it, forming haloes of flight, noting how the cave the fierceness of the ocean has battered out of its rock is like an archway spanning the width of a cathedral. This sense of the spiritual that surrounds the place is underlined by some of the rituals and stories associated with it: how each man leaves a cairn of stones behind him when he steps from its shoreline; how there is said to be an ancient temple found there; the legend of Brianuil and how she was found dead there with a cormorant nesting in the rib-cage of her skeleton.

There is much too in the gannets they have come to hunt there that inspires its own sense of wonder. There is the way the chicks can paddle for days on end, reaching, perhaps, the northern coast of Italy on their journeys. One even left Ireland and turned up in Brazil. There is the fidelity they show to both place and each other: returning to the same nest every year; mating with the same partner. There is the power of their vision; the sweep and power of their dive. Glimpse their aerobatics on a clear summer's day and one can easily see why the Cornish word for 'gannet' is *sether* or *sethor* – both terms that can be literally translated as 'archer'.

And then there are the changes that have come over the gannet these visitors have come to hunt since the days the storytellers of classical times first told of the mythical love affair between Ceyx and Alcyone, how the chief nesting grounds of the seabird appeared to have moved farther and farther north since then, drawn to the fish and plankton-rich waters of the North Atlantic washing round these islands' coastlines.

It is true that gannets have flown – and on rare occasions nested – in that direction for many centuries. Their flight-paths continually spinning, in ever-increasing circles, they cross over the land's edge from time to time. In this way, they make sure they retain their bearings as the more than two-yard span of their wings takes them sometimes across vast distances, from far-off North Africa to the islands of the North Atlantic in late February or March each year, for all that a number are a constant presence in these parts. It was the sight of these wings, tied tight as white ribbon among cloud, that made the Anglo-Saxon invaders who occupied so much of the southern end of the British Isles from the fifth and sixth centuries onwards marvel at their flight in their runes and poetry, calling the oceans they glided over so effortlessly the 'gannet's bath'.

Yet, while the Anglo-Saxons may have seen these birds in passing, there is little doubt that the gannet has in recent centuries chosen to nest in greater and greater numbers off the British coast. Nowadays there are 28 large gannetries in Europe. The British Isles is fortunate enough to play host to almost 13 of these, with a grand total of around 70 per cent of the world's population of gannets living within its waters. Scotland has the greater share, with eight 'settlements' around its coastline.

Some are relatively recent. For all that their bones have been found in the archaeological dig at Jarlshof near the southern tip of Shetland in the far north of Scotland, showing that they were eaten there from the Bronze Age through to the Iron Age and Viking times, they are late-comers to the cliffsides of these islands. Offering proof that the birds are shifting ever further north, they first settled on Shetland, for instance, during the years of the First World War with two colonies: one in the small island of Noss; the other at the tip of Shetland's most northerly island of Unst at Hermaness. Their search for 'real estate' in that area seems to be continuing, with birds nesting in recent years in more distant parts of the Shetland archipelago, both in Fair Isle in the far south and Foula in the west. Each of these locations shows the strength and resilience of the bird as it seeks new places to occupy and inhabit.

A number of these gannetries have more well-known locations than the rest. There is the Bass Rock, which nestles off the East Lothian coast, close enough to the nation's capital for many to be familiar with its size and shape. There is also, as noted, Ailsa Craig – known as Paddy's Milestone – between the Scottish and Irish coasts. There are the Skelligs in south-west Ireland, home to some 40,000 gannets today but once populated too by monks whose soft words of prayer must often have been forced to compete with the cries of gannets and other birds. And there is, of course, St Kilda, with its stacs and skerries; its epic tale of emigration and depopulation occurring against a backdrop of white wings and bird-cries, the relentless music that accompanied the lives of people there.

Yet its Main Street is empty now. Its young men no longer

climb the cliffs of Hiort and Dun to capture birds and harvest their eggs. The only place remaining where the lives of men and bird truly blend together in the way they have done for centuries is Sulasgeir, lying some 40 miles off the Butt of Lewis.

In some ways, apart from its geographical position, Sulasgeir is not as impressive as some other spots where gannets gather. At around a half-mile long and possessing cliffs that are a mere 200 feet high, many claim it has none of the sweep and majesty of St Kilda, where the summit of Connachair reaches an impressive 1,397 feet. It lacks the eerie, haunted quality that makes the Skelligs look as if they might belong to the film-set of a Dracula movie; the knowledge that hermit monks once occupied its crags, hewing steps and stairways out of stone, adding to this illusion. Sulasgeir is, in contrast, not unlike the many hundreds of skelligs, skerries, crags, islets and *eileanan* found all around the British Isles – from Cornwall to the tip of Unst in Shetland. Even on a good, clear day, you are halfway there before you can even see it rising out of the waves. Its very name suggests the narrow limits and justification for its existence. The word 'Sula' refers to the gannet, or 'solan goose'; 'sgeir' emphasises the fact that it is simply a 'rock'.

And one can gather other opinions in order to underline the negatives that could be associated with Sulasgeir, the apparently overwhelming visitors' view that all, in this case, that glistens may simply be guano. Its human significance, in terms of the structures standing on it, seems especially slight. Most of its five buildings are rudimentary bothys with drystone walls, probably erected by the Nessmen who come to Sulasgeir every year to hunt gannet, but mainly providing shelter for the fulmars nesting there. Lying to their east is the one exception – the building known to all as the *Teampall* or 'Temple'. For those accustomed to marvelling at magnificent churches and cathedrals, it is

likely to inspire only derision and contempt. The 'temple'
or Taigh a' Bheannaich (or Blessing House) seems at first
glance simply a huddle of stones, many of them toppling in on
each other as they give way to the onslaught of what must
be some of the worst weather on Europe; its roof collapsing
under the pounding of wind and rain. Fourteen feet long
and eight feet wide, it was believed by the archaeologist
T.S. Muir believed it to be an early Christian hermit's cell;
he based this conclusion on his conviction that there was an
altar-stone below the small window at its eastern end. There
does seem to be some evidence for this. The beehive structure
is certainly better constructed than the bothys on Sulasgeir.
It is far less higgledy-piggledy, with much greater attention
paid to the course of stones laid down there to form its
walls: each one with a place and a place for every one. Yet
'temple' . . .? While it may be the case that Nessmen or a
hermit monk, alone on Sulasgeir sometimes for a considerable period, may have used the building for religious
purposes, the word seems a considerable exaggeration,
caused, perhaps, by someone's imagination being stretched
and overwhelmed by the sweep of gannets overhead.

Muir, however, seems to have regarded little else in
Sulasgeir as sacred. Considering it 'barren and repulsive',
he was also dismissive of its scale, noting during his visit in
1860 that while the highest point is 229 feet above sea level,
its low and narrow centre is only 20 feet above the ocean.
This allows any person who walks there to be showered by
the Atlantic for, 'in the winter-time, the serpent wave must
be evermore lashing from side, and cutting up the whole
mass into so many . . . merest of particles'.

This is the crooked back of the island. Underneath it, the
sea has tunnelled stone, creating a sea-cave that runs from
one side to the other. It is as if, year upon year, Sulasgeir has
been robbed of its very marrow, leaving only a thin covering
of rock for the hunters to step precariously on – a group of

part-time 'Blondins' from Ness in the Isle of Lewis balancing on a taut and rigid tightrope above the Atlantic swell.

It is this cleft in the rock that even leads J. Baldwin in *Traditions of Sea-bird Fowling in the North Atlantic Region* to consider the possibility that the name 'Sulasgeir' is not as noted above but derived from this feature of the island. A 'sula' in Old Norse and Shetland Norn 'was a forked or V-shaped wooden frame on which a fishing handline was wound'. He notes that the mountain Suilven in Sutherland, with its distinctive outline often seen from the shores of Lewis, Sule Stack and Sulasgeir all share this feature. He ponders whether or not there is something significant in this, or even if the word is Scandinavian at all. Perhaps it might originally have come from the Gaelic word *sùil* or 'eye', a tribute to the sharp sight of the gannets that now occupy much of its southern, higher end.*

Yet even there the birds do not escape the whip and stroke of salt. Sròn na Lice on the rock's shoreline was swept clean of its nesting gannets in a storm in June a number of years back. Even below its summit, with its giddy 229 feet, can be found many caves and geos – the latter a Norse and Gaelic term for an inlet made by the sea. This is because the island is composed of hornblende gneiss, a stone that can be weathered and transformed by the power of waves. On its surface, there is hardly any soil – for all that a few plants, such as scurvy grass, chickweed and thrift are found there. In T.S. Muir's view, it is simply, 'a high, horrent, and nearly herbless strip of gneiss, or other suchlike adamantine matter, scarcely [in his measurements!] one-third of a mile in extent'.

Not to be outdone, the amateur geologist John Wilson

---

* There is even wide disagreement about the spelling of that name. Some write the island's title as two separate words, 'Sula' and 'Sgeir'; others spell it as, say, 'Sulisgeir' or even 'Sulisker'. For the sake of consistency and to avoid confusion, I have chosen to refer to it throughout as 'Sulasgeir'.

Dougal, visiting the island in September 1930, complains of 'the soaking showers of rain which beset us as we ranged, hammer in hand, over the rough rocks' – though in his case, his misery was tempered by his joy at finding some 'flinty rock there'. Malcolm Stewart, whom we will read more of later, turned up there that same year to suffer what he felt were the symptoms of chronic insomnia engendered by the cacophony of birds. He mutters discontentedly about how: 'One who spends a night in or near the bothys of Sulasgeir will without doubt be rudely awakened by cries and considerable commotion issuing from the walls of the buildings.'

It is still a condition suffered by the men who go to Sulasgeir today. When I spoke to him, my guga-hunting neighbour, Norman Murray, complained about a time when he awoke with a flock of birds flapping in his face. On many other occasions, the sleep of the men has been disturbed by earwigs trekking across their nose and cheekbones, with most plugging their ears to prevent them gaining entry there. One time my second cousin Angus Murray informed me that, while eating a boiled egg, he had discovered half an earwig inside it. 'What bothered me most was wondering where the other half had got to,' he grinned.

When compared to the writings of J.A. Harvie-Brown, however, all the above visitors' views of this seaside location seem idyllic, almost as if they were filched from the pages of a holiday brochure, focusing on the more positive aspects of a short vacation in a sunlit edge of the world. He complains of Sulasgeir's 'foetid hollows and dark-green spray pools', which he finds 'usually covered with green slime and feathers, and old saturated nests'. He believes that:

> Our visit to Sulasgeir in 1887 will ever be remembered as one of the most remarkable visits of our Hebridean peregrinations during many years, more especially if we look to

the ghastly lonesomeness and geologically disintegrated nature of the whole place; almost pathetically sad in its collection of rough stone huts, the solitary wretched sheep, and the remains of another and the heads of defunct Gannets strewn all over the surface.

Clearly, for all that Harvie-Brown might be shining a light on Sulasgeir's more murky corners, the island would still be a difficult and challenging landscape for any human existence – one which only someone aspiring to sainthood might suffer for long. This type of individual may have come in the shape of Brianuil (or Brunhilda), who, as noted earlier, was said to have lived and died there. (She is said to have gone there to have escaped the incestuous desires of her brother St Ronan, who lived on the island of North Rona, some 12 miles to the east of Sulasgeir.) Or he may have come in the form of a sheep-stealer, for legend has it that those convicted of that particular crime were sent there as punishment, saving the cost of a hangman's rope. If that were the case, the culprit had little to do but chew on the bones of the available wild fowl, stare out at nearby sea-rocks, such as Bogha Corr and the slightly larger Gralisgeir about half a mile away, and wait for the inevitable arrival of death.

What makes Sulasgeir remarkable and distinctive, however, is that far from being the destination of convicts, free and intelligent humans choose to step there – and when they do so, it is not to undertake the modern practices of the ornithologist and naturalist, counting the flocks nesting within its shores, but to take part in the age-old tradition of taking a bird or two – or three or four . . . – home for the pot. In doing this, the men who gather there are connected to the ancient, classical world when the legend of Ceyx and Alcyone was first told, for it is not birds or rocks that make Sulasgeir unique. Instead, it is the continual return of its neighbours, the men of Ness, to its shores, year after year, representatives of a community who over centuries have developed a taste and relish for seabirds. At one time, they brought home a range of flavours with them – such birds as the fulmar, puffin, guillemot and shag. However, over time – and with the assistance, perhaps, of national legislation – their tastes settled on a single variety of bird. This was the guga – the young, fledgeling gannet of Sulasgeir.

And there is much more than just the bird's taste and savour to be reaped from their harvest during that time on the rock. There are tales and poems to be taken home and recorded too. Spend any time in the company of a guga hunter and they are soon to be heard. They speak about Sulasgeir in extremely different ways from the storytellers of old. One might talk, for instance, of the day a particular bird careered in his direction, its beak spearing his cheek.

'I didn't duck down quickly enough, so its beak went into me, just below my ear. And, boy, was it sore. The worst cut I ever had while on the island.'

Another could tell of the time a lad accompanying them decided to have an outdoor bath early on a Sunday morning before any of the rest of his fellow workers woke up. Stripping off his clothes, he emerged from the only real pool on Sulasgeir to the customary cries of birds – and a chorus of wolf-whistles from the crew of a crab boat that had entered a sea-inlet below. Realising it was far too late to preserve his modesty, he simply waved back to the burly fishermen crowding round the cabin of their boat, his skin the same shade of pink as the cluster of sea-thrift nearby.

'If you had thought soon enough, you might have used them . . .' one of them jokes.

'Och, he'd only need a petal for that.'

'Or a stalk.'

They might also speak of the time a French yacht arrived

at Sulasgeir's only possible landing place, Geodha Phuill Ban, on the island's east side. Its passengers were greeted by a young Nessman trying to look as self-important as possible as he stood on the rock in his yellow oilskins, all besmirched with bird-droppings, an occasional feather adorning his hair.

'Do you have your passports with you, please?'

They could indulge, too, in mock-competitions, comparing the number of young gannets they could pluck in one morning. A gleam would sparkle in their eyes as they exaggerated the number of birds they had succeeded in stripping bare; their fingers and mouths blurring in lightning-speed, a blitz of white feathers left behind as their totals multiplied.

'I did 75,' one might boast. 'One day before breakfast.'

'*Thusa!* You'd be lucky if you did five.'

'The slowest hand in the north-west.'

Or else they might talk about a Gaelic song, such as the one Norman 'Conter' Macleod wrote when John Dods MacFarlane's late father, Murdo, presented the former Lionel schoolteacher with his own private gift of a young gannet. He received the following verses in return, praising both the kindness of his 'neighbour' and the unique nature of the bird's flavour:

> *Tapadh leat, a nàbaidh,*
> *Gun chuir thu gu mo làmhan*
> *An t-eun a tha cho àlainn air m' inntinn;*
> *'S ann agam bhios mo chuibhreann*
> *Nuair gheibh mi e air truinnsear*
> *Le fàileadh 'g èirigh aoibhneach gum chuinnlean;*
>
> *An t-eun as blast' 's as càilear*
> *Na bhloinig shultmhor làidir –*
> *Cò idir dhèanadh tàir' air ach truaghan;*

Mac an t-sùlair chiataich
As glaine nì an t-iasgach –
Cha tèid biadh fom fhiacail cho luachmhor;

'S nach toir mi taing le dùrachd
Do chàirdean fearail tùrail
Thug thugamsa mo mhùirn thar an t-sàile,
Is molaidh mi gu sìorraidh
Na Nisich tha cho ciallach
Tha tuigsinn gur e eun e bheir slàinte.

When they are doing this, they are taking part in a timeless tradition – one with a longevity that can be easily shown. Testimony to it can be found in the words of a remarkable traveller, Donald Monro, the High Dean of the Isles, who visited Sulasgeir, among other places in the Hebrides, in 1549. An important churchman, he travelled around his diocese, writing accounts of much he had encountered on his way. In words that recall, deliberately or otherwise, Shakespeare's *Tempest*, he notes that:

This ile is full of wild fowls, and quhen the fowls hes their birds [or chicks] ripe, men out of the parochin of Niss in Leozus used to sail thair and tarry 7 or 8 dayis and to fetche with thame hame their boatful of dry wild fowls with wild fowl fedderis.

Later that century, an anonymous writer declared that Lewismen obtained 'great profit' from seabirds, though he failed to mention Sulasgeir in particular or specify any species of bird. In his economic surveys of the Hebrides in 1764 and 1771, John Walker turned his attention onto the fine down of the eider duck: a bird only to be found in large numbers on a few islands at that time, including Sulasgeir. *The Old Statistical Account of Scotland*, published in 1797, shows that men from 'Niss in Leozus' were still sailing out to the rock over 200 years later. It notes that 'There is in Ness a most venturous set of people who for a few years back, at the hazard of their lives, went there in an open six-oared boat without even the aid of a compass'.

And they were 'venturous' in other ways too. Macdonald in the *Old Statistical Account* notes that there were two expeditions. One was the 'tacksman's boat', which 'when collecting produce from Rona usually went to Sulasgeir too for birds and feathers'. The others were – in many ways – the ancestors of those who go there still today; some landing and collecting birds while others kept the boat from harm, 'having no means to secure it'. At the turn of the nineteenth century, the tacksman took steps to ensure all this activity was his sole right and prerogative. The 'poachers' who arrived on Sulasgeir, apparently, landed not only there but in the law courts in 1811 and 1821. On the first occasion they were fined; on the other, they had to return to Sulasgeir on the tacksman's behalf, doing this in 1824.

This also affected the way in which the hunt was carried out in the early nineteenth century. In Dean Munro's account, it is apparent that the crew stayed on the *sgeir* for a time – not unlike the way they do today. In the *Old Statistical Account* it is clear that, for some years, some remained on the island while others stood guard on the boat, perhaps to keep an eye out for any members of authority who might appear on the horizon.

In the early nineteenth century, this seems to have been a typical arrangement. The organisation of the hunt and all the profits from its proceedings seem to have been assumed by the tenant of both Sulasgeir and nearby North Rona. In this, it appears to be not dissimilar to at least one other gannetry off the British coast. At the southern end of Ireland, where gannets were being sold at somewhere between 1/-8d and 2/-6d each (worth roughly £20 and £30 in today's money) in the mid nineteenth century, they went so far as to guard the Small Skellig with a boat-crew of 12 well-paid men. Tomas O'Crohan's *The Islandman* tells of a battle that took place between the Dunquin men and the gannet-guards:

> This time a boat set out from Dunquin at night with eight men in her, my father among them, and they never rested till they got to the rock at daybreak. They sprang up it and fell to gathering the birds into the boat at full speed. And it was easy to collect a load of them for every single one of these young birds was as heavy as a fat goose. As they were turning the point of the rock to strike out into the bay, what should they see coming to meet them but the guard boat. They hadn't seen one another till that moment.

It was at this point the action began, with the guards attempting to take the Dunquin-men prisoners, but, 'some of them sprang on board and they fell to hitting at one another with oars and hatchets, and any weapon they could find in the boat till they bled one another like a slaughtered ox'.

Despite the fact that there were only eight of them against the twelve guards, the Dunquin men won the battle, eventually arriving back in their own harbour with their haul of gannets intact. The men on the guard boat were not so lucky. When they arrived at their base, two of their number were dead, while the other ten were destined for hospital. O'Crohan ends cheekily, 'After that they were less keen on that sort of chase and the guard was taken off the rock . . .'

Yet this period did not last too long. There are signs, for instance, that it was in the early nineteenth century that the bothys, still occupied by the men today, were constructed – evidence that men were staying on Sulasgeir once again. One can only speculate how this change came about. There are, as far as this writer is aware, no signs of any direct physical confrontations between men from Ness and those in authority. However, with the rebellious tendencies of the people of Ness throughout the centuries, it is not beyond the bounds of possibility.

Through the passage of years, however, it seems likely that one aspect of the expedition has altered – the nature of their bird harvest. Certainly, as was true around the edges of much of the country, feathers and eggs played a more important part at one time than they do today. Dean Munro, for instance, calls the wild fowl they catch there a 'Colk, little les nor ane goose' and notes that the men collected not only 'wild fowl fedderis' but also 'utter fine downis'. His use of the word 'colk' suggests that the fowl they sought there was not the gannet but the eider duck – the bird featuring in Walker's account too. This may fit, too, with what we know of the gannets' slow increase and expansion north; the bird seems to be just about as common in Classical literature as it is in the lore and legends of the North. It not only forms part of the basis of the story of Ceux and Alcyone but is also found settling on the edge of Odysseus's boat in Homer's *Odyssey*. One of the Greek goddesses, Leucothea – also known as Ino – had taken on its shape to bring comfort to the wounded warrior trying desperately to make his way back home.

To many, even in the other traditional seabird-hunting communities of the British Isles, the Nessmen and their guga hunt must seem to belong to the age of Odysseus, a throwback to those long, hard, centuries when it wasn't possible to take the car down to Tesco's, ASDA or the Co-op to fill up the boot with foodstuffs and other goods. In many of these places, the ancient art and craft of fowling, whether for the gannet or any other bird, came to an end many decades ago. No doubt, as it did so, many men and women must have heaved a hearty sigh of relief. Into the kitchen bin was scraped the last remnants of the fulmar, cormorant or – whisper it! – guga. In its place was served a generous helping of chicken tikka masala, spaghetti bolognaise or pasta pesto.

Only Ness was different. Its people, aided by their representatives in Ross and Cromarty Council, argued in favour of a special clause to be inserted into the Protection of Birds Act 1954. This allowed the people of Ness – alone of all communities within the United Kingdom – the right to head to Sulasgeir to hunt the guga, taking 2,000 of the birds each time they journeyed there. Over a half-century, the uniqueness of their tradition was recognised by national legislation. Those who occupied the Houses of Parliament were convinced that there was something different about the Niseachs and the way in which the young of the gannet was central to their lives.

This recognition extends even more widely than this. It is only the men of Ness that are permitted, under a special licence, to hunt the gannet by EU legislation. It is an exception that comes with the full blessing of a number of groups that might in normal circumstances seem designed to oppose it – the Royal Society for the Protection of Birds and the Scottish Society for the Prevention of Cruelty to Animals. For a number of reasons, which will emerge in the course of this book, they recognise that the actions of the guga hunters are no threat to the existence of the birds out on the rock.

Yet even these acknowledgments beg as many questions as they answer. How and why, for instance, are the people of Ness different? Why do they persist in this annual hunt for seabirds? In their forefathers' time, there may have been an economic justification for it. It prevented people from starving. It kept the raven from the door. This is clearly not the case now. (In fact, one of the young men involved in the Sulasgeir expedition each year has told me that he actually loses money through taking part in it.) Why, too, do the people of Ness continue to enjoy the taste, while most of their counterparts in the coastal communities of Britain – and even within the Isle of Lewis itself – have long since pushed it to the side of their plates, replacing it with the culinary miracles of the modern supermarket? Is it, to paraphrase Mallory's answer when asked why he was attempting to climb Everest, simply because the birds are there?

Clearly, some of the answers to that question must lie within Ness itself. To do this, I must return – in my imagination – to an annual pilgrimage I used to undertake. This was to the Butt of Lewis lighthouse. Its doors in these safety-conscious days are now barred to visitors, yet some 30- or 40-odd years ago, I clambered up its steps, following the footsteps of the lighthouse-keeper, Donald John Smith – or the Bodach Dubh – as he went about his work, the long, stone steps continually circling till I reached its light. When I stood there on those rare summer days when the wind wasn't blowing fiercely or the rain had stilled, I could scan the horizon, noting the different landmarks, taking in as many different views as there were prisms on the glass that swirled behind my head, night after night. There was the Decca Station where James Morrison worked, relaying, among his other tasks, messages to the men of Sulasgeir when they travelled there each year. There was Sgeir Dhail, a barren, jagged outcrop which lay off the coast of my own village of South Dell and where I felt sure my own family might one day maroon me if I persisted in my current (mis)behaviour. There were, too, the Churches that dominated the life of the district; the sprawling stretch of houses that constituted what some people have called the longest village within the British Isles.

And long it certainly was. With only a few short breaks, it stretched from South Dell at – appropriately – its southern end to Port of Ness in the north-eastern corner of the island some five miles away. The almost direct road linking these two villages was criss-crossed by a tangle of other routes and roads. One leads to other townships such as Skigersta and the empty ruins of the former settlement of Cuisiadar in the east. There is the dip, curl and twist of Cross Skigersta Road. Another takes people to Eoropie and Knockaird, villages so close to me in my vantage point that I feel I can reach out and touch them if I just stretch out my hand.

Behind most of the houses there are strips of croftland. Bordered now by fence posts and some 50 or so years ago by low walls of stone, it would take a major act of the imagination to summon up the way it all looked back in my youth, 40 and more years ago now. Nowadays, much of the land lies bare and grazed by sheep. A few decades ago, however, cattle tethered within its fields chomped away at long grass. Turnips, potatoes and oats grew tall and strong within its acres; the rich green of these crops only coming to an end when they swept down to the flat and open grassland of the machair. In summer, its dull green shade can be heightened and changed by a bright array of flowers: yellow bird's foot trefoil, white and purple clover, wild hyacinth, daisies, buttercups . . .

Yet if I imagine myself standing once again atop the lighthouse, other aspects of the scene attract the eye. There is the sheer expanse of the moor with its Atlantic blanket bog stretching over much of the northern end of the island. Again, much like Sulasgeir, it would be possible – if more than a little unfair – to describe it in an accumulation of an entire stack of negatives on the page. In *Lewisiana*, Mr W. Anderson Smith claims that in winter, much of the district is a 'howling desert' harassed by a 'bullying wind in its restless ferocity stirring up strife', notable only for its 'peats and ponds' with 'not a sign of a natural harbour'. In 1952, the writer G. Scott Moncrieff sums it up in the following way in his book *The Scottish Islands*: 'The heart of Lewis is hardly conducive to permanent residence. Much of it is a vast morass, a great wet plateful of cold porridge.'

One possible objection to these words is that it omits the colouring; the 'cold wet porridge' has been sprinkled with demarara sugar that resembles the coating of brown heather that covers much of its surface. It is a shade that only changes in the last days of summer, when it flushes purple for a brief, beautiful interlude as the heather comes to flower.

In other senses, the heart of Lewis is hardly majestic either. In these low-lying acres there are few swells or dips that might qualify as either hills or valleys. The almost-comically titled Beinn Dhail (or Dell Mountain), in front of my bedroom window, seemed to straddle the heavens when I was young with its 170 yards or so of dwarfish height. Muirneag at its southern shoulder was a veritable giant, its summit a startling 271 yards, just a little more than the highest point in Sulasgeir.

For all its flatness, however, it is deceptively difficult to cross the Ness moor. Eyes have to remain fixed and focused. Feet must be placed carefully, one in front of the other, as travellers jump from tussock to tussock, trying to keep both shoe and sole from being sucked down into a bog or having to cross a crack in the moorland's surface that may be a few feet wide. Black beckons continually below us as one hillock looks suspiciously like the last. It is all too easy to lose the most direct or even the most rambling way before reaching, say, Tolsta on the island's other side.

In some ways, the rent charged by this landscape can prove almost as costly as the high price paid by man to the waves. I recall this especially in my childhood, when my father used to come in shaking his head, complaining that we had lost one of our sheep out on, say, Allt Lèineabhat. The sight of an animal rotting on the edge of a bog was a common sight when one walked the moor. Gulls would have whittled the sheep down to the bone, leaving its skeleton bare and gaping.

There were times, too, when the landscape wrought the same effect on human life. One time when this occurred was way back in 1883. In mid-December a blizzard covered the north end of the island. It left three young men, Allan Campbell, John Macritchie and Angus Morrison, dead from exhaustion on their way home from Stornoway to the village of Lionel in Ness. On Friday, 14 December, they were found by a search party six miles from their destination and not far from a house that would have provided them with shelter.

Though they might have been blinded by snow on this occasion, there is little doubt that the very absence of landmarks on the moor has not helped many who set out there. Despite the way that previous generations marked their way home with cairns of stone and occasional boulders, mist could steal away a human life. A slip can take one too. For all that the end people meet there might be less dramatic than one occurring at sea, it can be no less deadly.

Yet it is largely the sea's hazards these pages must focus upon. From my imagined vantage point at the top of the lighthouse, it is clear how the land eases down towards the Atlantic. It is edged by the yellow sands of such beaches as those found on the shoreline of Eoropie, Habost, Swainbost and Cross – some of the most magnificent in the whole of the British Isles. And then beyond this there is wide, blue emptiness, bordered and brought to an end only by the greater, vaster emptiness of sky. Occasionally there can be seen, making its way past the Butt of Lewis, a bird that is able to master both these elements. Granted power in the heavens, the gannet can still succeed in thundering down like the spears ancient warriors must have aimed at Odysseus during the Fall of Troy, splitting waves to emerge moments later with the silver gleam of fish in the tight purse of its beak.

On one occasion, when writing his weekly column for the *Stornoway Gazette*, George Morrison used the 'dual-identity' of the bird as an opportunity for some humour at the Nessmen's expense. A neighbour to the district, native to North Tolsta on the north-east coast of Lewis, George wrote under the pen-name of the Breve – a term that used to be given to the traditional judges of the Hebrides which his clan used to provide. At all times, he deployed a sharp wit that sometimes focused on the effects that 'guga' had on the Nessman's digestive system. This particular year, for instance, he claimed there was the 'possibility of canning the fird [combination of fish and bird, which to taste, it is] if any tin out of Singapore can be found to contain the internal violence from the northern end of the isle'.

If we treat his new word with a seriousness which the Breve never intended, it is clear that there is more than a little accuracy in the term. The gannet is first and foremost a bird – the largest seabird in the entire northern hemisphere. It coasts across water, not within it. It is able, too, to undertake long journeys, not only flying to the African coast each year but regularly undertaking round flights of around 1,000 miles to feed its young. The adult bird's brilliant white plumage – apart from its yellow head and the black tips of its wings – seems designed to mimic both cloud and wave.

For the 'fird' is also designed to enter the ocean, becoming at one with that element. Though its wings are long, it is able to tuck them up as it plunges into water, narrowing and concentrating its force. It can pinpoint, too, the presence of fish with its binocular vision, its marvellous eyes, ringed with black, far forward in its skull to allow it to see prey. While some may see it purely in terms of its notorious 'greed', it is this power that in heraldry makes it a symbol of the prophet, able to see what may be hidden to others. On a family shield it can represent, too, one who 'subsists by the wings of his virtue and merit, having little or no land on which to rest'.

There is also the way its head is designed in such a way as to reduce the full impact of the waves as it dives from heights of over 30 yards, reaching speeds of up to 60 miles per hour as it does so. Its beak cleaves water. Unlike the fulmar, it has no external nostrils, preventing the force of waters from entering its head. It has air sacs inside both its face and – crucially – its chest. Both act as a cushion when it strikes the Atlantic with tremendous natural force.

One of the men whom we will meet in a later chapter, Alasdair Bàn from the village of Lionel, employed a different term to describe the bird scientists call *Marus Bassanus*. With its long beak and powerful white wings, he called it 'the Concorde of the air'. One can see exactly what he means.

Yet there is more to it even than that. It is also a depth-charge exploding fathoms below to shatter a shoal of fish into fragments, emerging moments later with a splinter to either swallow or bring home to its nestling back on Sròn na Lice on Sulasgeir. It is nature's white torpedo, a Nemesis for the fish that for centuries have thronged the waters that surround Sròn na Lice, Gralisgeir, Bogha Còrr, Sgeir an Teampaill, much of the tip of Ness . . .

And each year ten men of that district leave Stornoway Harbour in the early hours of the morning to sail out to where they nest. They sail through the relatively sheltered waters of the Minch, round the Butt of Lewis and north towards Sulasgeir – the point and purpose of their journey to gather some 2,000 gannet chicks. In doing this, they provide the chief ingredient of what must be one of Europe's most timeless and traditional foods, satisfying a taste that has been lost elsewhere but endured within one tiny north-western corner of this land.

1

Port in Calm and Storm

WIDOW-MAKER

The sea makes widows too many mornings,
compelling women to be trapped in black
through days when storm-clouds come without warning
and nets tugged tight turn loose and slack.
The sea makes widows too many mornings
when time and tide permit no turning back
and out of stillness, waves come storming,
strong men shivering before their attack.
The sea makes widows too many mornings.
For all the crew switches sail and tack,
there is no relief from weight of mourning
that storms pile thick upon mens' backs.
The sea makes widows too many mornings,
when daylight opens with a skyline crack
of sun too weak to give much warming
to homes aware of life they lack.
The sea makes widows too many mornings
when boats are wrecked on reefs or stacks,
when quays fall hushed and quiet, transforming
coloured threads into shades of black.

'What mean ye by these stones?' – Joshua 4: 6

'When people look at Port these days, it's impossible for
them to imagine what it looked like at the tail end of the
nineteenth century. It was an extremely busy place. There
were 400 people directly employed there. Five thousand
lives dependent on the fishing industry. Thirty-seven boats

there in 1892. Six men to every boat. Mostly catching ling. Ten thousand ling at one time, for instance, in one day. In 1900, there were 12,500 hundredweights of ling caught there during the year. Imagine that. And other fish too. Cod, skate and halibut. A whole array.'

As Norman Smith – the man most people know in the community as Tormod Sgiugs – talks about the northern end of my home-district, I think of the Port of Ness I am familiar with today and visited often in my youth. To be honest, nowadays his vision of its past glories is more than hard to imagine. The only remnant of their existence seems to be 'A' Ghlainne', the meeting point for the men of Port. Loaned to the district's fishermen by the Met Office in London in 1836, it is a barometer set into a stone pillar at a sand-coloured bungalow standing across from the road leading down to the quay.

Otherwise, it's a sleepy little village, only disturbed by an occasional collie padding from house to house, a vehicle full of locals or visitors making their way down to its glorious stretch of sand, or – sometimes at night – the boy-racers revving their cars along the road in one of the machismo rituals performed persistently within its boundaries for decades. And then there were the evenings men and women would queue along the breakwater in order to obtain a clutch of gugas, slipping them into plastic bags bearing legends like 'Lewis Crofters', 'James MacKenzie' or – more exotically – 'Marks and Spencer' or even 'Harrods'. Other than that, its stillness would only be broken by the cries of seagulls, harassed, perhaps, by a skua visiting the harbour, dipping and rising over the breakwater wall.

Yet if Tormod tells me it was an extremely busy place, it must be so. For all that he claims he is uneasy upon salt water, it only takes a few moments in his company to make clear he has a head more than full of the lore of sea. One can hear it in his conversation, bright and sharp and knowledgeable about the waves and its effects on his native island. One can even see it in his study. A filing cabinet in the corner is crammed with documents relating to the boats and businesses of Port of Ness, the village which his community of Lionel borders. There are papers, too, in what he jokingly refers to as his 'banana boxes'. There are a number of them – the word 'Fyffes' printed on the sides of quite a few – stacked against one wall. No doubt, even though he does not disturb them on this occasion, there are similar contents squashed inside – all part of his vast knowledge of the community to which he belongs.

A fit and slender man for his 80-odd years, his hair still thick and silver, he pauses for a moment to catch breath and thought before continuing the conversation.

'And that meant there were buildings that had to deal with these catches, preparing them for the Continental and Irish markets. You know where Beirgh is?'

I nod my head, having just learned where it was the other day. For most of my life, a single house called 'Bay View' has stood there, occupying a bare headland above the breakwater, much of it – as my friend, Dods, notes later – scored with folds in the land, called either lazybeds or run rig. I remember being told that this had been built by the brother of the entrepreneur and benefactor Murdo Macaulay, who made a fortune in Rhodesia, the country now known as Zimbabwe. Later, he established a Trust which had helped in the creation of the Ness Hall at my end of the parish and assisted the fishermen of Lewis in the purchase of boats. He had made, too, the education of those a decade or more older than me possible, providing Nessmen of that time with a bursary to go to university.

'There used to be shoals of fish left to dry out on its south-eastern tip, the flat ledges of rock that lie there . . . It was the women who brought the fish there, carrying them on their backs in creels the half-mile or so from the curing stations.

One of them was where Harbour View is today, just beside the road that goes down to the beach. They would be split there and salted in vats. After that, families would have the task of drying the catch, spreading it out on the rocks for the weather to do its work. And then, within a fortnight, the fish would be ready for the market, which was mainly Ireland, as for most of the fish cured on Scotland's west coast.'

He pauses again, drinking from the cup of tea his wife Cairstiona has just brought in.

'And you know where Bàrr a' Iàirrd is?'

'No . . .'

He tells me. It's on another point of land not far away, overlooking the beach and the inner harbour. For most of my life, it's been occupied by a peatstack and a Portakabin acting as a public toilet. Nowadays, they're building a small restaurant there, where visitors will be able to eat and enjoy a glass of wine while looking at the sands and sea below. It will be a welcome change from being blown about by the gale force wind on the summit as I was so often in my youth.

'You know what used to be there? And also in some of the croft houses close by? Storehouses. First of all they were used in 1895 for the material to build the harbour. Even wooden buildings to accommodate staff, the engineers and such like. Later they were used for fishing gear. The lines and sails that they needed. Where the Portakabin is used to be an old smithy, Henderson's place. All behind four thick walls. There's no doubt it was a thriving place. Depending on the direction of the wind, there would always be a group of men gathered there, viewing everything that was going on. And, of course, they would be a different sort of men from the ones that are around here nowadays.'

He tells a story to illustrate this. Sipping as he does so, he speaks of a time when some of the men were spending their evening fishing from some of the rocks that form part of the jagged shoreline of the district. A young lad, Angus, fell in. Gasping and heaving, spitting mouthfuls of salt water, he was eventually hauled out. Instead of gaining sympathy for his plight, all he received was one man jerking his head in his direction.

'*Aonghais, am faca tu cudaigean* . . . Did you see any cuddies while you were down there?'

'*Smaoinich*,' Tormod laughs, sipping his tea. 'What kind of men were they?'

If any man had the ability to answer that question, it would be Tormod. He possesses knowledge of many matters relating to the community he comes from. His life since he was a child has been caught up in it. His father, for instance, returned home in 1893 from Glasgow, where he was employed as a baker, opening a bakery at that time in Port.

'He used to spend all his time baking ship-biscuits for the men in the boats that were tied up here.'

For many years too, Tormod was the Ness correspondent of the *Stornoway Gazette*, writing the section of the 'From Butt to Barra' column that kept natives and exiles informed of what was going on in the district. Still an elder in the Free Church, the largest in the area, he takes the duties of that office very seriously. On the day we met, for instance, he travelled up to my own village to visit a woman there who had been largely housebound for a number of years. He was also for many decades a teacher in the Church's Sabbath School; a fact that is recognised by the wooden carving of an open book on a cabinet. As Secretary to the Ness Cemetery Committee, he works hard to ensure that both the new and old cemeteries in the district are kept in order. He is the one on hand to answer visitors when they arrive in Ness from the distant edges of the world asking: 'Can you show me where my ancestors are buried?'

In short, I am with a man who has a wide range of

interests, a continual questioning of the world, that his wife Cairstiona gently chides him about. '*Dè 'n diofar a th' ann aig deireadh an latha?*' she asks, a half smile on her face as she does so. 'What difference does it make at the end of the day?'

For all that he appears a serious-minded man, we share a similar sense of humour. A twinkle flashes behind his glasses when either he or I make a joke, sometimes even about the sea-sickness we share in common. Talking of a time he lay stretched out in the bottom of a boat leaving the harbour, he tells of how an older man responded: 'Throw him into the waters! He'd make good bait.'

Yet in many ways I feel dwarfed by him. There is the scale of his war-time experience. Too young to be part of the early years of the Second World War, he was involved in the Battle of Anzio in the first half of 1944. Later he was captured by the Germans in Florence on a date he remembers only too well – 30 November 1944. From there, he was taken to a Prisoner of War camp near Munich. It is a time he recalls without bitterness or rancour.

'The Germans knew they were losing the war by then. The guards in the camp were old men who did their best to treat us well, but they were as hungry as we were. After all, we had the Red Cross parcels they used to send. We used to give them bits of chocolate when the boxes arrived.'

I also feel awed by the immensity of his Christian faith. In this he reminds me of my father, prayer and the reading of the Bible punctuating the rhythm of his day. Central to his life, it is always evident in him, paradoxically both lifting him up and grounding him, for all that he only talks about it while saying grace over a cup of tea and scones. There is, more prosaically, the way he is able to place his hand on exactly the right piece of paper in the reams that surround him. His slight frame moves around the room, bending down to fetch a particular sheet or notebook from the bottom of the filing cabinet: a gift that fills me with envy when I consider the blizzard of white and scrawled paper that surround me in my own life.

And, of course, there is that detailed knowledge of the community, much of it gained while employed at the Decca Station in Lionel from the end of his war-service until his retirement. Some was gleaned, too, from standing behind the counter of the family shop. Near the crossroads in Lionel, it acted as the ideal location to garner news from Knockaird and Eoropie in one direction, the extremities of Skigersta and Cross Skigersta Road in the other. He displays the understanding he has gleaned from this again and again in my company, revealing an astonishing recollection of dates, names and figures. For instance, he tells me that Port was the centre of the hunt not just for fish and the guga – it was also a place where seals were harvested, taken from, among other locations, Sulasgeir's nearest neighbour, North Rona.

'In 1905, one of the boats returned with the corpses of 190 seals. The seal oil obtained from them was taken from Port to Stornoway.'

In the early days, these and other similar cargoes were shipped to Stornoway by trading smacks, former East Coast clinker-built Fifies with keels of between 40 and 50 feet. With names like *Grace Darling*, *Village Maid* and *Jessie*, they travelled sometimes to the Scottish mainland for goods such as timber. By the opening years of the twentieth century, this was changing, these boats becoming less and less required. One of the reasons for this was Port itself, its industry and existence justifying the outlay of expenditure needed to create a road to allow lorries to travel back and forth from Stornoway.

It was this, local historian Michael Robson told me later at his home in Port, that also explains much of the way the district is laid out, with houses shadowing the road between

Port and the village of Barvas for much of its length. 'It's straight just about all of the way. A direct route across the Barvas moor into Barvas and then another straight road to Port. Over time, the villages come out to meet it. Before then, the houses were much closer to the shore.'

He also goes on to tell me that at one stage another development was planned – a railway from Stornoway to Port of Ness with a branch-line leading to Carloway, situated near Loch Roag and one of the few natural harbours on the western edge of the Outer Hebrides.

'It was mainly for one purpose,' he explains, 'to take the catches from Port to Stornoway as quickly as possible.'

I shake my head in wonder; my vision of my native parish transformed by the thought of a train belching steam as it puffed down where the main road lies today, a guard shouting 'Passengers to South Dell, please disembark at the next station.'

It would be easy to conclude from this that Port of Ness harbour was a success, a thriving place that provided a great deal of work and industry for people. In the long-term this would, however, not be the case. Even at its zenith as a fishing port, it was already showing signs that would eventually lead to what in all practical terms, at least, was its final demise in 1900 or thereabouts. To show how this happened, it is necessary to examine the history of the port and how it first came to be. In addition, it is necessary to explore some of the fishing disasters that were also associated with these waters during much of the nineteenth century and beyond.

Tormod pushes a paper in my direction that helps me to do this. A long and detailed account of the kind which that newspaper has all too rarely carried, it is a clipping from the *Stornoway Gazette*, dated 3 October 1970. Headlined 'Port of Ness – a Lewis Fishing Village', it is an extremely impressive and detailed piece of work with the name of its writer absent, identified only by the single word 'Contributed'.

'It was written by John Murdo Macleod. You know, the boat-builder, the one who lives over in Stornoway these days.'

'Aye . . .' I know the man, and more especially his sons, both around my own age. John Murdo's own father was one of the legendary figures of Ness. When the ship the *Iolaire* was going down in Stornoway harbour, he was the one who dived into the waters with a rope, responsible for saving many of the 79 rescued men from that sinking on the first of January 1919, a day when over 200 men, largely from the rural, Gaelic-speaking areas of Lewis, met their end.*

I skim-read the article, aware immediately I must obtain a copy for myself. It tells of the many problems men encountered while attempting to build a harbour in Port of Ness. This was attempted on two occasions; the first quay completed in 1837, with its larger, longer successor coming into existence nearly 40 years later in 1872. Even when this was done, not too many years had passed before omens and auguries began to gather. All was not going well with the new structure. Sand – a perennial problem – silted up the harbour; the entrance was 'only accessible for a short period during each tide'. These were difficulties that would haunt the life of the harbour, persisting even until the present day.

Some proved almost impossible to solve. A few days after my meeting with Tormod, I am in the company of artist and poet Ian Stephen in his home in the former Sail Loft building on the harbour front of Stornoway. He talks for a time about the difficulties of the location of Port of Ness.

---

* Due to the inexact records kept at that time, there appears to be some uncertainty over the number of lives lost on that date. What is not in dispute, however, was the catastrophic effect it had on both Ness and other island communities for many years afterwards.

'In the pilots' books,' he tells me, 'people are warned that apart from in ideal conditions, they should keep about five miles away from the Butt. It lies at a point where two stretches of water meet, where the weight of the Atlantic meets the shallower waters of the Minch. And that means there's real force in both tide and eddy, particularly on days when there's any kind of north wind blowing. The seas can build up fast.'

I nod my head. Even a landlubber like me can understand some of this, how the next parish was in America and the Minch is a relatively narrow channel of water within which to cram the width of the Atlantic waters.

'Sometimes it's really hard to leave the harbour. You might have a good wind behind you, bearing you out, and the boat's stopped by the swell of the wave. It's made worse by the way there's sand below. It comes in with the tide, silting up the harbour.'

Again I nod, thinking of the various solutions to the problems of Port that have been offered over the years. In the last decade of the nineteenth century, a breakwater was built – and later extended by a further 50 yards – to shelter the approach into the harbour. Experience has shown it to be a waste of sweat, tears and concrete. Pounded by the Atlantic, the crumbling structure provides yet more proof of man's inability to challenge or control the force of the sea. Tormod shook his head when he looked at it, making a remark I have heard before on the lips of others: 'They built it in the wrong place. If only they had put it in Skigersta, a little bit further down the coast, it would still be standing. But they didn't think it through properly. They didn't think it through.'

Yet if the harbour provides proof of man's folly, the boats that sheltered there offer evidence of his ingenuity. The type of vessel used mainly within its waters to catch the ling that shoaled around the island's rocky foreshore was a locally built *sgoth*. Initially, many were small. For all that there were boats with keels of 20 feet by 1867, they were the exception and not the rule. This changed in the 1880s, with boats like the ill-fated *Christina* – which will be discussed later – arriving around that time. Its keel was 21.5 feet; its length was approximately 30 feet overall; the beam varied from 8 to 10 feet; the hold was 10 feet. Throughout the last two decades, improvements kept being made – like the great boats of the East Coast, the Fifies and Zulus, also changing rapidly at the time. In doing this, all those involved in these alterations, both fishermen and builders, had to keep in mind the conditions they were sailed in. In the words of the *Gazette* report, they could never forget that 'Tidal harbours, like open beaches, required boats of shallow draft and of light construction, as these vessels were frequently hauled up and down beaches, very often short-handed.'

And not just beaches. When arriving in Sulasgeir, the men had to haul these boats high upon the crags on Geodha Phuill Bhàin to prevent the sea from tugging them away from their landing point, exiling them on that rock until others became alerted to their absence – a process that in the uncertain waters of the North Atlantic might take some time. In this, they had clearly learned valuable lessons from their Norse ancestors, who had made their vessels light enough to draw them over a neck of land if such a task proved necessary, which meant less effort than they would expend at sea. For this reason, they were largely undecked, though some of the later models possessed a half-deck. The boat-builder mainly used larch for these impressive vessels; this light wood assisting them in this purpose.

There were others aspects of the boat that were impressive. According to the *Gazette*, the rig was 'large, simple and effective', enabling it to be big enough to 'catch the wind' if this was necessary, while there were other times it could be reduced to a mere scrap.

Perhaps the title of 'Sgoth Niseach' given to these boats may be a bit of misnomer. As John Murdo Macleod, the celebrated Ness boat-builder, confessed in a letter to me: 'Much as I would like to claim that the boats were developed in Ness, the evidence handed down to me through three generations of boat-builders cannot support that view.' The larger boats, for instance, were originally constructed in Stornoway, where there was already an established ship and boat-building industry at that time with a number of firms, both large and small, engaged in this task. Some of their creations were identical in terms of their design to the ones later made in Ness, drawing on a tradition that probably began in Scandinavia and the Baltic Sea, but was later found throughout the north of Scotland, from Lerwick to Loch Fyne. Their closest family resemblance can be found in the yoals of Orkney. They had broader bows than their counterparts in Shetland, necessary for the shallower waters of both the Minch and those around Orkney. The only difference was that in Ness the keel length was increased from about 17 to 21 feet after the quay was built and the boats set out for more distant grounds – the skills of families like the Macleods adapting the design for local circumstances.

Yet for all the skill that went into the making of the *sgoth*, there were times when all the craft of the boatmaker, and the courage and ingenuity of the men aboard these boats, was not enough to save them.

I am sitting in the Comunn Eachdraidh, the local history museum for Ness that stands in the village of Habost. It's a building I recall from my childhood as the local Co-op and a little time later as a shortlived knitting factory. Yet few of these memories are with me today. Instead, I am feeling a little numb as I look down a list of similar sounding names, all hailing from villages I have known for most of my life. As I do this, I scribble down a few of the details noted there. In the beginning, I perform the task roughly: a few words sketching out the terrible backdrop of death and loss that formed much of the history of the gannet-hunt over the last few centuries. As I go on, I write more and more, a sense of the great scale of these events beginning to strike me.

Some of them even pre-date the building of the first pier – not long after Mackenzie of Seaforth first wrote in 1834 to the Commissioners of the Herring Industry.

1836
Eathar an Phiobar – Skigersta
Five or seven men drowned.

There are only five names recorded, but when the Napier Commission interviewed him when investigating the conditions of the Highlands and Islands some five decades later, Malcolm Mackenzie, son of Norman Mackenzie on board, stated that seven men were on board when the boat went down. There is no note of exactly how or where this occurred.

1839
Eathar Chalum 'Ic Fhionnlaidh
Six men from Fivepenny on board. All lives lost.

Again, there is no note of where or how the drownings happened.

1847
Eathar Mhic Iain

The vessel contained six men, mainly from Lionel, of whom an individual survived: Donald Campbell (Dòmhnall Mhic Iain) from that village. I've also jotted down the name of one of the deceased, Donald Morrison from Knockaird. We are told how Campbell was found clinging to the vessel, claiming that Morrison had been with him moments before. What happened to him just before the rescue is one of these mysteries that frequently cling to deaths at sea.

To the general reader, particularly today, the scale of loss seems awesome: a litany of untold sorrows and grief. John Murdo Macleod, however, provides some sense of perspective on this, pointing out that the village at that time was the centre of the Lewis deep-sea fishing industry, involving some 400 or more boats. He notes that this amounts to 'a huge number of days at sea as against the ten or so days when they didn't return'. He compares Port, too, to other places – such as Newfoundland, where the losses were so great the entire fleet had, in effect, to be replaced every decade. A reporter attached to the Fishing Museum in Hull, he also points out, was amazed to discover that trawler loss reached an average of one every two months.

Yet there are other ways in which lives can be lost on the waves. Both piracy and the press-gang were, during these years, two of the greatest menaces found upon the sea. The latter certainly turned up at a number of houses, both in Ness and elsewhere, at this time. Some locals even took shelter on North Rona to escape a procession of naval officers heading towards their homes. In 1849 the crew of a boat from the village of Galson disappeared. The tale of *Eathar Ghabhsainn* is as strange and startling as any that occurred in the Western Isles, with that boat turning up empty and upright on the shoreline and only a bonnet worn by one of the men lying near its stern. Afterwards, there are rumours of Lewismen in the West Indies, and of how one man returned home. On discovering his wife was now married to another, he turned on his heel and went back to Stornoway – and afterwards the Scottish mainland – once again. It is a story – with echoes in the French tale of Martin

Guerre – that inspired me to write the title story of my short story collection, *Special Deliverance*.

And it is not the only tale of its kind. Tormod Sgiugs believes it may also have occurred to a Skigersta boat sailing out of Lewis during this period. Perhaps it is this that lies behind another impressively written – but probably inaccurate – story which appears in the *Stornoway Gazette* on 17 September 1981. The writer, Norman Morrison, notes that:

> [a strange] tale revolves around a crew which went to Sulasgeir about 150 years ago. No word was received and the men were again feared drowned. Many years passed and many of the widows had remarried when quite suddenly the 'lost' men returned. Apparently they had been victims of a kidnap gang which had shipped them off to Africa. The men remained marooned until British officials secured their passage home . . . While rather sceptical [about the tale], one can realise how such an account has reinforced the Sulasgeir link [with the community of Ness] and understand how a tradition built on such foundations is so much alive today.

At the time of *Eathar Ghabhsainn*, however, there was more than just the press-gang visiting these shores. In the eight years that follow 1849 and the two years that precede it, there were a number of tragedies, occurring both within Lewis and in the Highlands and as a whole. Many were spawned by a fungus officially named *Phytophthora infestans*. Innocent in itself, it is little more than a few strings of genes possessing the means to reproduce itself again and again. And so it does, managing to do so in clouds of spore forming on warm, damp days when it spreads from place to place, affecting the crops just planted, often by the poor in hope of being fed. In 1846, it visited Ireland. In the following year it headed north on its macabre tour, coming to the Highlands and Islands of Scotland. And everywhere it went, it left little souvenirs of its passing. It began with rotten leaves; putrefied stems; the stink of decomposition; a decay that reached down into the soil itself, making the fruit of that plant worthless. It showed itself, too, in the rumbling bellies and haunted, sunken cheeks of those suffering from want and need. It was, of course, that bringer of famine, the potato blight.

Clearly, this disease did not affect the Isle of Lewis or the Highlands and Islands as a whole in the way that Ireland experienced it during the 1840s. Famine relief in these parts seems to have been better organised. Rations of oatmeal were doled out to the general population. Perhaps, too, and more cynically, landlords were less likely to allow those who were, at least in name, Protestant, to die than the Catholic population of the larger island further to the south. It was also the case that in districts like Ness, there were often fish available – for all that they could not always be relied upon to find their way towards net or line.

As a result of all this, fewer died in the Highlands and Islands than in neighbouring Ireland. Many writers have questioned whether it was actually a famine at all, or just another in a series of agrarian crises that affected places like Lewis throughout the nineteenth century, and before and since. It may in itself have been a contributing factor to some of the sea-losses of these times, with men going out to sea due to desperation and want, their tiny crofts unable to feed their large families. Some boats likely braved the sea when common sense and the men's awareness of the waves might have cautioned them against it. It was also true that there were times men might have gone out in their vessels when their bodies were too weak to meet the challenge of these waters.

And so the list goes on . . .

1851
Eathar Iain Chuisiadar

One man from the now deserted village of Cuisiadar – where some of my own ancestors once lived – plus five Skigersta men.

This boat was a replacement for the Skigersta boat lost earlier in 1836. I count the 15 years that separate both dates and wonder at the toll that certain households must have suffered, the sense of loss and hopelessness they experienced at that time.

1882
Eathar Aonghais Chaluim Ruaidh

This is the tragedy that must have left its wake closest to my own home. Its crew were all from Dell, people my grand-father and grandmother must have known fairly well. Of them, two of the crew were from North Dell – including the skipper, Angus Campbell; one from Aird Dell; three near neighbours of my own family crofthouse in South Dell.

Proud, contented men, they were clearly looking to the future with a great deal of confidence. A new harbour was – by virtue of Sir James Matheson's assistance – about to be built in Port and they had a new vessel that would grace its waters. This was the aforementioned *Christina*, one of the first of the new types of *sgoth* with its 21.5 foot keel, approximately 30 foot overall in length. It must have drawn envious glances as it sailed for the first time out of the small wharf and harbour that was still all there was in Port back then.

And then it disappeared.

Even today people are unsure how it happened. The weather was calm; no sudden, unpredictable squalls dis-turbing the stillness of the waves that day. There is no evidence either of the *Christina* going aground on rocks. Eyes shifted with distrust towards the crews of the north-east boats that were fishing in that area. One gave voice to

that suspicion: the poet known as Bàrd Bharabhais, Donald
Macdonald, born and raised in South Dell. Arguing that the
crew had experienced sailors on board, he notes that the
boat was also in excellent condition:

> *'S ann Di-luain a sheòl sibh*
> *Le bàta bòidheach ùr,*
> *Na h-uile ni an òrdugh*
> *'S na ròpan anns na siùil.*

> It was on a Monday you sailed
> With an elegant new boat,
> Everything in order,
> With ropes secured to sail.

And then, following a verse that emphasises the calmness of
the waters, he makes a bald and bitter accusation. Condemning a Buckie boat for ramming the new Ness *sgoth*, he
declares:

> *Nach bu chruaidh am Bucach*
> *Nach do thilg e thugaibh ròp . . .*

> How harsh the Buckie men were
> That they did not throw you a rope . . .

Whatever the truth or otherwise of this reproach, there is no
doubt that it marks another depressing entry in the annals
of Port of Ness, yet one more incident in the catalogue of
those that occurred over the centuries.

Another happened in 1885; the drowning taking place
within the view of many who were most affected by it. It is
known as 'Bàthadh Chunndaill', and the people of the
village of Eoropie watched as the sea washed away two
boats occupied by their men. It is, perhaps, for this reason

that memories of the incident still stir in the minds of many inhabitants of the district of Ness, the drama of that day forcing people to talk freely about it in a way they find difficult to do about any other.

Among the related apocryphal tales I came across was one I heard from the lips of an elderly woman in the district. She spoke of a young couple who had just been married a short time before. Among the wedding gifts had been a pair of white wellingtons given to her husband. He was wearing them as he headed out, listening, perhaps, to the others joke when they compared his pair with their black boots.

'Oh, here comes the bridal party,' they might have said. 'A lamb among old crows.'

His wife probably waved in her husband's direction, his white boots splashing through surf as he helped the others push the boat out from the shore. The next time she was aware of him was when she was standing behind the walls outside her house, watching the men on his boat battling waters that threatened to swamp and sink them with their weight. For a long time, she knew he was still alive, recognising his white boots as he stood upright in the vessel, knowing at the same time that most of the others were gone. Then the moment came when she knew he was no longer there. She retreated into the house then, barely leaving it for a year or so afterwards.

John Murdo Macleod has pointed out that this tale is unlikely to be wholly true. At this time, men wore thigh-high leather boots rather than Wellingtons while fishing. Despite this, the fact that such a story exists shows the dramatic power the incident possesses for the people of Ness. It is certainly one that lives on still within the folk memory of its people.

According to most accounts, only one man – Angus Morrison, known as Aonghas Liath – was washed ashore. A man from Port identified his corpse by the initials 'AM'

tattooed on his arm. Together with others, he dragged the
body a short distance from the shoreline. It was after this
they went to the Free Church minister, Rev. Duncan Mac-
Beath, for advice. The clergyman asked one question.

'Is the body outside the reach of the sea?'

'Aye.'

'Then bury him where he lies.'

Today that grave is marked by a pile of stones beside the
beach – not far from where the sewage outfall pipes run. A
visitor, Captain Smith, regularly maintained these each time
he arrived in Ness, but until recently few could identify what
they signified – so much so that when the Council planned
to replace the pipes, it was initially proposed that the new
ones would run through Aonghas Liath's last resting place.
It was this event that may – at least partially – have
prompted talk of marking the events of that day in a more
permanent and respectable fashion.

According to Tormod Sgiugs, there was, however, another body that came ashore. Broken and battered, his
corpse reached land in Àrnaistean in North Dell. Again,
they decided to leave him there, his features too bashed and
brutalised to be recognised or even shown to his family or
widow – perhaps that legendary woman who gazed upon
her husband, watching his boots no longer standing upright
on the boat.

There were other tragedies still to come as the nineteenth
century came to an end and the twentieth century made a
beginning. In 1889, the *Diligence* and the *Look Sharp* sank
not far from Port of Ness Harbour. Twelve men died with
'forty dependents left destitute'. Ten years later, another
twelve men drowned. On 14 July 1900, six men died as the
Stormy Petrel went down . . .

And then my eyes move inexorably to the date they have
been steadfastly avoiding, a disaster in the 1860s, the most
terrifying single event of all. It is an incident that – together

with its chilling and depressing aftermath – deserves to be recorded within its own book. Both human imagination and understanding seem dwarfed by it, these pages much too slight and frail to act as a memorial to the terrifying immensity of what happened one particular day.

One can only presume that it was necessity that sent them out into the waters that morning.

The date – 18 December 1862 – is well outwith the usual fishing season in the north of Lewis. This begins in early January and continues till the last days of autumn, with a slight decrease during May and June, when many of the more able-bodied voyaged to Wick for the herring fishing. However, on this calm December morning, a number of boats left the harbour, perhaps going to the fishing grounds lying between north-east and north-west of the Butt, stretches of water called after those who discovered them – like Carragh Pìobair or Carragh Mhic Dhòmhnaill 'Ic Ailein – or landmarks, like Grunnd Mùirneag, named after the largest 'hill' at the north end of Lewis. All seemed commonplace and uneventful – though there was one man, according to Tormod Sgiugs, who had felt disturbed by the sound of the oceans that morning. Ruairidh Ruadh was to join the boat that day, but he paused in his tracks as he made his way across the beach at Eoropie. Putting his ear to the sand, he seemed to hear some deep and distant warning to which the others were deaf. An experienced fisherman, he warned them against setting out that day – advice that for some reason they chose to ignore.

Perhaps they might even have been smiling at the thought of his words as they shot their lines, anticipating heading home in the hour just before darkness with silver glinting and filling their decks. The glimmer of their catch would bring about a bright and shining end to the hunger that some of them might have been suffering for days, if not weeks, before.

And then the heavens cracked at noon. Some said it sounded like an earthquake, a huge, dark sound that echoed across both sky and ocean. The wind rose, beating against sails the men tried desperately to take down. Rain blew and smacked like a whip. Waves gathered round them. Some rose like hills and mountains, collapsing down on them a moment later.

All in all, five boats – with six men crewing each – went down that day, smashed and destroyed as they tried to sail back to harbour. Two vessels survived the storm by heading in the direction of Assynt on the east coast of Sutherland, one man dying of exposure shortly after his boat had touched land there. A member of my own clan, John Murray or 'Iain Ruadh' from Swainbost, is buried in a graveyard at Loch Nedd in that district. Almost 40 boats – the means of existence for other families – washed up on the beach were carried off by the wind and crushed into pulp and small pieces.

On the shoreline after that storm, which persisted until seven o'clock in the morning three days later, 24 newly-made widows put aside their coloured shawls and skirts and donned black to mark their loss. Seven felt new life growing inside their wombs and reflected on the fact that these children would never see their fathers. There were other youngsters who might have some memory, growing fainter and more insubstantial, perhaps, with each passing year. There were 71 of these children, each one needing to be fed even though the provider of fish for their meals, guga for their hungry mouths had gone.

And, too, there were the 31 relatives who were dependent on those who went out to sea: ageing, frail parents; brothers and sisters; the children of those who might already have lost a father to the sea, the result of single drowning incidents, a foot slipping when clambering down a rock.

They all spoke in whispers about how bad the events of

these three nights had been: how there had been nothing like it in the history of Port before. A wall of stones and pebbles was thrown up overnight on the edge of the village of Eoropie, where children run and romp around the playpark today. Someone told them that seaweed was splayed against the wall of Swainbost Cemetery, something never to be seen there at any time before or after. The tide had reached some five feet above its ordinary highest point. Farther along the coast, there were tales of ling, cod, colefish, hake and rockfish driven to shore in vast shoals. They lay choking and gasping on land, drowning in a different element from the one that had claimed the men.

The better-informed also added other pieces of information about how vast and wide-ranging the storm had been. Twenty-two boats had been wrecked in Assynt. In Easter Ross, huge swathes of forest had been felled. In distant Elgin, a place which claimed to have 'escaped the worst of the storms', the turrets of a church had been blown down . . .

News of that night's terrible events did not travel in just one direction; it also journeyed in another. People everywhere in Britain heard about the horrifying consequences of that night's events in Ness, responding with kindness to their plight. A Widows and Orphans' Charitable Fund was set up following the tragedy, raising over £1,860 for those most affected by it.

Little of this was given out. The estate factor, Donald Munro, used much of it instead to pay the rent the landlord was supposedly due. What money was handed to those who had suffered was done in a harsh and unequal way. It was this kind of action that led John Smith, the Earshader bard, to pay tribute to Munro in a Gaelic poem entitled 'Spiorad a' Charthannais' or 'The Spirit of Charity'. Anticipating his death, the work contains the following verse:

'N sin molaidh a' chnuimh shnàigeach thu,
Cho tàirceach 's a bhios d' fheòil,
Nuair gheibh i air do chàradh thu
Gu sàmhach air a' bòrd;
Their i, ''S e fear mèath tha 'n seo,
Tha math do bhiast nan còs,
On rinn e caol na ceudan
Gus e fhèin a bhiathadh dhòmhs'.'

Then shall the crawling maggot praise
The tastiness of your flesh
When it finds you placed
Silently on its table,
It will say, 'Here is a tender fellow
Whom the crevice creatures shall enjoy
Since he beggared hundreds
To fatten itself for me.'

As they watched this taking place, it must have been very easy for the people of Ness to conclude that both nature and their fellow men had been very unjust to them, that the only comfort they could gain was from their strong faith in God and the Church. There must, too, have been days when, as the publication the *Lewisman* reported in the aftermath of the sinking of the *Look Sharp* and the *Diligence* in 1889, 'the spirits of the Ness fishermen appear[ed] to be broken. All their lines still remain on the fishing grounds and with the exception of boats engaged in dragging for the bodies of the lost men, not one craft has put to sea.'

It was not the only form of despair felt by these men. They could also have felt dispirited and dejected when the Continental and – especially – Irish market for ling failed in the first years of the twentieth century. It brought an end to their opportunity to transform their native island, bringing the bright and shining wheels of modern industry to its shores, the chance of keeping the generations that followed them at the firesides where they belonged. There might have been a similar gloom when they saw how both wind and wave hammered and pounded the concrete structures man had erected, destroying, for instance, much of the Port of Ness breakwater in 1905; each toppled slab of stone like a gravestone for their hopes.

Yet most of all it was the deaths of their fellow-fishermen that must have made the men of Ness most despondent, making them surrender to an all-pervading sense of hopelessness time and time again. Though they were aware that heading out in these waters was necessary for their existence, each incident would have forced them to question the wisdom of ever stepping into their boats during months like January and February, or the strong winds of the spring and autumn equinoxes. There would have been days when they even asked themselves whether the capture of these fish was worth all the loss and sacrifice that was involved with it, whether the price paid by these men in their boats was extortionately high. In short, there were times when the 'spirits of the fishermen' would 'be broken' when they considered the nature of the work they performed.

In contrast, there was another harvest in which these men were involved that was relatively quick and reasonably rewarding, taking place, too, at a far kinder time of year . . .

2

Dods: A Man in Exile

GANNETS

Their plunge is like that instant
people fall in love,
when remote from all life's turbulence,
a word or gesture shakes us
from icy altitude,
veil of cloud,
and we swoop down to chase
that elusive moment
emotion breaks
within us like a sea-storm,
giving us the chance to seek
and capture dreams
shoaling round us
with the startling speed of quicksilver,
a bright seam threading through
life's impenetrable shadows,
these days existence seems
mysterious, unfathomable,
the deepest, darkest ultramarine.

One of the men whose life seems most to straddle the geographical division of Ness is the acknowledged leader of the district's annual Sulasgeir expedition, John 'Dods' Macfarlane. He has spent the majority of his five decades of life in my own village of South Dell, yet he remains un-questionably a man of its northern end, specifically the township of Port of Ness, the place that has traditionally welcomed home the tired group of ten or so travellers from their time out on the rock.

His loyalty to that village is more than evident from a glance around his house. Its front window may look out on his late father-in-law's home at the opposite side of the road, an old traditional crofthouse with a tall, salt-battered tree swaying in the confines of its garden, but his sitting room carries more than its share of hints and suggestions that the man of the house might prefer to be somewhere else, viewing places like the hills of Sutherland or the waters of the Minch he is able to glimpse from his childhood home in Port instead. In his new home, a few mementoes of Sulasgeir are always in sight. A tiny ornament of a gannet sits on top of a video recorder underneath the TV in the corner of the room.

And on the other side of the room, his passion for the rock is even more clearly in evidence. Its wall is dominated by a large, framed black and white print of men sitting round the smoky shadows of their bothy on the island, the glow of a peat fire at their feet. It is immediately recognisable for two reasons. It was given him by the writer and photographer John Beatty, in gratitude for his help in the publication of *Sula – The Seabird Hunters of Lewis*, published in 1992, and appears within its pages. Despite all my years away, I also recognise many of the men within it – Dods, Murdo Campbell, Kenny Murray, Finlay Morrison and Angus Murdo Gunn. Smoke obscures their faces as most clutch mugs of tea. In defiance of the well-worn proverb, two appear to be contemplating the old traditional kettle dangling on its chain above the flames, waiting, perhaps, for it to boil.

His allegiance to his home village is also clear in the picture that sits above his fireplace. It is a large coloured aerial photograph of Port Nis, or Port of Ness. One can see the breakwater that prods – broken but still defiant – in the direction of the Atlantic; the seam of golden sands that lies at the foot of the village cliffs. It marks the border between some of the crofts and the waves that threaten to overwhelm them. Each year the sea wins a few more inches in this long battle, eroding part of what at one time was called – and still is by some – Cealagmhol, the other Old Norse name for 'Bay of the Hill', by which the community is known. Sometimes a number of fence-posts can be seen, still trailing wire but fixed into mid-air – evidence of the scale of the battle that has been lost over the last few years. Spiralling upwards, they might seem to the uninformed like nets set in place to catch one of the fulmars nesting nearby, some idle practice for a gannet-hunter during the eleven months or so he is away from the shores of Sulasgeir.

The photograph also shows up a number of contrasts between the village where Dods was brought up and the township he lives in today. The majority of the houses in Port look towards the ocean; most houses of Dell gaze away from it, out into the moorland, perhaps to keep a weather eye on some of the sheep that might still be grazing there. There is, too, the length of the crofts lying behind the houses. In the case of my home village, most are about eight to nine acres –in wind-blown land like this, hardly in themselves enough to feed a family.

And in Port?

Dods springs to his feet. Eyes shining under thick black eyebrows that over the last few years have become tinged with grey, his finger indicates where the family croft lies, just beside the road that takes people to Eoropie, Knock-aird, the direct route to the Butt.

'About four or so. Less since they've done a little work on the road.'

'Not much. And is there much common grazing near the village?'

'You're seeing most of it there.' He points out a bare,

green stretch on a cliff-top – the place called Beirgh – that overlooks the harbour. 'You can see if you look closely there's lazybeds on it.'

'Aye.' It's something I'm very familiar with. In places like Dibadale, a cropped swathe of land on the coast near the southern end of my village, or behind Eoropie, underneath the Butt, there are many examples of this. The earth rises and falls in the shape of waves, too regular and symmetrical to be natural. According to historians, this was because the people in these parts cut wide furrows in the soil where their crops were to be planted. Apparently, these were designed to allow them to dig in vast quantities of animal manure and seaweed to help increase their harvest and to permit rain to run off marshy land, making it dry enough for growth to be possible.

'I don't think they're right believing that.'

'Why not?'

'Well, who'd plant in these places anyway? Just beside the sea. The salt spray would ruin everything you'd put there. And what's the need of ditches in place like that?' He taps the photo again. 'Most of the water would just run off anyway. Straight into the sea.'

'But why did they do it then?'

'To improve the grazings.' He picks up a sheet of paper. One minute he holds it taut and tight. The next, he pushes it together, forcing folds to appear in perfect imitation of the lazybeds I have seen so often on the island's edge. 'You're doubling up the ground by doing that. Giving yourself a little more grassland in places where there isn't very much to begin with.'

I put up a few token arguments in order to contradict him, but all my words seem weak and feeble. His observations chime and echo with all that I have ever observed on the coast of Lewis but never really thought about before. The lazybeds do seem to be on headlands, in places where they are most likely to be blasted and burned by salt. Finally, I give in, asking him if he has ever suggested this to the experts in that particular field.

'Och, they just ignore me. I'm not a scholar after all.'

Yet the following day, I test out Dods's argument with a woman who comes from North Tolsta on the other side of the island.

'He might be right, you know,' she declares, 'That's where the lazybeds are out our way too. Out where no crops could ever hope to grow. Where only sheep could safely graze.'

We laugh at her joke, but at the same time we're both impressed by Dods's insight, the sharpness of the observation he has produced by looking closely at the island that surrounds him. Whether he is right or wrong, it seems to me that this view has come from the eyes and mind of a man who is prepared both to see and think for himself, someone who has the nerve to challenge the views of those who might wrongly consider themselves to be his betters.

There is no doubt that he is one who always refuses to be patronised, his opinions as definite and well-defined as his features. His head, once complete with thick dark hair but now, as he jokes with his daughter-in-law, thinning at its centre, shakes vigorously when he disagrees with you. His eyebrows can come down like shutters on his eyes. His thin lips can become tight and expressionless. He pauses for a while sometimes to think of some retort to some remark you have made. In my case, it is often directed against both my politics and profession.

'Och, you teachers! You would think that. I've never met one of you who ever voted anything but Labour!'

There is also in that small frame of this, often so lithe and restless, much that conceals a great deal of both physical and mental strength, a tenacious refusal to be intimidated by anyone or anything, even a force of nature like the storms that must howl around Sulasgeir while they are out there on occasion. I saw this some 30 or more years ago when he first went out with Mary Joan, the woman from our village who would eventually become his wife. He would be one of those who would try to break up the occasional fights on the dance floor of the Ness Hall.

'Right, lads! *Mach à seo! Ma tha sibh ag iarraidh sabaid, mach air an doras siubh!* Out the door with you if you want to fight!'

These traits were obvious, too, when he undertook the thankless task of donning the black garb of a referee at some of the football matches at various locations on the island. He would stand up to men much taller and more physically forceful than he was, taking out a red or yellow card slowly and carefully when the moment demanded, refusing to consider for an instant backing down.

'Right! You're off!' he would declare, whistle perched on his lips.

His litheness is an advantage too. It can be seen even in the way he sits, tense and ready to shift into third or fourth gear at a moment's notice. It is no surprise that among the other services both he and Mary Joan offer to the community of which he is an important part is teaching dance lessons. He is the one who takes them through the steps of a Scottish Country dance with which they are unfamiliar, directing people with fingers, feet and voice.

'One . . . two . . . three . . .'

In short, he is a man of tremendous commitment and energy, often directing this towards the welfare and well-being of the people of Ness – one of his chief complaints was the way that some of them refuse to go out in the evening, failing to support a local event.

'I've told one or two: if we were all like you, the Social Club would have closed long ago.'

His working life is probably one reason for this. He was

one of those who went to school in the sad, lost days of the Qualifying Exam, when real opportunity seemed to be limited to the few who mastered the world of books. Possessing a more practical intelligence than many of his classmates, Dods left school at the age of fifteen. At around this time, he went to work in a fishing boat – following a trade that his father Murdo had known before him. Dods was there when I first met him, dressed in yellow overalls and on the deck of one of the many vessels that crowded Stornoway Harbour in the late 1960s. Some of the lads with whom I went to school knew him well. They came from the villages like Port, Lionel, Adabrock . . . Some of then – even me – had relatives who were fishermen. Between him and us, however, there was the divide that always exists between young lads who are still at school and those who have experienced the world of hard graft, wide as the gulf between quayside and a fishing vessel straining determinedly at its rope.

Yet occasionally a shaft of wit would pass between us; a joke, either in English or Gaelic, would be exchanged . . .

Both the same dry wit and the continual switching of languages are still in evidence when I spend time in his company these days, our hours together moistened perhaps by a glass of whisky or two. His eyes gleam when I tell of a relative of mine who settled in Port and disliked it so much that he kept returning to Dell in the hope that he might once again obtain a home there.

'Och, the man must have been mad. Mind you, most of you are up here.'

Or he talks of a man who always wore the same pair of brown trousers when he spent time on the island, year after year after year.

'One fellow said he looked like an Aberdeen Angus heifer, every time he bent down to squeeze inside one of the bothy doors.'

He also recalls his days as a young rebel. When psalms were sung and the Bible read aloud in Gaelic every morning and evening, one or two of the younger ones would spark each other off in mischief if proceedings went on too long. On one occasion, burning embers were scraped in the direction of an older man's trousers when he knelt in prayer, causing a great deal of smouldering and smoke when it came into contact with the gannet oil with which his clothes were soaked. On another, a camera was pointed at the same man when his eyes were squeezed shut in prayer. The button was clicked. The camera flashed. Through it all, the old man continued to mumble his prayer.

It was only after he had said his final 'Amen' that he made any comment on what had happened. 'There was strange lightning there a few moments ago. Just a flash and no rumble of thunder.'

His wits are sharp in other ways too. He talks about his childhood, growing up in Ness in the late 1950s and early 1960s and the want he sometimes experienced back then.

'There were three sources of food back then. Fish, mutton from our sheep and the guga. And there were times when we ran short of them. I remember once crying to my mother with the hunger and her telling me: "Wait until your Dad comes home from the fishing. We've got nothing to give you till then."' He sighs, thinking of that time. 'That was the way it was back in those days. And we weren't alone in being like that. There were lots of people in the district like that.'

I nodded, recalling my own experiences as a child some years later, when I would complain to my father about not having a TV set in our home, unlike some of the other lads whom I grew up alongside. I would bemoan the fact that I had to go and visit other houses to watch such cultural highlights as *The Man from U.N.C.L.E*, *Champion the Wonder Horse* or the European Cup Final between Celtic and Inter Milan. 'Why can't we be like everyone else?' I would mutter. 'Most people in the village have one by now?'

'We can't afford it,' he would say. 'When we can, we'll get one.'

In contrast, we were one of the first homes to purchase a new Tricity freezer. My father didn't like the smack of salt which, clearly, families like Dods's father, Murchadh Mhurdaidh's household stored their food within. It was a taste he had probably lost during his year in exile in Glasgow and East Kilbride. Soon that chest was full of lamb chops, loaves and vast quantities of fish – all put at risk these stormy nights when the wind would whip the only 'trees' on our landscape, tearing the cables strung along the branches of the electric poles down. Often these times coincided with the failure of the ferry to cross the seas from Kyle of Lochalsh or, later, Ullapool, giving us a good excuse to get rid of the frozen stores we had hoarded away for a stormy day.

It was, of course, even worse in our fathers' time. As a young student, I recall searching the pages of the *Glasgow Herald*, looking for any information that might be available about my native district. There were a few entries from the 1930s about want and hunger occurring in the district. Apparently, after a few years of the harvest failing and poor catches being obtained, a few lorryloads of venison were driven to the parish and given out to those who were suffering. Rightly or wrongly, I have an image of my dad as a young boy stretching out his hands for this food. Both he and his younger brother were born in the early and mid-1920s, and were slighter figures than the older members of their family – a fact that may or may not have been caused by a lack of food.

There is also still standing within the village today a monument to the poverty of earlier times – in the vicinity of the house and shop of an old spinster, Effie Murray, who used to live there with her sister and brother. A legend above one of her doors, fastened by a heavy padlock even in my youth, used to be repainted, neatly and precisely, by one of the exiled village-men returning each year from his home in the Central Belt. It read something on the lines of 'E. Murray – General Merchant – Licensed To Sell Tobacco and Methylated Spirits'. Another villager, Alasdair a' Bhocsair, pointed out the stone wall that used to stand around a field she owned to me one day when I went past, comparing it with the one constructed around his own family home.

'What's the difference between them?'

I noticed it right away. The wall around his home was built in an exact and uniform pattern, each stone lodged in exactly the right place. In the one circling Effie's old field, the rocks suddenly switched direction and pattern, heading one way and then another. At the far end, they had even toppled, falling down into the long grass.

'Good,' he said in his usual slightly clipped fashion. 'That wall's the work of many different hands. That's because it was the work of people who wanted to pay off their debts to the shop, doing that with labour rather than cash.'

Clearly, these more desperate times were over by the years when both Dods and I grew up but, filtered through our parents, they had an effect on us too. In Dods's case, it laid the foundations of the businessman he would become after his years on a fishing boat. He knew poverty and was anxious to shield himself from its effects. When I recall him next, he was married to Mary Joan Mackay, one of the few girls I grew up alongside, since there was a surplus of boys existing in that generation in South Dell. He was a father, too, to his son Bobby, now living in even more distant exile from Ness far south in Calanais, the centre of one of the Highlands and Islands' most well-known landmarks, the Callanish Stones. He also sold fish from one of the many mobile shops that travelled through the villages of Ness, making a living wage from the various business deals he made at that time. (This is a concept that a journalist from the *Guardian* appeared not to grasp when writing a report on the guga hunt for his paper a few years ago. He described Dods as running ' a mobile phone shop on Lewis'. One can imagine the conversations he thinks Dods must have with old men and women in his van. Samsung or Nokia? Vodaphone or Orange? And his customers gasping for O2 as they try to reply. 'I only came here for some haddock.') Honking his horn to summon them from their homes, both he and the people who come to him often swap bits and pieces of information together with the portions of ling, herring or mackerel he doles across the counter.

'*Càil às ùr?*' they might ask. 'Anything new?'

And either he or they would tell of some loss or piece of good fortune that had occurred to some household within the district. Such information about death or birth is the common currency of life in villages like these. Passed on from neighbour to neighbour within their island homes, it is exchanged as readily and eagerly as pound coins in the mobile shops that still occasionally trail through Ness.

It is the knowledge of the community he has gained through these years that has assisted Dods in his role as the man-in-charge of the Sulasgeir expedition. He is familiar with both the weaknesses and strengths of the families that come across his way. When asked how Dods and the other hunters choose the newcomers to accompany them, a gleam appears in his eye.

'No one is ever asked to come.'

'No one?'

'No. They come to us instead.'

'And how do you pick them from these ones?'

'We know which ones are suitable and which are not,' he smiles in reply.

From a glance at that wonderfully atmospheric photo in

Dods's home, however, it is possible to work out exactly the ones in the past who were most likely to be picked. Both their Christian and surnames – Murdo Campbell, Kenny Murray, Finlay Morrison and Angus Murdo Gunn – have, like my own, a long pedigree in the area. While names like Angus and Kenny are found throughout the Highlands, two of the forenames cluster in what is probably their greatest number in Lewis. 'Murdo', for instance, has its origins in the Gaelic *Murchadh* or 'sea-goer', while 'Finlay' comes to be in these parts due to the arrival of an evangelical preacher, Finlay Cook, many years ago in the district. As a result, it is perceived even within Lewis itself as a Ness name.

Together with, among others, the Macleods and Macaulays elsewhere in Lewis, the Morrisons are seen as being a Norse clan. Historically, they were based in the district, with, reputedly, their traditional centre being in the old fort at Dun Eistean, near Eoropie. The Murrays are not newcomers either. They have been around since the mid-seventeenth century, the days when lawbreakers were given 'sanctuary' in Ness by the Breve, linked with the Morrison family and the most important judge in the Outer Hebrides (hence the name of the legendary satirist from North Tolsta whom I mentioned earlier). As for the Gunns, Campbells and Macdonalds, all members of the group featured in *Sula: The Seabird Hunters of Lewis*, their names have been on class registers since schools were opened in these parts – and in the annals of the parish long before.

Yet one can be even more specific than this. In front of me, I have the list from 1983, signed by Alasdair Bàn, the previous holder of the licence to go to Sulasgeir. The addresses of the guga hunters form, in the most part, a tight circle around the northern tip of Ness. Of the ten taking part, three come from the village of Port of Ness; three from Lionel; one each from Skigersta, Adabrock and

Eoropie. The only one who comes from anywhere outside that web is Dods, the exile living in South Dell. Many of them, too, had fathers, brothers, uncles who made the same trip. These include men like Angus Murdo Gunn and Bobby Ruadh, two of Dods's right-hand men.

Another clue to what kind of men can be considered 'suitable' are the trades these men follow. In *Sula – The Seabird Hunters of Lewis*, they are described as 'coming from all walks of life in Lewis: joiners, fishermen, weavers, a lighthouse keeper, engineers and an electrician joined together . . . in a close-knit team'. Even at the time, the first part of this statement was open to argument. It is even more so now. There are fewer young men in Ness than there were 20 or 30 years ago; the population having continued its long and steady decline. Yet again, there is talk of my former primary school in Cross closing. A high percentage of those leaving school go onto further education, unlike the men in the years when Alasdair Bàn, and even Dods and I, grew up. Like the majority of workers everywhere in the United Kingdom in these times, most Nessmen now occupy white-collar jobs. They work in banks and offices; the Western Isles Council, Comhairle nan Eilean Siar, with its inevitable bureaucracy is the largest employer in the area. Generally speaking, these are not the men who set out to Sulasgeir. As one of the more recent arrivals on the rock put it to me, 'We don't need these people. We need ones who are used to physical labour and don't mind a little bit of sweat.'

There is little doubt that a great deal has changed over the 20 years since that list was compiled, in much the same way as Ness itself has changed. Nowadays, while it still matters that a man's blood is strong, it is even more important that his muscles are stronger. There are so few young males around that men from remote South Dell – some without any historical connection to the area – are made welcome to the team. Gaelic is heard – marginally! – less often. The prayers, psalms and readings from the Bible that precede the day's work are a little shorter and more hurried than they were decades before – though they still take place, echoing over the rock as they did centuries before.

There are, however, a number of factors which Ness today has in common with the district of decades before. One of the most important is Dods, more the lynchpin of the team than ever. It is his business skills that help organise the expedition. He makes the arrangements for it to take place, ensuring that correct forms are completed and provisions put in place for the journey.

'Sixteen kegs of water for drinking . . . Sixty bags of peat . . . Twenty to thirty bags of salt . . .'

There is, too, an order of meat from Cross Stores – all vacuum-packed these days instead of stored in salt, as in earlier times. There is flour, potatoes, tea, some butter to help them make scones, and duff – the traditional pudding of Ness – some vegetables . . . Dods laughs and talks about how priorities have changed in the 30-odd years since he first stepped on the island.

'In the '60s, cigarettes were all important. There was one time we ran out and this fellow started smoking tea-leaves in desperation, anything he could get his hands on . . . He would have tried to use sea-thrift if he thought it would have worked . . . Imagine his reaction when he found 20 fags in the bottom of a bag after he went ashore. He was dancing on the quay in annoyance . . . There was also this other time, when we were young lads, that we put earwigs in this man's pipe tobacco. And goodness knows there were more than enough earwigs on the island some years! Anyway, he smoked it quite happily. Just the thing. Didn't notice there was anything wrong . . .'

(Many of Angus Murdo Gunn's memories of his early years on the rock also centre on tobacco. One year, when they stayed some time longer on Sulasgeir than they had expected to, there was an economic crisis centring on this product. He recalls paying the most inflationary prices for cigarettes and using turf from the peat instead of tobacco to make 'roll-your-own' cigarettes.)

Once Dods has stopped chuckling at the memory, he continues with his list, trying to recall where he left off.

'Sleeping bags . . . Ropes . . . Poles . . . Ideal milk . . .'

Again, Dods interrupts himself, recalling another story.

'There was one time we had this fellow acting as the cook. I recall this day watching him taking a knife and hammering again and again at the lid of the can. When I asked him what was wrong, he looked very worried. "We'll have to go home," he said. "It looks as if this milk has turned. Nothing but lumps in it. Don't know how we can get by without it." It was then that one of us picked up the can he had been trying to open. "Ambrosia Creamed Rice", it said on the label.'

We laugh again, especially because the gentleman at the centre of the story had a close connection to my own family. While he is relaxed, I decide to ask one of the two questions I have been saving for him all night. The first one had been directed to me by a gentleman in Glasgow who had quizzed me about the guga hunt one night. I remembered not answering him very well. Aware of my own ignorance about the subject, I stammered and stuttered in reply, taking refuge in the pint of beer that had been before me at the time.

'How would you defend yourself against the charge that your actions are endangering the survival of the bird?'

'Och, we're doing nothing of the kind. If anything, there are more birds now than ever. There are around 8,000 pairs of gannets on the island and we take 2,000 chicks. Yet the fact is that for all that these birds live for 20 or so years, their survival rate as chicks is very low. Only 5 to 6 per cent of them are going to survive anyway. And if they lived, there would be too many. There's little enough room left on the rock as it is.' He pauses for a moment, taking a sip from the cup of tea that Mary Joan has just provided. 'Otherwise, there would be a huge population explosion, and they're already fighting over sites. Some of them very fierce fights, too, with no quarter spared.'

It is at this stage in the evening I tell Dods of a book, published in 1951, I had just finished reading while researching the gannet colonies of the north of Scotland. Written by Andrew T. Cluness, it had been entitled *The Shetland Isles*. In its pages, he points out that at the beginning of the twentieth century, even ' a stray solan was an object of interest' in the nation's far north. Fifty years later, there were two large colonies in the Noop of Noss and Hermaness. The author then takes on the role of prophet, declaring that they will soon 'make the islands their principal breeding grounds' as they are unmolested there, unlike at the Bass Rock or Sulasgeir.

'Well, he got that wrong, didn't he?' he chuckles.

'Aye.'

'There's no danger of the guga dying out in these parts at the moment. Or anywhere else.'

'Just as well for you,' I say, referring to the way Dods has taken a slide-show around many parts of Scotland, talking about the way he and his fellow-Nessmen cull the young gannets. Though I have never seen it, I can imagine he's excellent at doing this. His enthusiasm for Sulasgeir has already been on display so many times during the evening.

'Yes. I really enjoy doing that.'

'And what about going out there, Dods? What do you really enjoy about that?'

His brow furrows for a moment. 'Well, Donald, do you know what I enjoy most about that? It's that sense I have of following in the steps of my ancestors. Of going over places like Sròn na Lice, Sgeir an Teampaill, Mullach an Eilein and thinking to myself I'm going over the same places they did and doing the same things they did when they were here. It's like being away from the ordinary world, the world of here and now. And you know something, Donald?'

He looks at me expectantly.

'That's not a feeling you get in many places these days.'

'Not even South Dell?'

And then he lets me into a big secret, coming out with a remark I can't imagine the Dods of ten years before even thinking, far less confessing.

'Och, it's not such a bad place. I'm happy enough here. In fact, I don't think I would go back to Port these days. I know the people here nowadays too well to want to live anywhere else.'

Yet for all our protestations, it could argued that men like Dods and I are among the rare Nessmen who are in exile from our ancestral lands. Most of our neighbours have – as I have noted elsewhere – long and well-established connections with the area. Bearing surnames like Morrison and Macleod, they have been there for countless generations. This is not the case with men whose second name is, say, Gunn, MacFarlane or even Murray. While we have been here for a number of centuries now, we are comparatively recent interlopers to the district of Ness. And while I cannot dare to speak for Dods's kin, it is certainly true for my family that our arrival was in fairly inauspicious circumstances. It occurred some 400 years ago when one – if not more – of my forefathers became involved in a touch of skulduggery and derring-do in the Dornoch Firth area of Easter Ross; an act they performed not under my present unsullied identity, but under the darker and murkier name of Macphail.

Or to be even more specific, John Roy Macphail. Together with William Murray, a man who later became known as 'An Gobha Gorm', a celebrated blacksmith in Ness, he was involved in a bizarre assassination attempt on three members of a prominent family in Dornoch during the early years of the seventeenth century. Their targets were the brothers William, Thomas and Charles Pape. They were a family resented by many in Dornoch, especially for the power and influence exercised by them in the area. They held important positions in the region, with William and Thomas ministers in Dornoch and Rogart respectively. Charles was Sheriff-Clerk of Sutherland. According to the folklore of that time, they made full and sometimes improper use of the authority they had been granted.

Add to this mix another ingredient – one that fuels a thousand quarrels even today. There seems little doubt that John Roy was a man who liked his drink. In fact, he enjoyed it so much that he was prevented from consuming any more by the mistress in charge of a local hostelry. She regarded him as a 'brawling fellow' and, as if to underline the truth of her description, a heated argument arose within or outside her premises. It was one that led to the assassination attempt on members of the Pape family in the local churchyard later that evening.

Knives were drawn; tempers triggered. By the end of that evening, the Sheriff-Clerk was lying dead among the head-stones and his two brothers also appeared to be fatally wounded (they recovered later). By the following morning, the chase was on. One can only imagine the uproar that occurred. Shouts ringing out; bells doled and clanged; alarms raised; a terrible hullabaloo was created. There is nothing, after all, that disturbs authority more than the killing of one of their own, and here were three of their number attacked near the church walls. John Roy and his accomplices fled the area in fear of their lives, knowing that more than church bells would swing if they were captured.

It is at this point that they are rumoured to have escaped across the North Sea to Holland, part of a great deal of movement that occurred during the seventeenth century between the Low Countries – including the Netherlands, Belgium and even parts of northern France – and the eastern coast of Scotland. (We can see this in names like Fleming, Moyes and many others in areas like Fife and Edinburgh and the presence of a man with the surname Maakay in the orange shirt of the Dutch national football team.) One reason for this is that the United Provinces – as that area was known then – was regarded as an extremely tolerant place. According to some, it was the only part of the world where no one ever troubled a man over whether he was a Muslim, Christian or Jew. In what was at that time one of the great trading empires of the world, he was judged simply on the kind of human being he was.

Side by side with that liberal view of the world, it was also Calvinist with – in some parts of the country – much of the same strong sense of the Sabbath that is found in the part of the world where Mackay and Murray later settled. According to folklore, they reached Lewis by obtaining a boat and heading in the direction of the north-west coast of Scotland, rounding the Butt and landing on the beach at Tràigh Shanndaigh in Eoropie. They settled there, doubtless marrying local women. There is little doubt either that they were valuable acquisitions to the community, especially William Murray, the man that came to be known as the *Gobha Gorm* or the 'Blue Smith' – a nickname he gained from the blue scars on his face, caused by sparks from his fire. The iron he hammered out on the anvil of his smithy was reputed to be of far greater quality than any of his rivals'. Allegedly, this was because of some magic ingredient he added to the flames. However, the truth is that its strength was much more likely to have been obtained from the coal he imported secretly from Easter Ross. (Brora, a short distance from his own native township of Dornoch, was the only real coal-mine that ever operated in the Highlands.

It opened in 1529 and only finally closed four centuries later in 1968 – at that time being one of the few independently run coal mines in Britain.)

In landing in Eoropie, these men took advantage of the sanctuary that was granted to those fleeing the justice of the times to arrive in Ness. In 'The Early History Of Ness – an Interpretation', a paper written by the historian Domhnall Uilleam Stiùbhart and published by Comunn Eachdraidh Nis, we are told of this tradition operating within the district where those who had arrived there '*am freasdail lamh dearg*' – or 'in consequence of a red hand' – were granted protection by the Macleods of Lewis.

Apparently, there was similar protection on offer on the other side of the Minch in the parish of Durness at the tip of north-west Sutherland, with one man, at least, leaving Lewis to settle there after being responsible for a number of murders on the island.

The sense of being different that policy might have engendered has sometimes produced a way of thinking that, perhaps, has marked Ness's own perception of itself for centuries. It has occasionally been remarked upon by others. Sometimes it has even inspired its own brand of fiction, centring occasionally on the guga hunt itself. There is the legend, for instance, that the boat bearing Bonnie Prince Charlie to Scotland passed a vessel crewed by men from Ness. One was setting out in a journey that would end in the blood and defeat of the battlefield at Culloden; the other was en route to Sulasgeir. Rumour has it that the Nessmen refused to join the Young Pretender to the throne on board his ship. However, they were the first Scotsmen to see him, acknowledging him briefly as his boat sailed in a southerly direction to the opposite end of the Outer Hebrides. Prince Charles Edward Stewart would find willing recruits in that part of the world. Some would be left behind when he fled Drumossie Moor. Others would accompany him when he fled that part of the world for France.

There are many myths about the island, though a number come from the pens of visiting journalists. One was a Canadian journalist called Halton who, after spending a few days on the island, wrote an account of the worship of the sea-god Shony that occurred there. He reported how he had seen a group of Nessmen wading into the sea to pour ale into the waves and increase the bounty of seaweed for the island's crops. After this, according to him, they spent the night dancing around the church in Eoropie, behaving in much the same way as Martin Martin reported them as acting some 250 years before – though even then, he had the grace to point out that the practice had died out long before 1700. In another report, appearing in the *Sunday Times* in the late 1970s, another journalist recorded, stony-faced, the rumour that there were more blow-up dolls in Ness than in any other part of Britain – further proof if yet more were required that one should not believe every fantasy conjured up over a glass of beer or whisky.

Yet occasionally the people of Ness have earned headlines for themselves. A number of these arose, naturally enough, in the two areas of life which the journalists of the Central Lowlands have always been fixated on when they write about life in the Western Isles – drink and religion. Unique to Ness is the tradition of the bothan – the speakeasies-cum-shebeens that existed in a so-called 'dry' district from the end of the Second World War to the tail-end of the 1970s. They were illegal drinking places on the edge of villages like Eoropie, Adabrock, Habost, Swainbost, Cross . . . Regularly raided by police as they were, the courtroom trials that took place afterwards provided entertainment for years for consumers of Scotland's tabloid newspapers, even supplying much of the material for cartoons like the *Daily Record*'s Angus Og. Their readership would titter to themselves as they read about the illegal stocks of Dewars and Trawler Rum supposedly stacked within the bothan walls, piled underneath its floorboards or occasionally concealed – precariously! – within the rafters of the building.

And all this was made even more hilarious for mainland readers because this hard-drinking took place against a background of what was perceived by some as grim piety and moral rectitude, a stern and conventional Calvinist society. However, this is to overlook the fact that the Church in Ness was fashioned by its own brand of 'rebel' – who, in the context of much of twentieth-century life in Britain, are as out of step and awkward as any of the 'bothaneers'. They retain the Kng James Bible and reject the accompaniment of any musical instrument in their worship.

In doing this, they are following a long tradition. It was in the sprit of rebellion, after all, that religious groups like the Free Church were created. In Ness, as in much of the Highlands and Islands, the Free Church was born in response to the way in which the Established Church was perceived as being in favour of both landlords and the state at the time of the Clearances. Unlike most institutions in the nineteenth century, it was seen as being both radical and democratic, opposed to any of the powers that presumed themselves to be so.

There are times in its history when this aspect of Ness life has generated its own acres of newsprint. A particular cause of this was during one of the interminable religious disputes that have blighted and scarred the district's history. Around the turn of the nineteenth century, Ness even earned the dubious honour of being the last place in Lewis to have been visited by armed police and a warship. This occurred when the Free Church, born after an earlier Disruption, was in itself 'disrupted' as the result of a union with the United Presbyterian Church. In Lewis, unlike the rest of Scotland, the majority of people rejected this arrangement, remaining in the Free Church as, by and large, they do today. In Lewis, too, the quarrel between the two sides was deep and bitter, with neighbour turned against neighbour, father against son.

No more so anywhere else in Lewis than Ness, where, apparently, the Free Church congregation barricaded the building against those who had gone into the union, refusing to obey an interdict granted against them by the court. The *Stornoway Gazette*, in its issue dated 24 December 1937, records what happened in that period, reporting how:

The tension which existed at that time necessitated the stationing of four police officers at Ness, and when feeling was at its height, the police station and Manse were damaged, the windows of leading figures in the disputes were damaged, and cornricks set on fire. Eventually HMS *Bellona* was despatched to Stornoway with eighty constables recruited from several Scottish forces, and under the command of Sheriff Squair. Every available conveyance in Stornoway was commissioned to bring the police from Stornoway to Ness but fortunately there was no clash, and after spending a night in the Church at Cross, most of the police were withdrawn , and the ill-feeling passed off and a more reasonable spirit prevailed.

It was a story that one newspaper, *The World,* summed up in a little poem in its pages:

NEWS FROM NESS
Eagerly to church you press,
(Holy Ness!)
To your minister's distress,
(Wilful Ness!)
You the union would suppress:

(Bitter Ness!)
Came *Bellona* HMS,
(Lawless Ness!)
Soon your errors you confess:
(Gentle Ness!)
And this comment we express –
(Foolish Ness!)

It could be argued that 'wilfulness' is a characteristic that has always marked the people of Ness. This wilfulness can be seen in the number of distinctive Presbyterian churches within the community – four at the moment, and counting! It can be seen in the tenacity with which it clings to Gaelic, for all that throughout the last century the forces of history were opposed to its survival, attempting to grind it out of existence.* A similar 'cussedness' can be found, too, in men like Dods continuing to uphold the ancient tradition of the 'guga hunt' when all the prejudices and assumptions of the urban world would compel him to bring it to an end. The men and women who argue for this forget that his knowledge of his local environment is based, not on any glib or superficial understanding, but an awareness of the generations of experience which men like him have gained from living in a place like Ness. One can imagine that if those opposed to the hunt ever came into contact with him, their prejudices and ignorance would become so obvious within five minutes that their conversation would grind swiftly and embarrassingly to a halt.

Evidence of this strong tie between man and rock can be seen in one of the stories of Angus Murdo Gunn from Lionel. As a child, he recalls his own grandfather in his 80s being told that someone had pulled out of the expedition at the last moment.

* There is more than a little irony in this. Ness, as the most 'Scandinavian' area of the Western Isles, was also the last place to hold onto another island tongue – a variety of the Nordic language, Norn.

'That means we're a man short,' his informant declared.

A few moments later, Grandad disappeared, only to return a few moments later from his bedroom with a pack of his belongings in his hand. It took a great deal of time and argument to persuade the old man that his years of going to Sulasgeir were over, that, perhaps, his feet were a bit too old and faltering to take part in the hunt.

Clearly, men like Dods and Angus Murdo have an intimacy with their own locality that few nowadays in our contemporary existence can dream of possessing. It is an intimacy that cannot be found in books or any internet search engine. Instead, it is accrued over generations, taking time – not only Dods's own but that of those who have gone before him. The geography and history of the land thrive within him, born in moments like one back in 1919 when his grandfather Murdie, or Murdo, Macfarlane was among the guga hunters crewing the *Guide Me,* which had a close escape that year. There were five others with him – including three Campbell brothers from the district.

Labourers working on Lord Leverhulme's (ultimately unfinished) road around the far north coast of Lewis – some of whom must have lost relatives over the preceding years – watched the *Guide Me* below them as it sought to master the waves that were threatening to overwhelm it. They dreaded the thought of more men being drowned that day as they saw it nearly being swamped as a 'broken sea passed over the tarpaulin covering the birds'. Murdie and the other men baled out the boat with water barrels as they struggled to keep it afloat, looking like insects to the men on land as they tussled and wrestled with the force of the sea. They could only look on as 'the mast thwart slackened and was lashed by a chain', praying as they hoped the crew would win a battle that had too often been lost by the men of their community in recent years.

And then the moment must have come when the men on

shore either cheered or simply sighed with relief, when they realised that Murdie and the other men were safe and sailing to shore with their rich harvest of gugas – for all that their vessel still bore the scars of its struggle. When the *Guide Me* was later broken up, it was found that her keel was badly broken, marked by damage that probably occurred at this time.

It wasn't the first such drama that had occurred over the previous years. In 1912, the survival of the men who had voyaged to Sulasgeir had been uncertain for a time. In 1916, the *Thelma* and the *Good Luck* had arrived safely on shore, but only after a long struggle with the waves. Throughout these years, too, in the Great War that lasted between 1914 and 1918, there had been the awesome toll of young lives lost at sea in places as far apart as Orkney and the Dardanelles – the names and dates scrawled in black between the covers of the family Bibles opened daily in island homes. And, of course, there was in everyone's minds the memory of the *Iolaire*, with its over 200 men lost some months earlier, at the beginning of 1919.

The fact that men like Dods, Murdie's direct descendant, returned to sea and Sulasgeir on many occasions after experiences like these occurring in their family and the community as a whole shows that sometimes men can be more resilient than their vessels, that blood and spirit can be tougher to crack than wood . . .

3

Men on Rock

A WOMAN CONSIDERS A SEABIRD HUNTER'S MARRIAGE PROPOSAL

White brought about her wedding;
a surf-like-whirl that sent her reeling
in days following his return.
The thought of him shivering on that rock,
wind and water crashing on his back,
forced her to slowly learn
how much she'd come to care for him,
his quiet strength, sure-footed ways;
her head swirling like his own one must have done
when he balanced those few inches over waves,
fearing slips, small hesitations like one she made
the first time that he asked her – afraid,
she slowly shook her head.
But now she drew back words
that restrained her like a rope tight-tugged
and trusted life to him instead;
a weighing-up of hopes and fears,
this sharing of both days and nights,
like the way both smiles and tears
mingle in those hours a bride wears white.

'Mattresses. Sleeping bags. Plastic sheeting. Tarpaulin to spread over the roofs and help keep the earwigs away . . .'

Norman (or Tormod) is giving me a similar list to the one that Dods provided when I spoke to him a few days before about the trip to Sulasgeir. Before I arrived, Norman had been indulging in the type of conversation the people of

South Dell had been involved in for centuries – talking about one or two sheep that had wandered off the moor in recent weeks. He and his next-door neighbour were puzzled about their whereabouts, wondering where on earth they might have gone. I listened to place-names I have heard in these talks since I was a child echo once again.

However, for once, the conversation didn't last too long. I had come to speak to Norman about the 12 years he had gone to Sulasgeir. Only the second man or so to go out and hunt the young gannets from a village traditionally associated with sheep rather than fishing, he is undoubtedly also the longest lasting 'guga hunter' in South Dell. Norman only stopped going when his new job on the oil rig prevented him heading out to the rock.

'Do you miss it?' I asked him.

'Aye. I do. I enjoyed my time there with the boys.'

And it is clear from a short time in Norman's company that the 'boys' must miss him too. A quiet, amiable individual, he is an excellent worker, neat, precise and industrious in all that he does. His employers out on the North Sea where he has worked the last few years have appreciated this fact. Maintaining lifeboats on oilrigs, he was only there a short time before he was promoted to the post of senior service engineer – recognition not only of the care with which he undertakes his work, but also of his tact in dealing with others. In his spare time, while he is at home, he is also a volunteer member of the Ness Fire Brigade. Its star is visible on the front of his grey sweatshirt, and he takes great pride in telling me he has worked in that service for 20 years or so.

'You must have seen a few things during your time there,' I say.

'Aye . . . And one or two I'd prefer not to have seen.'

His exactness is clear, too, in the way he spends much of his time checking the engine of his car, making certain that it is ticking over. It is apparent in the manner he paints the gates and fences around his family home, ensuring each tiny nook and cranny is covered by his brush. It is even obvious in how he has waited until his early 40s before contemplating marriage. Engaged to Christine MacAulay, a girl from the village of Breasclete, whose brother is already married in this village, it is a step that, cautious at all times, he plans to take next year.*

Remembering how I used to come across him in the local pub during his early 20s, girls flocking around him, I tease him about this.

'You must have had plenty of offers.'

'Perhaps,' his blue eyes gleam, 'but I was always wary of them. And in one or two cases, I was quite right to be.'

He winks while I laugh, enjoying his humour.

His care is even apparent in his speech. He talks accurately and quietly, making his points precisely and unobtrusively, weighing up each word to ensure he is communicating its meaning clearly. It is, perhaps, this that makes him seem more youthful than one would expect someone with his four decades to be. For all that he spent a number of years selling meat as a butcher going around Ness in a mobile shop, there is nothing brash or loud about him. Instead, there is a tentative quality, reinforced by his wisps of fair hair, pale colouring, the nervousness of the smile that appeared when I asked him to talk about his years going out for the guga.

'Och, no. There must be someone better than me around to do that!'

There wasn't. I knew when I asked him that this would be his response – a modest and diffident reaction. There is even

---

* By the time of publication, this event had already taken place. Tormod and Christine MacAulay were married in Stornoway on 14 March 2008. Congratulations and good luck were sent out from the majority of those in the district – with the exception, according to his brother, Calum, of Tormod's first love: the New Holland tractor he has spent much of the last year restoring.

a similar reply when I ask him if he sings as well as his
father, the man I knew as Dolly Chaluim, a former merchant seaman who died a number of years ago and whose
voice was appreciated by many in the district.

'No. I can hardly sing a note.'

I suspect he may be maligning himself but I have no way
of knowing, learning to appreciate him instead for the virtue
I know he possesses – the plain, concise way he explains
what the men do when they reach Sulasgeir on the boat.

'We leave Stornoway on the boat at just after midnight.
Depending on the weather, we arrive in Sulasgeir just after
five o'clock in the morning, tying up in the geo, making sure
it's safely anchored there. And then the unloading begins.
That takes about four hours or so. It's quite a load.
Mattresses. Sleeping bags. Plastic sheeting. Tarpaulin to
spread over the roofs and help keep the earwigs away.
We hold that down with fishing nets and heavy stones.
Tools. Boxes full of food. Nowadays much of the meat is
vacuum-packed. Keeps it fresh. There's even some curry
sauces now. Not just corned beef like the old days! Some
fishing rods to help vary the diet. A car battery for the radio
and a mast for the signal. Sixteen kegs of water for drinking
. . . Sixty bags of peat . . . Thirty to forty bags of salt . . .'

I point out that in the past, the men only took one keg or so
of water, relying on rain to keep thirst at bay. Sometimes they
would use the scummy water that gathered in rock-pools if
there were rare occasions when the rain didn't come.

'That's certainly changed.' He said. 'Nowadays we always leave four behind us when we go. That's in case the
unlikely happens and someone ends up being marooned on
Sulasgeir. It would need to be boiled, though, before they
ever drank it. One of our lads took it and his stomach was
upset for a long time after it.'

'Poor soul.'

He ignores my interruption. 'The last thing to be brought

ashore is a rubber dinghy. We tie that up at the geo in case of emergency, hoping that it never has to be used. And then after we have a cup of tea we begin the real work, hoisting some of the smaller items up the cliff-face, making a chute and hauler to help us with the bigger things – like the bags of peats, for instance, and the kegs of water. They're lighter than they used to be, made of aluminium instead of steel or wood, but they're still heavy enough.'

'How do you make the chute?'

'It takes around half a day for four men to do that. We leave the materials for it on the island each year, all stacked and tidied away beside one of the bothys. The chute's just like something you might find in a gold rush somewhere, in the days when they were panning for gold. It's made of wooden planks, around 38 yards long and a half-yard in width. It's all nailed together and fixed on good, strong legs. And then we use this woollen dolly on castors, with a hauling line to keep it in place, to whirl the larger objects up and down. We start with the heaviest and most precious thing we take on land with us. The water barrels. Without them we couldn't survive. Then the other things are brought up. The peats. The mattresses . . . We do this as carefully as we can. Some of the men can remember a time when the rope snapped and a barrel went hurtling down towards them. Some of the older fellows have never raced as quickly as they did that day. Anything to get out of the way . . .'

For years before the introduction of this system, the men had to haul everything up the crags. Slowly, painstakingly, wearily, the whole exercise would take place inch by sweaty inch. It was worse because at that time the squad consisted chiefly of older men, lacking the strength to do this with anything like the eagerness of youth. It is a change that Norman recognises.

'The problem years ago was that some of the men were too old going there. They hung on to their places year after year, long after it would have been more sensible for them to let it go. It made no sense. The younger the squad, the fitter they are. The loads are far easier for young men to carry than for the old.'

Nevertheless, as Norman would be first to recognise, it was the wit and intelligence of the older men that made life much easier for the younger squads who go there today. In particular, it was the work of William Macleod or 'Uilleam Iain Mhurdo' from Port. Employed for years in the Post Office, he was the one who recognised the value and worth of some of the work practices he experienced there and how they could be adapted for the hunt. It was his ingenuity, together with some of the 'left-over' materials from his employment, that lay behind the design of the chute. He was, too, the architect of another form of technology used on the island – the 'Blondin'. Again, the Royal Mail played its part in this development, named in tribute to the first man ever to cross the Niagara Falls by tightrope in 1859, his fame clearly spreading even as far as Ness long after that time. Admittedly, the men of Ness never perform quite the same stunts with their tightrope as Blondin did all these years ago. It is never employed to allow a man to stand balancing on a chair on a single 3-inch hemp-cord, over 1,000 feet long and 160 feet above not only a thundering flood of water but a crowd of 100,000 people as well. Unlike him, they do not cook meals suspended there or carry others on their backs across its width.

Yet in terms of their lives on Sulasgeir, 'Blondin' probably engendered the same sense of awe and amazement as that tightrope-walker must have caused when he first stepped out over Niagara. Again, William used the tools of his trade to develop the pulley-system that stretches now over part of the island, supplying surplus gear like hooks, mailbags and wire to create a method by which the young gannets can be taken from the edges of the island across water and into the centre, where the plucking can occur. It was not an immediate success. When the weight of these birds was first placed in a bag, dangling on its hook from the wire, there would be a loud banshee-like screech as it headed, perhaps, to the central collecting area they call the Factory – a progress that ended with another loud shriek, an oath, perhaps, or two, as the procedure ended in disaster. It was all evidence of the fact that, as Alasdair Bàn recalled in his conversation with me another evening, 'there wasn't a brake on Blondin first of all'. That had to be developed later – the problem solved when it was decided that Blondin was henceforth to become a form of transportation not dissimilar to the one that operates a funicular railway. One package goes one way; one travels the other. By this means, balance is maintained. A brake is set in place. Gravity does much of the hard work in bringing the bird to the centre, for all that there are occasions when even it goes wrong and the sacks land on the rocks below.

It is to the edges that the men go first the morning after all is set in place for their stay on the islands. Dods and one of his compatriots, often the tall, well-set figure of Angus 'Bobby Ruadh' Morrison, walk slowly around the Sgeir, trying to see in which area most young birds are ready to be slaughtered. They take their time doing this, making their way carefully across a rock-strewn landscape where even the mere act of walking requires precision and balance. They judge the weather – which places it would be safe to go on a certain day when the wind might be over-strong and gusting from a particular direction, or the rocks might be slippy beneath their feet. They note down, too, the numbers in the various nesting-places and also where most are ready to be killed. These are identified as the 'tre-tim' or three tufts; the guga that has lost most of its down and not yet turned completely dark. The latter, blacker bird – slightly older than the rest of the chicks and having acquired the colouring of a year-old bird – has lost much of the fat many in Ness prize upon their plates while those still covered with down – the younger ones – produce little meat. The others wait for an end to their deliberations, watching them make their way around the island.

Much of both this and later parts of the expedition is directed by the most experienced of the guga hunters. Clearly this includes Dods, who has journeyed to the Rock for a number of decades now, but also others he praised during his hours in my company. These include Angus Murdo Gunn, Wee Ally Macleod, Murdo 'Am Bèibidh' Morrison and Bobby Ruadh. Mainstays of the group, they help ensure that everything is being done properly, that people are safe and the right numbers of birds are being killed. They check the last figures incessantly while they are working, ensuring they keep within their quota.

During this journey around Sulasgeir, they are often surrounded by small cairns of rocks and stone fingers pointing skywards. These were set in place by their ancestors, the men who visited the *Sgeir* before. Each time they journey there, they place one more stone on top of the rock that lies at its foundation. The final stone on the peak of their offering is the one that marks the splitting of the ways, the last parting between man and rock when a hunter turns his back on Sulasgeir for the last time.

These towers of stones are almost ever-present in the northern landscapes of the world. As I noted before, they are on the moorland of Lewis, a way of providing landmarks across the long and indistinct centre of the island. (According to a neighbour, my great-grandfather, the man they called 'Stuffan', set one in place – a white pinnacle of rock which he carried for some distance across heather before finally setting it down on some small mound that rose a little above the monotonous, level, low-lying land of the moor.) They appear, too, in the Faroe Islands. Known as 'Stone Forests' in these more northerly parts, their strange foliage of gneiss and quartz stands impervious to cold or rain.

And they are in Iceland too, dotted around the landscape. Nowadays half the Icelandic population lives around the nation's capital, Reykjavik, but at the turn of the nineteenth century, when the celebrated American folklorist Nelson Annandale visited that country, they were a far more scattered – and less prosperous – group of people than they are today. Since the period between 870 and 930, when the country was first settled, human existence there has been fragile, with periods of famine regularly reducing the number of their population. The land is largely infertile. Driving from the airport in Keflavik to the nation's capital when I visited, it was easy to feel that I was still travelling across the Ness moor, for all there was clearly volcanic rock strewn on either side of the road. Only the sea around the island is a rich, if unreliable, resource. Not for nothing does the country's most celebrated novelist, Halldór Laxness, put these words into the mouth of the central female character of his novel *Salka Valda*: 'When all is said and done, life is first and foremost salt fish.'

And seabirds too. Icelanders have in their past (and even today in some cases) enjoyed a wide range of them – from puffin to smoked cormorant; eider duck to guillemot (either black, bridled or ringed); three or four different types of gulls, kittiwake or . . . gannet. This shared palate is hardly surprising. With the exception of a plume of volcanic smoke or two, there are similarities between the Hebridean and Icelandic environments. Both are peripheral; both partly dependent on the sea. There may even be similarities in the ethnic mix – a mingling of two separate traditions, Celt and Norse. A recent study on 'Blood group variation in the Isle of Lewis' published by the University of Aberdeeen discovered that the people at the northern end of the Hebrides were unlike much of both western and eastern North

European populations, though they showed 'a common but distant ancestry with Icelanders'.

There are more connections than distant blood-ties, however, between Hebrideans and the people who live even farther north. Nelson Annandale spent much of his visit gathering folklore from an area called the Vestmanneyjar, a small group of rocks and islets lying six miles off the coast of South Iceland. In his own words, the islands 'owe their name to the fact that in the ninth century a party of Irish or Hebridean slaves who had murdered their master took refuge in them for a while'.

The more romantic might be tempted to suppose that some of those who fled there were native to Ness. This is especially the case when we discover that in 1838, when Annandale went to Sulnasker ('Gannet Skerry'), the fowlers made special prayers before they ascended the rock. They also left money and 'iron nails and other trifles' on a cairn they called the Skerry Priest which represented a legendary giant who – at one time – lived upon the rock. He had first shown them a way to climb the skerry and would call on them for centuries when he wished them to come and take the birds on Sulnasker. At these times, they were certain of a good catch, a fine harvest of their equivalent of the guga. Yet if they ever arrived without his invitation they would obtain no birds, 'and some disaster generally overtook them'.

Annandale goes on to make further connections; some of which might directly relate to the hunters' practice of placing a stone on a cairn each time they visit. He notes that this custom might be linked to 'the belief that certain rocks are haunted by a giant or a spirit, who must be propitiated or overcome before the birds on the cliff can be taken'. He claims, too, that this belief 'was at one time common in Scandinavian Europe [and] the Hebrides, where the birding season formerly commenced with an elaborate ceremony of propitiation'.

According to him, this could be related to the 'dangerous

occupation' of capturing birds that breed on cliffs, a way of giving thanks to ancient gods and ensuring that life and limb are protected while stepping out on crags and ledges to catch wild sea-fowl.

There is little doubt that the guga hunters are particularly skilled in rock-climbing – a fact acknowledged by the celebrated climber and Ullapool doctor Tom Patey, who was the first man in modern times to manage a similar feat to one performed by a man from Ness, Donald Macdonald from Lionel (known as Dòmhnall Seònaid) way back in 1876. In 1967, Patey managed to arrive on the crest of the Stack of Handa or Stac an t-Seabhaig, a 126-yard high tower of sandstone that stands, at its narrowest, some 26 yards away from Handa Island off the north-west coast of Sutherland. He succeeded in crossing this traverse by means of a 196-yard nylon rope that stretched taut across the top of the Stac, spanning from one side of the geo that partly encloses it to the other

It was the bird-life that skirled and soared around its cliffs and stack that Donald sought, rather than the physical challenge. Flocks and multitudes are to be seen at the Stack of Handa. They include, according to Hamish Haswell-Smith's *The Scottish Islands*, 12 species of nesting seabirds including razorbill, kittiwake, puffin, shag, and a huge 'population of guillemot – at 100,000 strong, the largest colony in Britain'. In order to harvest these birds, Donald crossed this gap in the style, perhaps, of the original Blondin, pulling himself the length of a rope across an 80-foot chasm dividing the stac from the island of Handa, some 2 miles in diameter and at that time a place populated by some 200 souls. Only the strength of his arms and legs kept him from wave and rock below, a triumph over the tug of gravity described by the naturalist and historian Tom Weir in one of his many articles. He notes that the men of Ness:

. . . had summed up the geography of the big inlet around the Great Stack and seen that if a long rope were walked round it, then pulled tight in a straight line, it would pass over the nearest bit of the Great Stack. Donald Macdonald was the fowler chosen to make a landing on the stack once the rope was in position. Donald hooked his feet up and locked them together so that the rope took his weight, then hand-slid his horizontal body along the rope.

From this point onwards, Donald succeeded in setting up a block-and-tackle rig to allow the others over to harvest the puffins and guillemots nesting on the face of that stac – an accomplishment so miraculous that some mountaineering journals ascribe it to the mystical people who once settled St Kilda, as if they were the only race of men capable of such an act. They do this blindly in the face of all the evidence, giving Donald Macdonald's name yet failing to note that none of that surname ever lived among the MacQueens, Fergusons and other families who once lived within the houses of Village Bay.

In his tribute to Donald MacDonald's achievement, the celebrated climber Chris Bonington linked the people of Ness with those who had once lived in that most westerly isle of the Hebrides. Praising both groups, he noted that 'making this crossing was indeed remarkable, but when you think of it, islanders were all amazingly agile and venturous on the sea-cliffs, harvesting these birds'. It is, perhaps, worthwhile to put this Tyrolean – the technical term mountaineers use for crossing a traverse by this method – in context. In the following decade, the sport of mountaineering was in its infancy; Nape's Needle in the Lake District still just about to be climbed.

But islanders climbed cliffs and crossed chasms, not as a pastime but in order to obtain food to eat. Those who clamber the rocks of Sulasgeir today do so for much the same reasons. The people of Ness – and sometimes those beyond its borders – relish the taste of the guga and the bird must be captured and brought back to their plates.

In my family house, Norman explains the procedures that lie behind the killing of the birds. He takes his time doing this, seeking to make sure I understand the entire process that is involved.

'There are a few things that are essential during our time there. A good, strong pair of boots with grips to avoid slipping on the rocks. Rope to keep you tight and harnessed, sometimes to one another when you're making your way across a tricky ledge. And the catching pole.'

'What's that like?'

'It's a long pole with a spring-loaded jaw on top. Once they used to have a pole with a noose attached to its end, but they stopped using that a few years ago.'

I nod. I suspect that it was William Macleod who developed this too; another innovation courtesy of Her Majesty's mail.

'It's this we use to catch the young guga, snatching it from its nest and lifting it across to another man who strikes it dead with one blow from a heavy stick. A moment or two and it's passed to some other guy. This time the bird's head is removed, taking care to leave a long neck. The whole thing takes place as quickly and painlessly as possible.'

It is amazing how speedily the men move when they do this. Grouped together, they form a tide of yellow oilskins and multi-coloured boiler suits that disturb the adult gannets with their slow and steady progress across the rocks, making their way, perhaps, in the direction of Sulasgeir's automatic lighthouse, where many nests can be found. White wings flocking above them, they surge through the birds, killing some 200 or so in around half an hour. A short time later and their harvest of sea-fowls is collected together. Sometimes a

Blondin is used to carry them from these points. At other times, they are brought to a central place by hand.

The birds are plucked at places like Mullach an Eilein, the high point of the island, the following day, after rigor mortis has set in. There is a reason for this choice of location: the wind is at its strongest here, allowing the plumage to be stripped away easily. Sometimes, though, on the still days that occasionally occur out on the rock, fans are used. Powered by tractor batteries, their thrum accompanies the rhythm of fingers, the sound a constant undercurrent to the flurry of downy feathers falling like soft snow on the heads and shoulders of the men. And throughout all this, there is little talk – only the intense concentration of individuals hard at work.

Silence and speed are central to the entire operation. If the birds are left too long, decay sets in fast. It is a process that may be hastened if rain arrives, something that happens all too often on this edge of the Atlantic. Hence there is hurry and haste till the next stage of the operation is reached. If all goes well, the plucked birds are hurtled once again into sacks attached to the pulley wire of Blondin. Their destination on this occasion is the so-called Factory. Part of this involves the peat fires that, depending on the direction of the wind, are placed on a number of stone hearths in various locations around the island. The breeze puffs up the flames, ensuring they are high enough to singe any remaining feathers from the bird. One man cracks the young gannet's wings, allowing it to be held above the fire. For an instant it seems to dance, swirled back and forth by the man's fingers, a 'phoenix' transformed into a bird that is just about fit to eat. An instant too long and the skin will burn; a moment too short and it will possess something like the stubble of a beard, the odd, spiky bristle of a quill. Throughout this, too, the fat of the young gannet is feeding the peat-fire flame, sparking and sizzling occasionally. After this, the remaining down is scorched into dark ash; the webbed feet curling in the heat.

'This is when I always wear goggles in case anything gets into my eyes. You scrape the down off then scrub the ash clean off it,' Norman says, 'before passing it across to one of the guys who's got a blow-torch in his hand, using it to burn off the remainder of the feathers. After this, it's cleaned again, with any new ash removed. It's after this that the wings are cut off, sliced clean with an axe. That's not the end of the butchering though. We split the bird from end to end, removing the neck and tail, rib-cage and stomach . . .'

'That would sound ghastly to some people,' I say.

'Och, I suppose so – but then any form of butchering would. People these days just want the meat on their plate. They don't want to think where it might have come from.'

Thinking of my own sanitised, middle-class existence, I can only plead guilty to the charge. Most citizens of the modern, industrialised world would no doubt stand aghast at the 'blood-dimmed tide' accompanying such slaughter, the broken bone, gristle and coils of intestines left behind after the task is done. Apart from times when the likes of celebrity food heroes like Jamie Oliver and Hugh Fearnley-Whittingstall campaign against the brutalities of the chicken farm, we have become a people all too unaware of the truths of our own food production. We do our best to ignore the way the average battery hen lives only for around 40 days, in a cage measuring no more than an A4 sheet of paper. We pay no attention to the fact that out of the 855 million birds bred in this country every year, the majority are kept in sheds of 50,000 or more, or that a high percentage suffer serious problems with their legs, or hock burns due to the ammonia rising from the urine puddles on the floor.

Instead, we pretend our meat arrives pre-packed in the supermarket without the slightest whiff or tinge of the slaughterhouse to which the animals are consigned. It might be possible even for some to think that their Christmas turkey does not come from the flesh of any bird – far less one that has had its beak removed and spent its existence squashed together with other birds before being slaughtered. In our antiseptic world we are incapable of judging that, in comparison with the way many farmed animals eke out their existence, the killing of these gannets is both speedy and humane. There is also the fact that, given the survival rates of these gannets into adulthood, only something in the region of 5 per cent will make the transition from the dark figures of a chick into the white plumage of the mature bird anyway. Nature, in itself, is far more brutal than any guga hunter.

Oblivious to my reflections, Norman continues his slow and careful description of the 'process', telling of how the men make four neat cuts behind each fold of flesh in the bird's long neck, to create small pockets. 'That's for the salt that will pickle and preserve the bird,' Norman explains, 'and then we leave out the dead gannet on the tarpaulins, waiting for the next man to stack the birds.'

Another traditional skill of the islander is employed at this time. The gugas are built into a shape that closely resembles the brochs that were once found on much of Scotland's coastline; a legacy still seen in places like the Mousa Broch in Shetland or Dun Carloway in Lewis. These round towers, however, are not fashioned from stone, but instead from the brown scoured skin of fowl. Built on a foundation of flat stones covered by a plastic sheet, the gugas are laid out first of all like the rim of a great wheel; each bird's legs turned to the centre, the flap of its long neck like a seal turned round to prevent salt dribbling out. Behind this outer wall, another band of meat is set in place. The wall moves closer to its centre, a process that will continue until that point is reached and there is no break or dip in the bottom layer. On top of this, the men add another tier, making sure that each single bird is placed precisely and accurately in the correct position – a triumph of the wall-builder's art. And so it goes on, slowly and inexorably. Each guga is twisted and turned, taken out and examined to ensure the level is right, while at the same time, the strange circular tower continues to rise, an unfamiliar broch of some 2,000 birds beginning to rise on the surface of Sulasgeir, as if these men were seeking to build a miniature replica of Mousa or Dun Carloway out of the flesh of birds.

During the night the tower is shrouded by a tarpaulin to protect it if it rains. Too much rainfall and the brine would be diluted, lessening the preservative qualities of the salt sprinkled on these birds that are now ready to be eaten. Despite this, small glistening pools can be found the next morning at its foot, with residues of the coarse white grains with which each tower has been speckled. It is this loss that leads the men to dab their fingers into the small pockets of salt each day before they begin, checking the strength of the brine with their tongues to make sure it maintains its strength and quality. If it is too weak, more is added before another level is placed on top. Too strong and most of the time they can be sure the rain will weaken the strength of their pickle.

With each day the tower grows, yet when the boat arrives to collect the men, the broch is dismantled quickly. It stands for a short time while a number of other tasks are performed on the island, begun almost from the instant that the trawler sailing in their direction to take them home is glimpsed on the horizon. The tarpaulin and netting are stripped off the roofs of the stone bothys, folded neatly away within their walls. Pots and pans are brought to the shoreline for loading on the boat. The car battery. Fans. Blow-lamps. Empty water barrels. Luggage packed for home. They stack this on the rocks as the small boat – or 'punt' – is sent out from the trawler

And then the most precious part of the cargo is brought down to the landing place. Birds are placed, one after another, in the chute. Very quickly, they slide to its foot, their progress downward helped by the layer of fat and grease that quickly coats the chute. Each one slithers down speedily; gathering pace and momentum from the oil covering the dead fowl. A mattress is placed at the foot of the wooden chute to prevent the birds hurtling into the sea.

'A soft landing . . .' Norman grins. 'Stops them being bashed and bruised.'

It is these birds that are thrown first into the bottom of the punt. It is a task that has to be done as quickly as possible – the swell of the tide as it rises and falls against the rocks telling the men that time is swiftly passing. The cargo of birds is then taken out to the fishing boat; each one thrown onto the deck, almost as if they were in flight, before being stored in the hold to be taken home.

Meanwhile, the last annual rituals of the hunt take place. Men go and place a stone on top of their cairns. Once the last guga has skidded from the mound to the shoreline, the chute is folded away and put aside to be used the following year. Eventually, as the fishing boat heads for home with its full cargo on board, the island, too, fades and disappears, complete with all the memories of the actions that have taken place on it during the season. For some, like Norman in the year before he went to work on the oil rigs, it will be for the last time.

It is clearly a period in his life that Norman feels nostalgic about, recalling the laughs and moments he shared with others there. However, he is unlikely to go as far as one old man who, unable to go to Sulasgeir any more, dived into the hold of the boat when it arrived at Port of Ness Harbour.

'He covered himself in guga grease. Bathed himself in the stuff.'

Chuckling at this thought, he added another.

'Mind you, I bet none of his neighbours sat beside him in the kirk for ages after that. You should have smelled my boiler suit when I got home. It needed a few packets of Fairy Snow before it'd stop knocking you down with its stink over half a mile away. Aroma nan Gugas, indeed!'

Perhaps, though we never discuss it, Tormod might feel less nostalgic about Sulasgeir if he had experienced some of the events a number of his predecessors went through on the island. One of the most dramatic of these occurred in late September 1952, when the *Mayflower* voyaged to the island. On board were a number of men who all shared the surname of Morrison. They included brothers Donald and Angus from Adabrock and Cross Skigersta; 24-year-old Hector from Eorodale and Murdo Morrison the blacksmith, who also came from Cross Skigersta. The last man was a walking illustration of the Nessman's fondness for obscure nicknames. Known as Jellicoe a' Ghladstoin, his first nickname was clearly a tribute to the First World War naval admiral; the people he belonged to received their family nickname from the nineteenth-century Liberal Prime Minister, William Gladstone.

In an account recently published by the Ness Historical Society, the youngest of the men, Hector (in his 70s at the time), gave his account of the events that occurred during their stay on Sulasgeir. He begins this tale ominously, noting that the night they set out was the darkest he had ever seen. 'No moon or stars – just sheer blackness.' Nevertheless, he did not feel dismayed. It was only meant to be a short trip – 'a day raid'. The *Mayflower* could carry 400 birds and they were expecting to have that total in their hold by the end of the following day, heading home then. As a result, they began harvesting the birds as soon as they arrived. There were fairly slim pickings available. Many had already taken flight by the middle of September.

They also had faith in their boat – a vessel based not in Port but in Skigersta, that other village that has an important role in the history of the *Sgeir*. Constructed in John Macleod's yard in 1948, it was, with its 16-foot keel, one of the smallest boats ever to take part in the guga hunt. It was powered by a four-stroke Ford inboard engine. A development relatively innovative at the time, it was, however, well-tested and reliable enough for their eight-hour voyage. They also had Hector's mechanical skills and a dipping lug sail on hand if anything went wrong.

They also had companions on their voyage, on the fishing boat the *Mairi Dhonn*, which arrived in Sulasgeir a short time after the *Mayflower*. Aboard this boat was a varied crew of 12 men who came not only from Ness but other places. They included a young Donald Macaulay from Breasclete, who later became both a Church of Scotland minister and Convener of the Western Isles Council, and George Clark, an Edinburgh-based businessman whose family are connected with a famous footwear firm. Among the Nessmen was 79-year-old John Macleod, the man from Port of Ness who was responsible for the saving of so many lives on the *Iolaire* on 1 January 1919. As there were so many of them, they were able to work quickly, managing to load 800 on the boat before the weather forced them to move further out.

This was not so easy for the men of the *Mayflower*. They had the birds ready on the ledge when the wind turned south-east, blowing directly into the geo where their vessel was anchored. Doubtless, they must have suffered more than a moment of regret when they became aware of what was happening, wondering why they had not hauled the vessel high up on the rock when they arrived or whether they had been wise to arrive there so close to the autumn equinox.

It was, after all, not the first time the *Mayflower* had been in trouble. Three years earlier, they had experienced a narrow escape when they had been trapped on Sulasgeir

for a number of days by winds of 70 miles per hour or more.
(On that occasion the storm had blown from the east,
keeping the geo in shelter and their vessel relatively safe.)
They had arrived home courtesy of a Norwegian tanker that
had towed the *Mayflower* home to Skigersta. In the process
of rescuing the Nessmen, down to their last tin of salmon
and few slices of bread, the Norwegians' own small boat
had been smashed by the waves. By the time they were back
on shore, even the welcome flavour of the guga had began
to pall for them. Murdo Morrison showed how grateful he
was to the tanker crew for helping them the moment he
stepped ashore. 'We would like to thank the Norwegians,'
he declared to a *Stornoway Gazette* reporter, 'they went to
great trouble, especially the lads who were in the boat that
got smashed.'

On this occasion the weather was just as dramatic – if not
more so – as it had been that previous time, for all that its
force blew from a different direction. The crew of the *Mairi
Dhonn* decided there was little point or purpose in remaining sheltered in the bay. Conditions were becoming such
that they had no choice but to move into open water.
Knowing the other men were likely to be safe on the island,
they decided to head for Stornoway, some 50 miles away, to
raise the alarm. Their voyage was made yet more necessary
by the fact that the ship's radio had failed. They had not
been able to send the message those at shore had expected at
midnight. With rain and wind thrashing, the silence from
the boat was even more ominous than the darkness Hector
had noted on the voyage out to Sulasgeir. Not for nothing
was there a headline dark with foreboding on the front page
of that week's *Stornoway Gazette*: '*Mayflower* and *Mairi
Dhonn* – Caught In Gale At Sulasgeir'.

Over the next few nights, that sense of 'being caught' on
Sulasgeir was growing stronger and stronger for the men of
the *Mayflower*. Although they knew that it was essential for

their own safety, they clearly must have felt more than a little dejected as they watched the *Mairi Dhonn* sail away. The weather was becoming more extreme through Tuesday night and Wednesday. In addition, they were struggling to save the boat anchored in the geo. The backwash of the waves rolling into the geo was gradually flooding the vessel. By the fireside of his home in Eorodale, Hector recalled the effort and feelings of that day:

'We fought hard to save her though the night on Tuesday and into Wednesday, but the conditions were such that we couldn't hold her. Every painter we secured was broken by the motion of the sea – eventually we just let her ride out on the swell. I don't remember being cold, though. Mostly what I remember was seeing her capsize on Wednesday, though we could still see her the following day floating in the cove. And feeling so helpless about what had happened. All we could do then was retreat to the bothy and huddle in there.'

Having planned only to go out on the rock for a short raid, they were now marooned with little food or provisions. Their supply of water was now on the sea bed, having gone down when the boat turned turtle in the geo. Both their fuel and food came largely from the same source – the guga they had just harvested. They threw the dead birds with the few peats they had brought with them onto the fire and watched them spit and spurt fat on the flames, their sudden, small eruptions combining with the roar of the storm continually in the background. Their cooking of the same bird also suffered from a small problem: 'We were just using the same water to cook every meal. You can imagine what that was like after a few days. Fortunately, there was a galvanised bucket left behind there and we cooked the birds in that over the fire. It was the lack of water that was our main problem. By Friday, our lips were beginning to swell.'

In his account of the incident, Donald Morrison put it even more graphically. 'It was the same as the Ancient

Mariner,' he explained, 'Water, water everywhere and not a drop to drink.'

Yet there was help on its way. A few minutes before midnight on Wednesday night, the *Mairi Dhonn* had lurched into Stornoway, alerting people to the *Mayflower*'s predicament. It appears, however, that some time passed before the authorities were informed. The Station Officer at Stornoway Coastguard, Mr Price, complained of this in the *Gazette*. 'I wish someone would tell us about these things,' he declared to a journalist. 'It was just by accident we heard about it. Someone mentioned casually in the house that the men were on Sulasgeir and that they seemed to be in difficulties.'

After the Coastguard was informed, however, matters began to change. At six o'clock the following morning, the fishery cruiser *Minna* left the same pier to bring home the stranded men. It was not a task they were capable of. According to the *Gazette*, there was 'still a heavy sea running and it was impossible to send a boat across to take the men off'. They had to content themselves with a few semaphore messages flagged across the short distance at the marooned men, telling them they would return later. One of the men, Donald Morrison – or Dòmhnall nan Twins – answered, having learned how to semaphore during his time in the RNR. As a result, the *Minna* returned to its usual duties. Given the strength of wind and weather, it had little option but to do this, for all that their retreat must have even further disheartened the men.

It was the crew of the Stornoway lifeboat that changed the situation, leaving the harbour around midnight the following day. Despite the fact that coxswain Malcolm Macdonald had never been to Sulasgeir before, they arrived at seven o'clock the following morning. The *Minna* was there alongside them, watching events as they took place. Neither boat could come close to Sulasgeir because of the heavy swell. Surf broke over the rocks at the entrance to the geo, reaching 15 feet or more.

Using a loudhailer, they shouted over the noise of wave and wind towards the men, asking them to go down to the ledge. It was not a suggestion that those stranded felt inclined to accept. When they were asked later why, they were quick to give their reasons: 'If they didn't get us back off, we would never get back up the cliff again. It's over 100 feet and we'd sooner be where we were than be stuck there.'

The lifeboat dropped anchor, waiting for the tide to fall. It was when this happened an hour or two later that the rescuers backed the boat into the geo. There was still a strong surge running through the water, no place to tarry or delay. When the lifeboat had got as far in as possible, incurring damage as it did so, a lifeline was thrown to the men. One after another, they tied a rope around them, ensuring it was as secure as they could make it. One of them even secured a gold watch he had borrowed for the voyage on a string around his neck.

They each dived into the sea, doing this as carefully as they could to avoid being hurt by either the smack of rock or the ocean. The men of the lifeboat hauled them safely aboard – one of their crew even snapping their photos as they were dragged through the waves. They sat then on the deck, their fingers wrapped around warm cups, and reflected on the skill of the men who had saved them and all, too, they had left behind them after their short time on Sulasgeir. Some of their clothes and food were on the bottom of the sea; other items, including the stack of gugas they had gone to the rock to reap, were still on the shoreline.

'We'll get them next year,' Murdo Morrison told the reporter he met in Stornoway Harbour. 'We'll get them next year . . .'

4

Alasdair Bàn: A Life on the Margins

THE CORMORANT TRANSFORMED

For years, I swam within shallows,
twisting round the narrow, shadowy sides of stones,
diving from ledges into spindrift,
my plumage stained by each soiled fringe of foam,
as I rummaged through poor offerings washed up
near land; slim pickings from a shoal
spread out for my dark head to sift through,
meagre morsels I could swallow lean and whole.

The last year has brought in changes.
Once a beggar dressed in black, I find
my wings have brighter, lighter raiment,
white feathers buoyed and lifted by the wind,
and now I peer down on the Atlantic from a height –
transformed; a bride of Christ; fledgling reborn
and granted new perspectives as I soar,
gifted with great insight in each gathering shoal and storm.

Alasdair Bàn is one of the few men in his 70s I have ever
encountered who has a continual gleam in his eyes.

It can be sparked off by many aspects of his life. There is
evident pride in his four children and many grandchildren,
photographs of whom decorate the walls of his and his wife
Agnes's home in Lionel. There are tales of his years on
Sulasgeir, the sense of comradeship; his voice becomes
hushed when he speaks of the birdlife that crosses the

Atlantic to spend sometimes a few brief moments on either his native island or the rock he visited on so many occasions.

At one time he speaks about McGeoch, the Inverness policeman and part-time naturalist who was the first man from outwith the parish to go out with the Nessmen to Sulasgeir, filming them for a programme that would eventually be broadcast on the BBC during the early 1960s. He talks of how their guest managed to teach the old and seasoned hunters much about the birdlife that surrounded them in that part of the North Atlantic; how he pointed out a rare red-necked phalarope that was sailing on the waters, handing Alasdair a set of binoculars to enable him, too, to see the creature; how he succeeded in catching a goldfinch that had been among a flock landing on the rock during the night. Trapping one within a jar, he slowly revealed it to Alasdair, slowly and carefully ringing it before letting it loose into the heavens once more. When Alasdair speaks about that moment, he does it with a rare sense of reverence and tenderness. One can almost hear the stillness of his breath when it occurred.

Another moment he speaks about is the year a mother and her two daughters were diving for crayfish in the bay. When they emerged, shivering from the Atlantic chill, Alasdair offered them a cup of tea.

'Yes . . .' one gasped in answer, conscious that the men who stood near them offered no threat or danger and curious about what they were doing on the rock.

It was an answer that the young lady quickly withdrew when she saw the state of the bothys the men were living in. One glance around the huddle of clothes, the conditions of the camp, and she stuttered out a reply to the repeated offer.

'Well, maybe not . . .'

Her mother intervened. 'No. Make that certainly not.'

Yet the three of them sat among the men, talking about

their lives back home in the Black Isle, not far from Inverness. No doubt they were marvelling at the shyness of some of them, the talkative nature of others speaking to the first members of the female gender they had seen in a week. It was then that Alasdair spoke.

'Let me show you something . . .'

He reached over to the tea-chest that acted as their 'bedside cabinet', hauling it away from its position set against the wall.

'Look.'

He showed them a Leach's petrel, a tiny swallow-like bird with dark head and wings, a white body that lay nursing its egg, crammed into a corner. It was a flock of these birds that, perhaps mingling with storm petrels, had once or twice flocked into their bothys during the night, swirling and dipping above their heads.

'Oooohhhh . . .'

'Ahhh . . .'

'That's beautiful.'

'Wonderful.'

A short time later, they left the bothy, smiling and laughing, complete with the sense of wonder with which their host, the man they have come to know as Alasdair Campbell, his real name, had provided them – so much so that a short time later, the mother, Barbara Jones, wrote in to the pages of the *Stornoway Gazette* about the awe and astonishment they had experienced among the seabird-hunters that day.

Yet there is little doubt which bird makes Alasdair marvel most – and that is the one that he went out to hunt for 22 years of his life, from 1957 to 1989. More than any other man I have spoken to while undertaking this research, he is the person who seems to know the bird in the greatest detail. He speaks about the one blue egg gannets lay within their nests and how it takes 40 days to hatch and 90 for the chick to fledge. He tells me about how one adult stays with the chick while the other hunts.

'Though it will leave the nest if left alone too long,' he adds.

He speaks about the elaborate courting rituals with which one will greet the arrival of another on its nest, how their necks twine and curl, as if forming the half of a heart someone has carved into stone, how their beaks fence with one another like a gentle clash of swords, creating the most tender dance of devotion, an astonishing duet of delight.

He talks, too, about what that couple's chick will feed upon – sand eels, herring, mackerel, whatever is available – and how the nature of that fish changes as the young mature. In the beginning, it is almost liquid, a grey, runny mixture. A short time later and the feed has taken on the consistency of porridge, passing from beak to beak upon the ledge. And when the chick is almost ready to be left alone, heavier than its mother and swaddled by fat, it might be a full unbroken mackerel that is doled out by the parent, slipping whole from one mouth to another.*

Alastair's clear blue eyes register his own amazement when he talks. A smile appears on his relatively unlined face. Speaking in Gaelic, he declares: 'Well, Donald, you've never seen anything as miraculous as that.'

Yet there can be outrage too – and it emerges most when he describes some of the modern trials with which the birds have to contend during their time at sea. He shows his annoyance at what have been termed 'the ghost fishermen',

---

* Alasdair is not alone among the guga hunters in displaying this kind of tenderness towards the birds. At least two of the guga hunters, Dods and the late William Macleod, took it upon themselves to feed and care for young gugas stranded in Ness after being blown off course during their first attempts at flight. Both men looked after the birds for weeks, keeping them close to their homes before finally taking them to the edge of the land and letting them go. What their wives thought of this strange behaviour has never been recorded.

pieces of plastic, such as coils of string from nets cast out on
the waters, that the birds now use as the basis of their nests.
(Alongside them, there might even be kitchenware like pot
scrubbers or sieves floating in Sulasgeir's direction on the
tide.) Worse, there are times when the gannets' throats, legs
or wings might catch on them, condemning the bird to a
slow and awful death. His response to this would always be
to cut them free; a task he'd complete together with his
fellow-Nessmen, an act of mercy and release for the birds,
saving their lives.

'Otherwise, it would be a terrible way for the poor
creatures to go,' he declares.

There was also in the 1980s a phenomenon that disturbed
him even more than that. Stepping on the rock, he was
aware that around 20 young birds were badly deformed.
Their heads were twisted; beaks pointing backwards instead
of forward. A shiver comes across Alasdair as he describes
this. He was obviously extremely disturbed by the sight.

'What caused it?'

He shrugs. 'I don't know . . . It could have been some
kind of poison. Chemicals, perhaps.'

While sitting there, I think of the terrible legacy of
Chernobyl, but for once in my life, I say nothing. 'What
did you do?' I ask.

'We killed them. It was a kindness to them. Much better
than the slow and lingering deaths they might have suffered
otherwise.'

His face registers the sadness it takes on on a few occasions
during the course of the evening. Twice it occurs when he
is speaking about two deaths that occurred in connection
with the island. One happened when, in 1981, they were
waiting for the fishing boat, the *Ripple*, to take them from
Sulasgeir after three weeks on the island. All packed up
and ready to go, they stood for ages on the landing place.
Time ticked on. They kept checking their watches to see if

their impatience might manage to hurry the vessel along.

'I wonder what's keeping it . . .'

'The sea's flat calm. It can't be that.'

Eyes looked out to the horizon to confirm once again what they knew before. The sea was exceptionally quiet that afternoon. Some gannets fished in the distance; their wings in the water like white lilies in a still and unflurried field.

'It couldn't be a nicer day,' someone said.

Then they noticed a boat and helicopter coming in the distance from north to south, the fishery cruiser not far behind it. At first, they thought there was no problem: some stores being landed, perhaps, for a crew in North Rona. It was only when they saw an inflatable pass by the island at speed, heading south, that realisation dawned.

'Something's wrong,' someone said.

'Aye. No doubt about it.'

It was a little while later that they discovered what exactly happened. The three crewmen of the *Ripple* had set sail from Stornoway earlier that day, making their way out of the Minch and into the most placid waters they had experienced on that often stormy crossing for many years. The whole occasion had been so relaxed that one of the fishermen, Kenneth John Carmichael from Stornoway, had taken a cup of tea with him as he stepped out on deck, no doubt contemplating the beauty of the day around him, the sunlight glittering like fish-scales on the water.

He was never seen again – the only evidence of his passing a spilled cup of tea on deck.

'It was a terrible shock.' Alasdair says, shaking his head. 'There was nothing we could say. Nothing we could do. Only put our hands in our pockets to give something to his widow and children. But it wasn't enough. At a time like that, nothing is ever enough.'

The only other time Alasdair pauses for a while is when he mentions someone who shared his own name, Alasdair

Bàn, during our conversation. His namesake was the only man who has ever died on the island, way back at the beginning of the twentieth century, Alexander Morrison or 'Alasdair Bàn' – originally from North Dell but living in Lionel at the time – met his end there. Given the risks involved both in reaching Sulasgeir and their labours once there, it seems an unlikely fact that there was just one human lost upon the rock.*

'But it's the truth, isn't it?'

'Aye. It is. He's only the man we know of, anyway. I must confess every time I step near the grave where they left him for a short while, a shiver runs through me.'

'It must be harder for you than anyone else. Sharing his name and all.'

Alasdair Bàn smiles in answer, not wanting to claim that. 'Maybe.'

'How did it happen?'

It was Norman Smith – or Tormod Sgiugs – who replied in most detail to that question, in the conversation that took place a few days later in his home. Opening the drawer of his filing cabinet, his hand plunges in to emerge with some notes.

'No one seems to know for sure,' he muttered. 'There's a lot of different stories about how he died. Some say he had a heart attack while he was there. Others even that he choked on a gannet bone. There was a postmortem carried out way back in 1904, but no one seems to know the results of it. At least, I haven't found them yet.'

Yet he has other details from the account, which he obtained from Port of Ness Post Office. Leafing through

---

* There are also reports of 'the death of another lad who lost his foothold on the cliffs, and that was many years ago' mentioned, for instance, in an otherwise excellent *Stornoway Gazette* editorial dated 1 February 1955. However, as far as this writer can ascertain, there appears to be no evidence for the existence of this incident.

its pages, frustratingly incomplete, he finds the appropriate
entry, the family nicknames enclosed in brackets to distin-
guish one man from the next in an area where people share
both first names and surnames. Added to the endless
sentences, it is as if our forefathers were combining in a
plot to confuse later generations seeking ways of untangling
the roots of their family trees. In order to add my own layer
of perplexity to all this, I have decided to remove all this
information from the entry. In a small community, there are
times we all need to be protected from the behaviour of our
ancestors. The ripples from a single incident can last a long
time in a settled pool, washing away – quite undeservedly –
the reputations of the living:

> September 21st 1904
> D M****** (*******) and crew (name of village) came
> from Sulasgeir with the news that Alexander Morrison
> (Alastair Bàn) one of the crew had died on the island on
> Monday the 18th and his body was left on the island as they
> could not take his body home because of the bad sea. He
> was buried in a cave in the rock.

The names of the crew members and the villages they hailed
from were added after this.
'And so they left him there?'
'Not for long.' Tormod's finger slides down the next few
terse entries, settling on those a few days later:

> September 23rd *Village Maid* and friends went for
>   remains.
> September 24th *Village Maid* arrived with remains.

I later discovered that the tale did not end there, culminating
instead in years of friction between different households
in the district. Accusations would be thrown, a sense of

grievance nursed. A conversation with the eminent Gaelic scholar and my fellow Niseach, Dr Finlay MacLeod, sheds a little light on why the incident left behind such a bitter legacy. Reading aloud a report published in the *Highland News* on 1 October 1904, he told me that the men on the *Forget Me Not*, register number SY 230, had been conducting a raid on Sulasgeir, intending to stay on the island only for a short time before returning home once again. It was during this time that Alasdair Bàn died. In response to this, they rolled his corpse in a blanket and tarpaulin, securing his grave from the attentions of others with turf and stones. After this, they sailed back to Port. In the words of the report, they 'brought home their spoils but left the remains behind'.

In his time with me, Dods wondered aloud about the reasons for their actions. 'It might have been their fear of bringing a dead body back with them, the smell of it tainting the birds. Or maybe they just decided the room would be taken up by a few more gugas. Who knows? Times were desperate then. It's difficult for us to judge them.'

According to the *Highland News*, however, they blamed 'heavy seas' for their actions in the same way as they did in the Post Office records. There is little doubt that they were greeted with an even greater storm on their arrival. Relatives were 'highly incensed', as were many others in the community. It was for this reason that a crew made up largely of the friends and family of the dead man went out in the fishing smack, the *Village Maid*, to obtain the body; its skipper rewarded with a new suit for his part in the errand by the deceased's brother, who worked as a tailor in the community.

On the day after their return, the entire incident had its own grisly postscript. It involved Dr Ross – the local doctor in Borve and an uncle of the former Conservative Chancellor of the Exchequer, Iain Macleod – and his son, Jack.

They carried out one of the most bizarre postmortems ever in the history of the north of Scotland. It took place on a Sunday within Swainbost cemetery with – allegedly – a number of the village children peeping at the procedures taking place from behind its walls. Occasionally, some were even said to have been sent down to the stream to obtain fresh water to assist the men in their task. It is also claimed that Dr Ross was interested in brain surgery and used the occasion as an opportunity to provide a little elementary instruction on the topic for his offspring.

There are probably a number of reasons why this strange event occurred in this time and place. Given the strong feelings engendered by the event, there may have been the suspicion that foul play was involved. If so, it was important to either dispel or prove this story – and as quickly as possible; gossip, after all, loves nothing more than a vacuum. The body was also clearly degenerating at a rapid rate, clearly affected by both the time that had elapsed since the man's death and his burial. Perhaps, in those times, this might even have prevented the process taking place indoors. The presence of the young boys nearby can probably be best explained by the extreme nature of the incident. Not even the strongest Sabbath stricture was going to prevent them watching this take place. They might even have been on hand when the good doctor delivered his verdict, duly reported in the pages of the *Highland News*. Alastair Morrison had died as a result of fatty degeneration of the heart or what would be termed 'cardiomyopathy' today. The first death ever to be recorded on Sulasgeir could have occurred at any time, anywhere.

In contrast to this detailed and thorough account, Alasdair Bàn barely mentions the subject of his namesake's end, half shying away from it. Referring to his 'empty grave', he notes:

'It's where we leave the fishing rods. On the stones around where they buried him.'

It's at moments like this that I am reminded of the gentleness I have always been conscious of within Alastair since we first came across each other when I was barely 12 years old. His son Iain was in the same class at school as me. During that time, the young boys and girls from Ness who had passed the Qualifying Exam went to the Nicolson Instant in distant Stornoway – some 24 miles away from my home, a few more from Alasdair and Iain's house in Lionel. Due to the distance, we stayed in the Gibson Hostel, sleeping in the same dormitory. There were five boys from Lionel School, including Iain; two from Cross Primary, including me; and one poor soul who had wandered in, looking bemused and perplexed, from distant Bernera, many miles south down the west coast.

That expression was still on the Bernera boy's face five and more years later – and with little wonder. Goodness knows what he must have made of it all – all those late night conversations about Fivepenny, Adabrock, Port, Lionel and the heady excesses of Cross Skigersta Road. As someone from the far-flung outpost of South Dell at the southern end of Ness, even I was baffled by some of the tales. After lights out, talk would begin about the north of Ness. There would be mention of local characters and their strange personality traits, place-names which sounded odd and unfamiliar to me, conversations about heroes, too, like Murchadh Mhurdaidh, Eve, An Gaisean, Aonghas Bàn, the men who stepped out each year to climb the cliffs of Sulasgeir. Soon a new mythology was being created for me, one connected to the guga that – courtesy of my relatives in distant Port and Adabrock – would arrive on my plate a few times each year.

Two of the boys from the northern end of the district had fathers who regularly went out to hunt the guga. One was Murdo Maclean's father, Calum a' Bhodaich. The other was Alasdair Bàn. (Another who went out occasionally some 20 years before was my own relative, Angus Murray's father, Roddy.) Of the two men, it was the latter whom we came to know best. There were a number of reasons for this. First of all, there was the Morris Traveller van, with its wooden frame, that used to turn up sometimes at the hostel. There were the occasional Friday evenings when we squashed into its back seat, getting a lift home with him. There were the years, too, when he ran the Ness Youth Club on a Saturday night, playing table tennis with us in the Hall, gathering money for both membership and the top ten records that used to blare out of the Dansette at the edge of the stage.

'Mama, weer all crazee now!' it used to proclaim.

No doubt there were occasions when he used to look at his own son and me with our long hair, wide flares and platform soles and come quickly to the conclusion that it was all too sadly true.

Yet most of all, it was the fact that he retained some of the liveliness of youth that was the source of the greatest appeal for us. The majority of the boys had fathers who had taken on that role for the first time either in their mid 30s, like my own father, or perhaps even later, when middle age was approaching and their spirit and their footsteps were already slowing down. In contrast, Alasdair's son had arrived while he was in his 20s. As boys, we could sense the difference. There was the way he had fair hair – thinning now in his 70s – while the majority of the men who occupied the fireside chair at home were either grey or balding. There was his relatively unlined face – which has still gained only a few more creases today. There was a jaunty quality to his step, a quick wit and a way of relating to us – one lad to another – that none of the other dads possessed.

'Hey, Donald,' he would say. 'How are things?'

In short, it was easy to imagine him undertaking all the physical challenges men were meant to perform in

Sulasgeir – scaling up to Mullach an Eilein with a heavy load on your back; sleeping in stone bothys built at the turn of the nineteenth century; working hours without cease; scaling cliffs with ease, tied only to the man tied to the ledge above. One aspect of his personality that would, however, have escaped us at that time was his sensitivity, particularly to nature. We would not have been aware of this during our teenage years. Way back then, birds, for instance, fluttered and flapped at the far edge of our consciousness. Many of us would have been hard-pressed to tell the difference between a sparrow and a sparrow hawk.

For any urban-dweller, whose life is far removed from the realities of a rural existence at the periphery of Scotland, two aspects of Alastair's life must seem a contradiction – his intense love of wild life and the way in which he spent so many of his days hunting young seabirds. 'How could any man who feels so strongly about birds behave in such a way?' they might ask. For anyone who responds in this manner, the complexities they might see as existing within his personality are not yet complete. If one looked solely at a summary of his career, Alasdair might come across as a conservationist's worst nightmare. He also worked in the South Atlantic as a whaler for a number of years in his earlier life.

It is something I was unaware of before that evening, though I did know, for instance, that like my own father he had spent time at sea (in the Merchant Navy in his case; in a minesweeper in my dad's wartime experience), and as a weaver. I had seen him crouched above his loom in the shed beside his bungalow on many an occasion. His pedals would still for an instant while he grinned in my direction.

'You looking for Caesar?' He would mention his son's childhood nickname, showing some kind of youthful solidarity with us. My own father, in contrast, would never use the name – 'Rufus' – which I had been granted during my first year of hostel life.

'Aye. Is he around?'

'No, but go down to Port. He's probably down there with Amos.'

I recalled too that at one time, around my final year of school, he worked on the quay in Stornoway, loading barrels of fish for what were known in these parts as the 'klondykers' – large vessels that took the local men's catches across to the continental market. Hard and heavy work, which Alasdair recalls as the most arduous he has ever experienced in his life, he worked alongside two of my classmates, his own son Iain and Donald Finlay Macdonald – known as 'Rasper' – from Cross Skigersta Road, protecting them from the full rigours of that labour.

'My clothes were sticking to me when I drove home that day. Wrung out with sweat.'

I could remember too – at a push! – that he had been a janitor at Lionel School for a number of years. (I recalled obtaining a key from him when I was doing some evening work at the school.) But a whaler? I scratched my head and failed to recall any time I had been given this information.

'When was that?'

He responds by giving me a brief outline of his early life. 'Well, for the first few years after I left school, I helped my brother with the loom. Then I went for a year or two to the Merchant Navy. It was after that I signed up for Christian Salvesen, working down in South Georgia on a whaler called *Southern Harvester*, getting their catches ready to go to Leith, the main whaling port in Scotland at that time.'

'What was that like?'

'Hard work,' he admits. 'But it had its pleasures. You know, it's the best way of getting round the world quickly, circumnavigating its southern end from the Wendell Sea to the Ross Sea.'

I laugh, think of Alastair 'cheating' in some sort of speedy

version of Jules Verne's *Around the World in Eighty Days*.
'And South Georgia? What was that like?'
  'A cold place. Loads of icebergs.'

He shakes his head when I talk to him of a man I had met
drunk in a Glasgow pub when I was much younger. From
Lewis, he had never gone back home after going down to
the South Atlantic for the first time at 17. In a drunken
rambling conversation, he had told me of a quarrel within
the family, how he missed his mother but had never been
able to face his own people again. Years later, I had written
a poem about him, changing the name of the village he
hailed from and the pub's location.

A WHALER'S TALE

Small heat in that glass he drains
or fag he sucks,
sitting in that bar in Leith
and damning the ebb of luck
that drew him to the Antarctic
on a whaling ship.
'Fifteen when I left Sandwick
on my first bloody trip.
And hell, I've no' been back there since.
No one there for me.'
Lives snapped up when his days were trapped
within the jaws of frozen sea.

Yet still, a tattoo's inked on fist
ridged and flaked by nicotine and cold.
A thistle's spikes, below which
the one word 'MUM' is scrolled
to show the bitterness he's swigged
since his days were flensed from kin –
washed up in a city pub
drinking to thaw the chill within.

'A few of them went like that,' Alasdair shakes his head. 'Away from home at the far edge of the world. Only men around for company. It's hardly surprising that some turned to the booze.'

Once again, I am struck by the man's compassion, his concern for others. When he talks a little more about the whaling, he mentions how inspectors were on board all the time, checking the catch for cows that were either pregnant or giving milk. Apparently, the men lost their bonus if there were any in that condition.

'Not that that made any difference to the whales,' he mutters.

His attitude to the killing of animals reminds me of my own father. Seeing this work as a regrettable necessity, he would always perform his home-butchering alone, never allowing anyone to see him doing it. For the occasional Sunday dinner, a chicken, complete with feathers that would be later plucked and burned off with methylated spirits, might appear in the window of the porch. Its death would be carried out in a quiet moment, when the rest of us were absent. There would be, too, the rare ewe or wedder (the term used for a castrated male sheep) he might kill. Dad would drag it into the barn on his own, tying its feet before hauling it onto a home-made table where the killing was done. It was always a private act for him, something he managed, sweating and heaving, to do on his own. Even when I was approaching adulthood, I was never asked to help him. It was as if he shied away from seeing his own actions mirrored in the eyes of another person, especially his son.

It is probably the same for Alasdair Bàn. He is a man who gains pleasure from observing and taking part in life, not bringing it to an end. In that way, crofters are very much unlike some of the aristocratic gentlemen whom one of my uncles worked for in places like the Grimersta Estate at the

southern end of Lewis. He used to take them out fly-fishing,
marvelling at the dexterity with which some of them fished
from the banks of a river or moorland loch, drawing one
after another at the end of the line. Or how the same
individuals used to hunt deer in the hills of South Lochs
or Harris. As the corpses queued up, some of them would
cheerfully confess how they didn't much care for the taste of
trout, salmon or venison. It was all, at the end of the day,
just sport for them.

This was not an attitude shared by many crofters who eked
out their existence in the crofts of Ness. They killed because
they needed to eat, relishing the taste of chicken, fish or guga
when it was served out on their plates. There were times
when, for instance, I saw men in the village clearly upset
when an animal was lost before its 'natural time' had come to
an end. My father's face would become troubled at the loss of
a lamb; another would show emotion when his dog had to be
put down after being struck by a car. There was the occasion,
too, when the eyes of one particularly tough relative of my
own moistened after his cow had become so ill that the
'Cruelty Man' had to be sent for. (It was the first 'funeral' I
ever attended – accompanying the animal on the back of a
trailer as she took her final journey down to the beach in
South Dell.) None of them ever enjoyed the experience of
ending the life of a fellow creature. It was for them one of the
more dreadful requirements of crofting life.

And so it is with Alasdair Bàn. For men like him, the
killing of animals, such as the gannet or whale, brings not
the slightest twinge of guilty pleasure. It is simply something
that has to be done, forced on him by the demands of both
his and his family's survival – a difficult act to manage in a
peripheral and economically vulnerable area like Ness. In
one of the few statements he makes in English in the entire
evening, he explains the difficulties of raising a family there
with all the financial uncertainties this involved.

'I looked on life here as a challenge. Relying on croftwork and weaving, the money we got from the guga helped us to survive.'

'It wasn't easy,' his wife, Agnes, adds, joining in the conversation. 'Many a time we were grateful for the cash we got from the guga.'

'It helped us get by,' Alasdair nods.

Yet sometimes even this wasn't enough. Alasdair speaks about one time when the seven acres of his own croft and the nine acres he later obtained from his father were insufficient to support his family. Tweeds, too, sent out from the mills, were arriving all too rarely for his loom – a perennial problem experienced time and time again by many in the industry. With his children growing up, he had no choice. He had to return to the Merchant Navy. After two years there, he came back home, remaining there ever since.

'I've always been very committed to the place,' he admits. 'Though it's got problems like everywhere else, it's still a great place.'

And then, a cup of tea and some biscuits later, the mood of the conversation lightens. He speaks of more occasions when visitors arrived in Sulasgeir. Once a Frenchman and his wife arrived on shore to be greeted by Alasdair Bàn and his comrades pretending to be checking for radiation after some imaginary nuclear accident had occurred.

'Mon Dieu!' he declared – or whatever Frenchmen say when they feel they are in peril for their lives – as the couple scurried back down to the landing place at the geo again, more desperate to leave the island than they were to arrive.*

* There might have been an uneasy edge to their laughter. This episode belongs to a period when the guga hunters feared that the men and women of Sea Shepherd Conservation Society might arrive to disturb their annual harvest. There were good reasons for their fears. The group – led by animal-rights campaigner Davie McColl – had made a succession of statements against the

Or the moment in the late 1950s when they were working late into the evening and a large trawler came nearby. Noting the large fires on the rock flaring into the darkness, the trawler took them as a signal of distress. Circling a short time, one of the crew took out a torch, pointing it in their direction. A Morse code message was flashed:

'A-R-E Y-O-U I-N T-R-O-U-B-L-E?'

His years in the Merchant Navy coming to the fore, Alastair Bàn lifted one of the torches the men had brought to the island to enable him to respond:

'N-O W-E-R-E F-I-N-E.'

'W-H-A-T S-H-I-P A-R-E Y-O-U?'

'N-O S-H-I-P O-U-T H-U-N-T-I-N-G G-A-N-N-E-T-S.'

There was a puzzled pause for a moment while the crew took in this information. Finally, their reply flickered back – perhaps a shade more uncertainly than usual:

'G-O-O-D B-E-S-T O-F L-U-CK T-O Y-O-U.'

Yet the greatest humour was when the men were by themselves. Sometimes this was even sparked off by adversity. One time this occurred was when he was sharing a tent with Aonghas Ailig and Alasdair's near contemporary, Aonghas Ghliocais, one year on Sulasgeir. Exhausted from his labours, Alastair remembers looking over in the direction of the last-named, an old friend, just before he went to sleep that night. The entire length of the man – some six feet or even more – was curled up in his sleeping bag as he tried his best to settle down and sleep.

An hour or two later, that sleep was disturbed.

---

hunt. In Orkney, they had also sabotaged seal culls by spraying pups with red dye. In November, 1981, this led to 16 protesters, all with addresses outside Orkney, appearing in court at Kirkwall, accused of a number of breach of the peace charges. Fearing the same kind of incident, it was little wonder that the guga hunters felt a little nervous about their visitors, whether French or otherwise, that year.

An hour or two later, a storm blew up and nearly blew their tent away.

They tried their best to hold onto it, Aonghas's long arms and legs stretched in all directions as he sought to keep it upright, doing his utmost to keep it fixed to the ground, while Alasdair and the other Aonghas scrambled, also aiming to maintain what remained of it in contact with Mother Rock while wind, rain and wave thundered all around them. Eventually, the struggle proved too much for them. A few rocks were placed on top of the billowing cover while the three men scuttled for shelter.

Aonghas Ailig reached the bothy first, clambering into a bed despite the protests that were being yelled by the six or so men who were already there.

'Hey!

'*Chan eil rùm an seo!* There's no room here!'

'*Teich air falbh!* Get out now!'

There was no possiblity of squashing any other men into the bothy. Alasdair and Aonghas Ghliocais looked at each other in bemusement, wondering where or how they were going to sleep out the storm. Finally, they squeezed into opposite ends of an alcove; Aonghas's long legs stretching out of their narrow confinement, invading Alastair's space. Each way he tossed and turned, there was one thing certain. Aonghas's toes were there before him, claiming each inch of room for himself.

(Angus Murdo Gunn has a memory, too, of another night sleeping in that tent. He recalls a collection of insects succumbing to the tug of gravity when they lay there, falling from the underside of the tent. He also remembers lying on his side one night, kicking his neighbour awake and watching the man's startled face peer at him in annoyance. It was hard, however, to take him seriously, as he was wearing a nylon stocking, pom-pom hat and pair of goggles on his head to protect him from small creatures in the middle of the night.)

Nights like these are clearly the ultimate test of any friendship, yet it is clear that, more than just surviving, the companionship between the two men thrived for many years. They had much in common. The bows of their respective whaling ships had crossed near South Georgia a few times a decade or two before. However, this all came to an end with Aonghas's early death in 1989. A shock to the entire community, used to seeing the familiar form of Aonghas Ghliocais striding from house to house collecting insurance premiums, it was clearly a turning point in Alastair's life too. From that time onwards, he decided not to go back to Sulasgeir. It wouldn't be quite the same place without his friend.*

Yet he and his wife Agnes often think back to the first time Alasdair went there, possibly the most dramatic of all his trips out to Sulasgeir. It was the last occasion men went out there in two groups. The others had been brought there by the *Viking*, a fishing boat skippered by Angus Mackay. It was planned that he would pick up these men later, taking them and their haul from the rock.

Alastair's crew had gone there in what was almost the traditional manner, taking an open boat, the 25-footer *Star of Hope*. The previous year had been the first time that particular vessel – complete with engine – had been hauled up the cliff at Sulasgeir. It was a feat that some said could never be managed, that a boat of its dimensions would either have to be turned around or left for the sea to smash into fragments on the crags. It was a prediction that proved to be wrong. With a great deal of strain and effort, they hauled it safely high and dry, where even the savagery of the Atlantic could do no real damage.

---

* Aonghas was the man who delivered guga to our house, doing so while collecting payment for our household insurance. It might have made an interesting advertising slogan – 'Pearl Assurance – the policies that appeal to the palate'!

It was something they planned to do again the following year, but first of all, they had to make sure the fishing boat was loaded and gone from its shores. They did this by using the dinghy, going out to the *Viking* time and time again despite the fact that there was a heavy swell and it was clear that stormy weather was on its way. Eventually, however, the vessel was ready to go. Alasdair waved goodbye as it sailed, thinking, perhaps, of his young wife and child who were at that time living in the village of Cross, a little south of Lionel. As Iain was at that time not quite one year old, there was within him all the impatience of a young father anxious to see what changes the passing of a few weeks had brought about in his son.

There was also another thought. His brother-in-law, Donald, was going to be married the following Friday and Alasdair was supposed to be the best man. Someone else was going to have to stumble their way through the words of a wedding speech, read the telegrams and good wishes that had been sent by friends, relatives and neighbours, while all the time Agnes would have to sit there, half-absent from the celebrations, wondering how he was getting on.

But all thought of that would have to wait. The weather was worsening with the wind blasting through the geo. Even the few brief moments it calmed, it was never clear that conditions could be trusted. Two and a half hours would be needed to take the boat down to the water's edge. In these conditions, two and a half hours was a long time to be able to anticipate the weather and the state of the tide in advance. One mistake in their prediction and the vessel – and perhaps even the men who wished to sail in it – could be lost.

Time ticked on. The men – known by such names as Jellicoe, Aonghas Bàn, Red, Shonnie Saidh, Aonghas Ghliocais and others – kept checking the horizon to see if human impatience could manage to calm the weather down. The answer to that question seemed always to be the same.

'Perhaps tomorrow . . .'

'We have to be patient . . . Better late than . . .'

Their gaze swept across the horizon to make sure the world was the same as before. The sea was still crossed with peaks and summits, white crests on every wave. Rain buffeted against them, drumming their yellow oilskins with its frenzied, lunatic beat. They strained to watch one of the gannets struggle to take off, clumsy as usual as it ran across the waves to do so. A few moments later and it soared high and magnificent again, secure in its flight from the rock. They hoped that the same might be true of them.

And soon . . .

Especially since they were aware time ticked on for those at home too, perhaps even more slowly than it did for those on Sulasgeir. Unaware of what might be happening, they also studied the horizon anticipating that they might catch a glimmer of their men returning home on the *Star of Hope*. No gleam ever appeared, their additional time on the island now extending to a fortnight. And during that period, fears multiplied. Anxieties increased. Eventually, a local postman decided to get in touch with Stornoway. His brother-in-law was with the crew and they were becoming alarmed about his safety. A short time later and the fishery cruiser was sent out to see if the men were all right.

In a strange twist of fate, it was also the same day the *Star of Hope* was taking to the waters. Due to the length of the time they had been stranded, they decided they should take any opportunity, leaving in an unorthodox way. They launched the boat while the wind was from the north-east, blowing directly into the open mouth of the geo. It was something they would not normally do, knowing the waters can be stirred more than a little by a storm gusting from that direction.

And then there was the voyage. Again, the sea-skills of men like Alasdair came to the fore. 'We were chased by the wind with a full boat,' he explains. 'We decided not to take a direct route to the Butt because of the way the storm was blowing. Instead we planned to go south-east, straight into its force as far as we could.'

He pauses, trying to justify to a landlubber like me the reasons for that decision. 'We knew that if we kept going in that direction, if the wind became stronger, the further we could turn. It meant going as far south as we could leaving the fierceness of that storm behind us, only to make it easier for us to turn later and blow us in the direction of Port.'

Unaffected by the storm, some five miles east of them, the fishery cruiser was heading in the direction of where they came from. When it arrived, it circled the island. Eyes strained to catch any movement on the rock, noting the absence of any life on Sròn na Lice, Sgeir an Teampaill, Mullach an Eilein, Geo Phuill Bhàin . . . Slowly, eventually, after they'd gone round its shoreline twice, they came to a bitter, bleak conclusion, one they relayed to the likes of James Morrison, working at the Decca Station in Lionel. His eyes must have given the bad news away to the friends and neighbours of the missing men long before any words came to his tongue.

'There's no sign of them . . .'

The men on the *Star of Hope* knew, however, that the fishery cruiser was out looking for them. From their position low down in the waves, they could see the ship in the distance. One of the men may have shouted or waved an arm in its direction but the larger vessel continued on its progress away from Sulasgeir, complete with its cargo of bad news, believing there was a good chance that the lives of the Nessmen had been lost.

There was, however, one man on shore who had spotted them. Raising his telescope beside his home in Eorodale, Hector Morrison glimpsed a yellow speck out on the Atlantic. Blinking in disbelief, he raised his glass again, only lowering it when he was sure he was seeing the men of the *Star of Hope*, all kitted out in their yellow oilskins. Hurrying down to Port, he could barely contain his excitement. One by one he passed on the good news to the people already gathering like crows on the headland, staring out to sea.

The men were alive!

'There was a very strange reception waiting for us when we neared the harbour,' Alasdair confesses. 'A big Shackleton swooped down above us. Then it turned around, circled in the air and headed back to Stornoway. One of us asked about the strange black shape on the headland. Someone said it looked like a huge peatstack someone had built there. Imagine our surprise when a moment or two later, parts of that peatstack started moving. One or two people breaking away from the rest as they raced in the direction of the quay. We knew then we were going to get the greatest of welcomes.'

'And just then I wasn't worried about the gugas we had caught. The only thing that was on my mind was to see Agnes and my son Iain after all the weeks I had been away from them. So as soon as we landed, I raced to the Bedford van I had left on the quayside a few weeks before, turned the key but the dashed thing wouldn't start. Dampness had got into it while I was away. I looked around in desperation and there was the district nurse, Katag Dhanaidh. '*An toir thu dhomh* lift?' I asked her. 'Could you give us a lift?' She just smiled and nodded her head.'

'The next thing I knew I was back in the village and feeling embarrassed about the whole thing. Our next-door neighbours were out working in a field of oats and Katag was out of her car and shouting;

'*Thàinig iad! Thàinig iad!* They've come! They've come!'

It was the greatest and warmest welcome Alasdair ever received after his time away – the one too that must still come to his mind when the young men of Ness are out hunting the guga, his thoughts straying among them during all the time they are there.

5

Taste of Guga

A SEABIRD HUNTER'S WIFE
STAYS HOME TO SEW

When he is away,
she tugs needle-point
through cloth;
steel flashing like spindrift
against rock

Or that white bird he hunts,
yellow head piercing dark
for beak to gleam with silver,
as great wings
tipped with black
rise from ocean's depths
to stretch and soar in flight,
the same way she pays attention,
thin thread in the evening light,
tight between the constant tension
of either making do and mend
or tearing up a worn-out garment
and bringing its thin comfort to an end.

Barabel Murray played a major role in entertaining my taste
buds when I was younger. While growing up in South Dell, I
used to spend some time visiting her son Alex Dan – one of my
near contemporaries. As we played a game of Monopoly or
draughts, she would provide us with a glass of orange juice
and a plateful of scones and home-made jam. There would be
times, too, when something even more exotic would be on
hand – a plateful of 'duff', the skinned dumpling with currants

that was the speciality of many of the housewives of Ness at that time, or a slice of Victoria sponge, perhaps.

'*Siuthadaibh*,' she would say. 'Come on . . . Eat up.'

Frailer now, Barabel no longer has the gusto that she had in earlier years. A short time before I visited her, she had fallen and broken her hip. Later, they discovered the bone had been set incorrectly and took her back for another operation. She is recovering from this when I see her. Still in her nightdress and dressing gown, she sits in her fireside chair with her Zimmer frame in front of her. On the mantelpiece, there is a glass of water and a clutch of tablets.

Yet for all her body's lack of strength, her mind and tongue still have vigour. She recalls for me old disputes that once occurred in the district, how a respectable lady from the community once appeared in the courtroom and disgraced herself by referring to the judge as 'Lord Loaf' throughout the proceedings. She also recalled how that same community had fed itself in former days, when the district relied on its own resources.

'There were none of these supermarkets then. No, indeed.'

Her silver hair, once possessing a reddish tinge, bobs as she talks, giving emphasis to her words. She has a rather staccato voice, too, her words clipped and emphasised. These characteristics combine to recall the forceful quality she possessed some 30-odd years ago, helping to create a sharp, vivid picture of her early life at the north end of the district where she grew up. For most of our conversation she speaks about food, showing an interest in cooking and baking she has possessed for most of her adult life.

'We used everything we had to get by. Everything we had. Even the head and feet of the sheep were used. *Ceann is casan*. We'd singe the sheep's feet in the fire, using the prongs to turn them over. Singe the head too. We'd split it then and remove the brain. There would be the intestines too. They would be used, every single part rinsed and cleared out to make *maragan* . . .'

She takes me back to my childhood as she speaks, watching my Aunt Bella working away in the shadows of her own kitchen to make the district's own version of black or white pudding. She would have the sheep's intestines curled up in front of her in an earthenware bowl, a few other ingredients, too, set out and ready to play their own part in this recipe. Sheep's blood, rich and crimson. Oatmeal. Some coarse salt. Pepper. Five or six onions.

And I'd watch with gory fascination as my aunt spooned that red mixture into the intestines, slowly and precisely, taking care not to spill or waste a drop. She'd squeeze it occasionally with arthritic fingers, ensuring it was all finely and evenly spread out, trying to prevent, too, any clots forming in the blood. And then when it was three-quarters full, she would take a piece of string and tighten a knot fast around it. It would be plunged into a large pan of boiling water bubbling on the stove, a witch's brew prepared with love and kindness.

Barabel reminds me of all this, including much I'd forgotten. She tells of how long it all took to boil – two hours or more, and how women like my aunt would prod the *maragan* from time to time with a knitting needle, letting the air out before they burst. If that occurred, it would be a tragic event for the woman of the house.

'I remember going into this house,' Barabel recalls, 'and the woman being in tears because she had allowed her marags to burst. And it was no wonder. People didn't have much money then. It was a waste of hours too. All that work and nothing as a result.'

And when the *maragan* were completed, they were stored away, perhaps in that same earthenware bowl mentioned earlier. Nearby, too, there might be this year's supply of the guga, the half-barrel of salt herring bought at the end of summer. Together with the salted meat of the sheep they had killed, they were what most families relied on to get by.

There were other delicacies Barabel recalled for me – ones

like *ceann cropaig*. Despite its grisly appearance, it was a dish that I welcomed seeing at the centre of the dinner table. I relished its flavour, enjoyed its textures in my mouth. No doubt visitors might find this hard to believe as they watch a ling's head being served, and see it grinning at all those who come to feast on it. Beneath its sharp teeth would be a mixture made from oatmeal and fish liver. Sometimes Barabel would add some carefully chopped onion to the recipe.

'It's something I'm told they did in Point,' she explained, 'And I tried it once and they all liked it. After that, I put some onion in every time I made it.'

And, of course, like the *marag*, it was boiled before it was brought to table, a culinary approach that was dictated by the fact that for generations very few homes in places like Ness possessed an oven.

'Only the police station and the lighthouse had one while I was growing up . . .' Barabel recalled. 'The posh people.'

And even when they came into existence, part of the Raeburn stoves that came to be added to homes in later years, they were still viewed as unreliable. These new items in the kitchen required to be stoked with peat – a fuel notoriously hard to regulate and keep at a constant temperature. Chickens, when they were killed, were rarely ever roasted. Instead, they bubbled and boiled on top of the stove, a sprinkling of rice or pearl barley, carrots and onions added to the brew.

Yet there was nothing unique in any of this. In fact, if one were to have written a volume entitled '*Une Courte Histoire De La Cuisine Nordique*' or 'A Short History of Northern Cuisine' to the uninitiated, it would contain a remarkably similar set of similar recipes wherever it was written. There would be the local version of *maragan* or *ceann cropaig*, and meals based on the head and feet of a sheep. There would be a large variety of both sea and other varieties of birds eaten too.

In fact, in one part of this small world, there is such a volume. Many recipes similar to the one I've noted above appear, albeit under exotic names like 'Hakka Muggies' and 'Crappin' in a book, *Cookery for Northern Wives*, published in the mid 1920s in Shetland. Recipes for snipe and starlings are also to be found there – a reminder of the fact that any small birds straying into coastal areas were considered 'fair game' by the natives. Such practices were even found considerably nearer the centre than this. Throughout most of Europe, small birds were eaten. 'Four-and-twenty blackbirds' might or might not at one time have been 'baked in a pie' but there is little doubt that a variety of small birds provided a welcome snack for both the urbanite and his country cousin until relatively recent times.

It was, of course, not only the birds themselves that were eaten but also their eggs. In Fair Isle, for instance, it was only the signs of a fall in the guillemot population that put an end to the practice of taking their eggs in the 1970s. In Lerwick, until recent times, the man responsible for cleansing the town's buildings of scorrie or seagull eggs enjoyed a roaring trade supplying certain of the inhabitants. I have discovered, too, one person in Shetland, a near-contemporary of my own, whose father used to take her gathering seabird eggs from the cliffs, long after the Protection of Birds Act was in place. In her own words, she describes how she 'minds well'

. . . scaling sheer cliff faces at the back of Brindister, in my parka with huge pockets to collect as many gulls' eggs as possible! I think my record for coming back up a cliff face was a dozen intact eggs. Dad would test them to see if they were 'birded' by putting them into a rockpool – if they float, there is air in, and they are no good to eat – they got put back in a nest. If they sank – we took them home. It was mostly gulls' eggs we collected, the Mallie [fulmar] eggs were white, and tasted very fishy, so we didn't really take many, as nobody but Dad would eat them. The gulls' eggs, however, were used mainly in baking – making a lovely sponge.

She goes on to note how 'Dad tried different ways of preserving them – I mind an old sink or tub in the shed filled with isinglass one year, and Mum used to crack 2 or 3 into a Tupperware tumbler and freeze them, to be used in cakes later.'

Puffin eggs from Suleskerry even formed a secret ingredient in the recipes of a bakery in Stromness in Orkney till the 1950s, their yellow yolks adding a brighter shade to its cakes and pancakes than would be obtained from the duller offerings of domestic hens. It was a practice that, as the Orcadian poet Robert Rendall reminds us, sometimes took its toll of human life – as it did so often among the high crags and cliff-faces of St Kilda. His poem of that title adopts the voice and viewpoint of a 'Cragsman's Widow' as he points out that the cliff-face, just like the sea, extracted its own rent from the men who clambered up and down its crags searching for the 'mallimak' (the Orkney name for the fulmar) or the eggs of the whitemaa or seagull.

> He was aye vaigan b' the shore,
> An' climman amang the craigs,
> Swappan the mallimaks,
> Or taakan whitemaa aiggs.
> It's six year bye come Lammas,
> Sin' he gaed afore the face,
> An' nane but an aald dune wife
> Was left tae work the place.
> Yet the sune shines doun on a'thing,
> The links are bonnie and green,
> An' the sea keeps ebban an' flowan
> As though it had never been.

Another islander, Liam O'Flaherty from Inishmore in the Aran islands off the west coast of Ireland, tackles similar material in the short story 'Trapped'. In this, he describes

Port in calm. *Iain Gunn*

... and storm. *Hugh Macinnes*

Sulasgeir coming into view. *Used by kind consent of Jez Blackburn*

The fishing boat arrives. *Angus Morrison*

Encountering some familiar landmarks. *Jez Blackburn*

How the waves have caved its rock … *Jez Blackburn*

... and created chasms. *Jez Blackburn*

Challenged by its dizzy heights. *Angus Morrison*

Above. The Teampall
and cairns.
Jez Blackburn

Left. Some the work of
men who returned for
many years to the rock.
Jez Blackburn

Greeting Sulasgeir's inhabitants. *Jez Blackburn*

Shades of black and white – the residents. *Jez Blackburn*

Above. Gannet and chick.
Jez Blackburn

Left. Some hunters – like Tormod – might have been detained by more pressing commitments, like his marriage to Christina.
Iain MacAulay

Left. Tom Patey following in the 'footsteps' of Donald Morrison, crossing the traverse to the Stack of Handa. *Sir Chris Bonington*

Below. The men of the *Mayflower* crew in the 1950s. *Stornoway Gazette*

Above. High on the rocks – the traditional mooring place for the hunters' boats.
Alasdair Campbell

Left. Alasdair Bàn (far right) and some of the other hunters who accompanied him on his trips to Sulasgeir.
Alasdair Campbell

Above. 'Eve', like the Gaisean on the front cover, one who often accompanied Alasdair Bàn on his voyages to Sulasgeir. *Alex Murray*

Left. Its feathers scorched, the guga transformed into a phoenix by Kenneth Murray. *Sheila W. Macdonald*

The men of 1912 – the year of the *Phoenix*. *National Museums of Scotland. Scran.*

Sule Stack, another of the hunters' traditional destinations. *Jez Blackburn*

The craft of seabird hunting was also practised elsewhere, such as Orkney.
Shetland Archives

The men of Shetland risking their lives for seabird eggs. From *Picturesque Shetland* drawn by Frank Barnard. *Shetland Museum*

The Faroese artist Samuel Joensen Mykines (1906–79) celebrated the gannets of his native isle in this painting of the 'Cliffs at Mykines'. *Estate of Samuel Mykines*

Practising the art and craft of an ancient tradition, modern gannet hunters – such as Bobby Ruadh – at work.
Kenneth Murray

Latter-day hunters scaling Sulasgeir's cliffs.
Angus Morrison

In conversation. *Sheila W. MacDonald*

In a flurry of feathers. *Kenneth Murray*

Salting the bird. *Angus Morrison*

Most of the present crew – including Dods, second from left – circling a cairn of birds. *Angus Morrison*

how bird-catcher Bartly Hernon experiences difficulties
when he sets out on the island cliffs with the wooden stick
he uses for clubbing fowl in his hand. Using exact and
precise description, he notes how 'All sorts of seabirds were
flying in and out. The whirring of their wings in the
darkness was a terrifying sound, because they were invisible
and did not scream.'

In this particular instance, the central character escapes
death, overcoming 'a curious longing to look out over the
edge of the cliff and throw himself down' as he does so.
While he does this, 'he kept remembering all the men of the
district who had been killed in the cliffs'. There is a gravestone on St Kilda which testifies to the truth of this; the end
of a young man's life marked with the simple legend 'With
Christ Which Is Far Better'.

Yet it may be that in certain waters, like those around St
Kilda, the hunting of seabirds may have been a less dangerous activity than fishing. Any human loss on the cliff-edge
was likely to involve only one man; not perhaps six as might
occur when a boat, for instance, attempted to land in
Village Bay. In his book, *Collapse*, American writer Jared
Diamond highlights another society, Norse Greenland,
where men seem to have preferred eating seabirds to fish.
His evidence for that view lies in the contents of the middens
archaeologists have uncovered in areas occupied by the
Norse settlers. He points out that 'fish bones account for
much less than 0.1 per cent of animal bones recovered at
Greenland Norse archaeological sites, compared to between
50 and 95 per cent at most contemporary Iceland, northern
Norway and Shetland sites'. His explanation for this pau-
city, however, is less convincing than his evidence, especially
when he argues that the Greenland Norse 'may have developed a taboo against eating fish'. There are other, more
compelling, reasons for the non-appearance of fish bones
in the household heaps. Mixed within hay, fish bones were

apparently fed to cattle at one time; their salty presence among the feed encouraging the animals to drink more and, as a result, produce more milk. They might also have decided that given the risks involved in fishing for a half-dozen, the menfolk were better with their feet remained fixed on the crags. This only meant one man 'going over'.

Like the St Kildans too, they might simply have preferred the taste of seabirds, finding fish a little pallid.* This may have been a more common view than it seems nowadays, when the practice of hunting seabirds has been all but abandoned. After all, it occurred even as far south as the north-east of England in the aftermath of the Second World War. I have also been informed that shags shot in Shetland were labelled 'Black game' or 'black ducks' and sold in London during that period. Fair Isle seems to have developed a small industry, sending these birds to restaurants during that time, until one day a terse letter arrived from their contact in the metropolis, saying: 'Send no more of your black ducks!'

It was certainly the case that a quick squint and scurry down a cliff-edge was a neat way of dodging the worst effects of rationing and adding a little extra variety to your daily meals – even if it was only in the form of seabirds. While people took pleasure in eating these in their own right, it is also true that the taking of eggs was also a technique that aided hunters in their search for birds. It often extended the time these seabirds remained on the border between sea and land, delaying that final take-off and allowing the hunting season to lengthen. While birds like the fulmar, guillemot,

---

* There were also people who held the opposite view, sometimes because they felt that human souls could occupy the bodies of birds. These included one of Scotland's lesser-known Antarctic explorers, Thomas F. Macleod from Stornoway. He accompanied Shackleton and Scott on their journeys south and refused to eat penguins for this reason. A similar idea is found in an old Manx tale where one man warns his brother not to eat a variety of white-coloured seabird with black-tipped sleeves because that's where his soul is likely to be. This belief has clearly never been widespread in the north of Lewis.

razorbill and puffin would not lay again if their eggs were taken, other birds, including the gannet, would produce another, remaining on the cliff till they nestled it into life.

There were also a variety of different ways in which the seabirds were killed. A number of areas used the long pole, complete with single noose – which the Nessmen adapted and improved, finding its basis in a device found throughout the Northern and Western Isles. Multiple nooses attached to a small wooden frame were floated out to sea in Iceland and the Faroes as a way of catching birds away from the shore. A similar model was used on St Kilda, but on land, capturing up to 50 at a time. Nets are the method of choice in the Faroes and some other places. They could be draped across the mouth of a cave – as in Harris or Skye – or spread across puffin burrows at nightfall. Shortly after dark the fowlers would return to wring the necks of the unfortunate creatures trapped there. The Faroese were also adept at catching puffins and, sometimes, fulmars by using hand-nets fixed to the end of poles. The hunters would lay the pole flat down the slope waiting for their quarry to come into close enough proximity for him to quickly stand, loop and twirl the net and scoop the bird out of the sky.

Other, less common, means included the use of baited hooks and boards. The latter might be trailed across the surface of the ocean, complete with a tasty silver bite that would encourage, say, a gannet to swoop down upon it, only for its beak to be trapped in the wood or the bird to be rendered unconscious. It was this method that Shetlanders sometimes used when they caught gannet; in their case, however, they probably only kept some of their white feathers for their fishing lines – shamefully throwing much of the remainder away. Those in the far north were clearly without the necessary discernment to be aware they had a gourmet meal on hand.

Stones might also be thrown – a method much disapproved of on Lewis. There were also, more fancifully, dogs trained for the purpose of catching and seizing birds. Sometimes, these were used simply for retrieving. In the Lofoten Islands and the Faroes, little dogs called the Lundehund were specifically bred to scurry down burrows, emerging from the darkness with, for instance, a puffin and, sometimes, eggs in their possession. In other places, they were trained to pounce on the bird just as it was alighting on its nest.* On Harris, apparently, fox terriers were trained for this purpose, capturing shearwaters this way. A stranger practice still operated on Ailsa Craig, where the keeper's dog pushed along the burrows, emerging with a half dozen or so birds clinging to its coat. It is rumoured that the inventor of Velcro got his idea from seeing how objects often clung to dogs' coats. It is not recorded whether seabirds were among the items he noticed.

There are yet other methods that seem to stretch belief to greater lengths than even the most taut rope tugged over a cliff edge. One that makes Dods, among others, snort with derision is a tale – featuring a worsted glove – that comes from Shetland. This was used, apparently, to deceive the sentry on the edge of a flock of resting shags into thinking the weather was stormy and the group were safe perched on the rocks. Water would be flicked into the bird's face, persuading it to fall asleep. Once this happened, the entire group was ripe for the plucking. Sand was also used to the same effect in North Rona, imitating hail or the effects, perhaps, of a sand-storm.

'I don't believe any of that,' Dods grinned when we talked about that. 'It's simply incredible.'

Close attention was also, it seems, paid to the sounds uttered by particular birds. The noise 'Bir, bir' emerging

---

* The Lundehund is surely one of the most remarkable dogs in the world: it has at least six toes on each foot, for a more secure grip on cliff edge and crag; it can close its ears, preventing either dirt or moisture from affecting its hearing; and has front shoulder joints that are extremely mobile, so it can bend its head back over the shoulders – an extremely useful ability when reversing out of a tunnel.

from a flock of gannets was apparently a sign that they were aware of approaching danger. It invariably meant that the fowler would be standing on the cliffs alone a few moments later, wings flapping all around him. The cry 'Grog, grog' was evidence of contentment. If it was heard, there was a good chance that a substantial proportion of the birds would be captured before take-off took place, particularly if the 'sentinel' or sentry bird was caught.

Yet the oddest method of all took place on St Kilda. Allegedly, men sometimes used to climb down the cliffs with a stretch of linen attached to their chests. Mistaking this strange form of dress for the guano-stained cracks and crevices guillemots call home or, perhaps, the unstained breasts of their partners in their nests, the birds would attempt to touch-down there, being swept up by fowlers when they landed. Occasionally, it also appears islanders attempted a slight variation on this technique, baring their chests or backs in order to tempt the birds down. Clearly this was a method that would only be useful in the rain-soaked northern edges of the world, parts where the sun rarely reaches to brown or tan the more concealed parts of the human body.

Almost as strangely, it is also the case that people in different areas seemed to prefer to eat different foods and birds. For instance, I have spoken to a number of Nessmen in their 80s, asking them if they had ever eaten gull or other seabird eggs. They all shake their heads, never having heard of anyone who had done so – apart from on one occasion, when guga hunter Murdo Deedo, or Murdo Macdonald, tried to sell a quantity he had found on the local sea-cliffs while he was still in Primary school.

Certain birds are also proscribed in the Bible, with warnings that 'they shall not be eaten, they are an abomination'. One translation of the Bible, the work of Anglo-Irish scholar John Nelson Darby at the end of the nineteenth century, omits the cormorant included in the 'abominations' in

Leviticus 11:17 and mentions the gannet instead. For all the biblical injunctions against it, however, there were other parts of Scotland where the cormorant was the principal bird on the menu, just as the gannet is on Lewis. The shag or cormorant – both known in Gaelic by the same term, *sgarbh* – is particularly enjoyed at the opposite, southern end of the Western Isles from Ness, in places like Eriskay and South Uist. One – hopefully! – tongue-in-cheek recipe for this particular bird appeared in a book that was first published in 1965 – *Countryman's Cooking* by the aptly-named W.M.W. Fowler. It begins as follows with the instruction: 'Having shot your cormorant, hold it well away from you as you carry it home; these birds are exceedingly verminous and the lice are said to be not entirely host-specific. Hang up by the feet with a piece of wire, soak in petrol and set on fire. This treatment both removes most of the feathers and kills the lice . . .' before coming to an end with the following advice:

Simmer gently in seawater, to which two tablespoons of chloride of lime have been added, for six hours. This has a further tenderising effect. Take out of the water and allow to dry, meanwhile mixing up a stiff paste of methylated spirit and curry powder. Spread this mixture liberally over the breast of the bird.

Finally roast in a very hot oven for three hours. The result is unbelievable. Throw it away. Not even a starving vulture would eat it.

The same might be said for the fulmar, the St Kildans' favourite – the source of much of their food, light and warmth. The first ones arrived on St Kilda some time around the beginning of the nineteenth century before nesting around much of the Scottish coastline at a later date. Nowadays these stub-beaked creatures, with their unsavoury habit of squirting oil at intruders, can be found fluttering on just about every stretch of shoreline in the country – including, as the guga hunters can testify only too well, the cliffs and crags of Sulasgeir.

And there were other birds, too, eaten by man at these northern edges of the world. Some regarded as treats included the Manx shearwater, razorbill and guillemot. However, the most popular seabird on the menu even until the present day is probably the puffin. In Iceland, the best restaurants feature recipes like the following – Mjólkursoinn Lundi, known to the English-speaker as puffin in milk sauce. To paraphrase Mrs Beeton, to cook a puffin a chef must ensure it: 'should be skinned or carefully plucked and singed. Remove the innards and discard. You can use the breasts alone, or cook the whole birds. Wash well in cold water and rub with salt, inside and out. If you are using whole birds, truss them. Draw strips of bacon through the breasts . . .'

And soon it will be ready for table, accompanied by a helping of boiled potatoes, vegetables and a caramel-flavoured sauce. It possesses, too, not the expected salty flavour but a strong, dark, gamey taste. Or so, at least, say some of these Icelanders who have tucked into these small birds on occasion – men like Adalstein Asberg and Gyrdir Eliason, writers from that country who accompanied a group of us both in their own country and on a visit to the Faroes a few years ago. There were others too – Orcadian writer Matthew Wright; poet Jen Hadfield; and Lise Sinclair, the writer and musician from Fair Isle. We were met there by a number of Faroese writers and musicians, including musical maestro Kristian Blak, who took us on a tour around his homeplace soon after our arrival.

It was a place that impressed me from the moment we touched down on the plane – a collection of islands in the North Atlantic that resembled Skye, with their sweep of high hills down to the ocean, the mares' tails of water spouting down their flanks, the swirl of mist always hanging below their summits. Yet there was much which was different from that Inner Hebridean island. They included the brightly coloured wooden houses nestling beside the sea's edge, clustering beside the Lutheran chapel that was the central focus of each community; the brave attempt to cultivate the most vertiginous patches of land, with hay, for instance, stretched out on fence-wire to dry beside a stubbled, sloping field; and, of course, the tunnels into which our mini-bus disappeared at irregular intervals, exchanging mist for a deeper, more impenetrable darkness.

These had been dug to link the communities – and many of the islands – of the Faroes together. Their engineers had scooped out tunnels under mountains and inlets of the ocean to make, for instance, a connection between the airport on the most southerly island of Vagar and the main town, Torshavn, possible. Commuters were now also travelling between far-off districts and the capital on a daily basis across freshly tarmac-covered roads – distances that would only have been possible by sea a number of years before. On their way, they passed the Stone Forests – those distant cousins of the cairns found throughout Lewis. They were towers of stone stacked precariously on one another, looking as if their foliage of small rocks would be shaken down in the next strong breeze. Kristian beamed proudly when he told me all of this, speaking, too, of his little music shop – called Little China – among the tiny, 'dolls' houses' not far away from the Prime Minister's office near Torshavn Harbour.

'I've too many CDs,' he said in mock-complaint, 'You can barely stand when you come into my shop. No room for customers.'

One sensed that he almost preferred it that way, overwhelmed by his enthusiasm for song. That much was clear, too, when he spoke of how he and his band had toured the West Highlands and the Western Isles a number of years before.

'Some of the places we went to then are very like the Faroes,' he declared, giving me the full uncensored version of the night he had performed at the Dark Island Hotel in Benbecula. 'I liked them very much.'

How much like the Western Isles the Faroes are only struck me when Kristian took us to a small community on the northern coast of Eysturoy. A black-and-white collie acted as our guide during our time there, padding down the road past a church and a small collection of houses on our way to the pier. Kristian was talking animatedly, his hand gesturing the size of the hills that held this district tightly in their clasp.

'This place never sees the sun for most of the year,' he explained.

And then he pointed out a pair of sea stacks that stood beside tall dark cliffs some distance away – as impressive as any I have ever seen before. One was further out and seemed marginally taller than the other; straight and perpendicular with seabirds whirling round its summit. Closer to the coast, its broken tip pointing upward to the heavens, was its companion. It seemed to be balancing precariously, its two stone legs gaping apart. It was apparent even to the most uninformed observer that some time in the near future, perhaps by the end of this century and after a winter's storm, the sea would whittle away the rock that kept it upright. Already, part had already crashed and fallen some decades before.

'Risin and Kellingen . . .' he said, 'The giant and the witch.'

'Is that what they're called?' It was clear even at a glance which was which – the giant was the larger one; the witch the one with its legs agape, its finger scolding the clouds for some misdemeanour or other.

And then he told me the tale associated with them – how the giants who lived in Iceland were envious of the Faroes and wanted to take them back home with them. It was for this reason that they sent Risin and Kellingen out to get them. They reached the most north-western mountain, Eidiskollur, and tied a rope around it. Fastening all the islands within its knot, Kellingen tried to stack them onto her partner's back. It was at this point that part of the mountain split off while the remaining section stayed fixed where it was, its foundations firm and unshifting. Nevertheless, they continued at their labours all night, failing to move the islands one solitary inch.

They were turned into rock themselves the following morning. A shaft of sunlight performed this change, transforming them immediately – like other giants who stepped into daytime – into these stacks on the coastline. They've remained there ever since, looking pensively in the direction of Iceland and home.

'That all sounds very familiar,' I said.

It was then I told him a tale from Ness – how the Vikings had attempted to drag the entire archipelago of the Western Isles from its foundations off the north-west coast of Scotland back to Scandinavia with them. They looped rope through the Eye of the Butt – a hole in the rock that the sea has gnawed out there – and pulled, using their longships to help them in the task. They hauled and sweated; swore and cursed; heaved and tugged, in their efforts to alter the location of the piece of real estate they had obtained, but without any obvious result.

Apart from some unexpected ones. These came in the form of some messages that were being relayed from the crew of some of the other longships that were supervising the southern end of this massive removal.

'Barra has broken away . . .'

'So have the Uists . . .'

'Harris is threatening to go . . .'

It was this bad news that brought the entire enterprise to an

end. The men on the longships sadly and reluctantly un-
fastened their rope and headed for home, unable to realise
their dream of having the Hebrides hitched up alongside their
own coast. One of the more ambitious examples of Scandinavian empire-shifting had come to an abrupt close.

This piece of folklore was not, however, the only aspect
of life in which the two groups of islands resembled each
other. The DNA of both groups of inhabitants stems from
the same mingling of the bloodstreams of Scandinavian
and Celt. Similarities can be seen, too, in our languages. A
Faroese linguist was thrilled to hear the few words of Gaelic
with which I introduced myself that evening as the writers
appeared in Nordic House on the outskirts of Torshsavn,
telling me, for instance, that our two tongues shared a
number of similar words.

'Àirigh,' he announced, 'Your word for a summer sheil-
ing. We use something like that word. Also *tunnag*, your
word for 'duck', is like ours.'

He could also, if we had thought about it at the time, have
mentioned similar eating habits. Mykines, the furthest west
of the Faroe Islands, is also a place where the men of the
community go to hunt the guga. Behaving in much the same
way as my fellow Niseachs, they head out for the young
gannets in early autumn. The only part of these North
Atlantic islands where they nest, there is even a folktale to
explain the arrival of these rare birds among them.

It is another that features two giants – one from Mykines
and the other from Vagar – who battled to gain ownership
of these two islands, causing a great deal of damage to the
landscape in the process. At the fight's end, the Mykines
giant forced his defeated opponent from Vagar to provide
three items for the people of Mykines. These were a large
piece of driftwood, a bottle-nosed whale and a strange bird
to nest upon its rocks. The following year came and these
were duly provided. Their arrival, however, was accom-

panied by a series of complaints. The driftwood was too gnarled and the whale too ugly. (It was said to resemble a local politician.) The giant from Vagar overheard the words and, irritated by the ingratitude, decided not to send either to the place again. Only the strange white bird kept arriving, appearing in greater numbers on the island cliffs every year. Before long, the people in the area began to acquire a taste for it . . .

The story must be among the few in European folklore that feature the gannet, for it is unfortunately the case that in most legends, particularly those from the north, the bird fails to make an appearance. It is absent from the fables of La Fontaine or Aesop, where fox and crow pad or flutter into view time and time again.* In English verse, it is only an occasional visitor, occupying the central role, for instance, in one of Mary Oliver's poems, and one by Edwin Morgan. And when it does, it only turns up in work that proclaims the bird's speed and majesty, the way it clashes into the sea with the celebrated American nature poet, Mary Oliver, noting how:

> they explode into the water
> like white gloves,
> then they vanish,
> then they climb out again,
> from the cliff of the wave,
> like white flowers.

In the poetry of the north of Lewis, however, the gannet suddenly gains superstar status. Not for these writers,

---

* In the modern English novel, it is clearly neglected – though the gannet might be one of the seabirds that appear in Will Self's *Book of Dave* under the guise of the 'prettybeak', 'bonkergull' or 'oilgull'. These are just three species of birds the young men of the island of Ham, a place in an imagined future, set out to capture on fowling expeditions to nearby stacks.

however, is there any great emphasis on their power or startling accuracy. Instead, other aspects of that great bird are featured in poems like the following:

> 'S ann air muinntir Nis tha fadachd
> Gus an tig an guga còir,
> Ach am blais iad aon uair eile
> Air a' 'mhenu' bh' aig na seòid –
>
> 'S e rinn balaich Nis cho tapaidh
> Ged bhios iad fanaid orr' 's gach àit,
> Ach tha neart an sùgh a' ghuga
> Is tha e blasta le buntàt'.
>
> Tha e math do dhaoine bochda,
> Tha e math do dhaoine slàn,
> Ceannaichibh e, bhalaich Shiadair,
> 'S ithibh e gu 'm bi sibh làn.
>
> Ann an ùine nach eil fada
> Mas e 's gum bi sinn slàn is beò
> Thèid mi fhìn is balaich Mhurdaidh
> Shùlaisgeir a dh'iarraidh eòin.

It was the former pupils of Lionel School, like eleven-year-old Murdo Angus Murray, writer of the above verse and now a guga hunter himself for some years, who appeared the most enthusiastic about the gannet, believing it to possess magical health-giving qualities. They seem to have been inspired by the bird's glories, writing about it time and time again in the pages of the annual school magazine, *Tàintean*. Like the young Christina Norma MacDonald in Primary Six, who tells of how 'When you taste it, it is smashing. It is ten shillings and, oh dear, it is worth it. They are very wet before you put them in the pan and before that you cut their legs off and go and frighten the little baby if he is bad.'

Or, perhaps, the following from the pen of the guga hunter-in-chief, the young Dods MacFarlane who, way back in 1964, was clearly already aspiring to his current role, his thoughts slipping away from his school-work while scratching his head and coming up with the following:

When you get the guga you will break it in four pieces and take the grease off and put it in the pan and when it is ready you put it in the plate and when we come down to eat it we had to say grace and I nearly died before I got it. When you try the first one it is good and when you try the second one it is not so good and in five minutes after it you are thirsty.

George Morrison – the Breve – writes several poems about the bird, charting, for instance, the progress of the Protection of Birds Act through parliament in the mid-1950s. For some time, the Nessmen were not permitted to go there by James Stewart, the Secretary of State for Scotland at the time. George imagines a poor Nessman mourning the fact that he will only have salt to eat with his Kerr's Pinks for a time to come:

> Bidh mi le salainn,
> Le salainn's mi falamh dhìot,
> Bidh mi le salainn
> Ag ith a' bhuntàta –
> Ho-ro ghugachain,
> 'S falamh mo thubaichean;
> Ho-ro ghugachain,
> 'S duilich leam d' fhàgail.

And then there is 'am Bocsair' (Angus Campbell). In his poem 'An Guga Niseach' he eulogises the bird in much the same way as Burns pays tribute to the haggis in his own celebrated poem, declaring:

An guga Niseach liath-ghlas,
Is milis e fon fhiacail;
Thar gach uile bhiadh tha e càilear –
Roghainn na fir mhòra
O Sgiogarsta gu Rògh'dal
Nuair gheibh iad air a' bhòrd le buntàt' e.

There is also a most surreal piece of work that connects the nineteenth-century English poet John Keats, the eighth-century Greek writer Homer and astronomer Patrick Moore with the guga. Written by former Crowned Bard John Angus Macleod, it formed part of the epilogue to an astronomy book relating to Stornoway and the Isle of Lewis, called *Reul-Eòlas* (which the monocled *Sky At Night* presenter wrote expressly to be translated into Gaelic).*
Based on 'On First Looking Into Chapman's Homer' by Keats, the poem captured the immortal moment when John Angus first tasted the guga. As part of a class exercise, a young Gaelic student in his college in Essex, James Yardley, provided the translation that follows it.

Air Mo Chiad Bhlasad air a' Ghuga

Coisrigte do Dhòmhnall agus Raonaid Mhoireach

Trì fichead bliadhn' 's a deich fad' air mo chùl
's na Hearadh, air a' Ghalldachd is aig Deas:
's an àitichean de bharrachd fuachd is teas –
nach iomadh biadh san àm sin mheal mo shùil?
A' chuid bu mhotha, chòrd iad ris a' bhrù;
ri diathad de gach seòrs' mo chàil rinn cleas,
'Ach,' arsa Dòmhnall, 'cuiream thu fo gheas
le sògh de lòn air 'm b' eòlach mis' o thùs.'

---

* Interestingly, Moore intended all profits from the sale of the book to go towards further support of the Gaelic cause.

Air cagnadh na ciad chriomaig fo mo dheud,
crith-thalmhainn ann an toinisg càil is blas:
's mis' Pàdraig Moore ag amharc na h-ùr-rèil
ga cruthachadh gu h-obann is gu bras:
's mis' Niall a' Ghàirdein Làidir gearradh leum
air uachdar fuar na gealaich – a' chiad chas.

On First Tasting the Guga

Threescore and ten years now I've left behind
In Harris, Lowlands and 'neath Southron skies,
Besides less temperate lands. These nomad eyes
Have feasted in their time on many a kind
Of pabulum; most did my stomach find
Congenial-diverse diets to appetise.
But, 'Though your palate's jaded,' Donald cries,
'My long-known gourmet fare will still spellbind!'

As in my mouth the morsel melts, I feel
Seismically stirred, so succulent the taste;
Like Patrick Moore am I, when stars reveal
Them twinklingly new-formed from stellar waste.
With 'one small step' I leap, as strong-armed Neil
First-foots Selene's surface chill and chaste.

To anyone with even a smattering of Gaelic, one thing is clear. Virtually all the Hebridean poetry that features the guga has one feature in common: it is the bird's flavour bards – from the Bocsair to Contair, young Murdo Angus Murray to the Breve – choose to praise. It wasn't prepared in the same way everywhere, though: on the island of Islay, apparently, any solan goose intended for human consumption was first buried for 10–14 days in peaty soil to remove the wild taste.

The citizens of Edinburgh also used to appreciate its savour until the final years of the nineteenth century, though the capital's supply tended to come from a nearby source, the Bass Rock, with its seven acres of rock and thin grass in the Firth of Forth. The presence of the birds there was first referred to in a document sent to the Vatican at a time when the nuns at a Cistercian convent in North Berwick were engaged in a dispute with the rock's owners. Apparently, their chief concern was the prospect of losing the tithe they received on the barrels of fat produced when the birds were culled during the autumn. By the eighteenth century, however, any privileges enjoyed by the Holy Sisters were long over. The Bass Rock was rented out to a tenant who grazed a flock of sheep and hunted the gannet in season. In what was clearly an early example of niche marketing and rebranding, his produce was sold in the butchers' shops of Fleshers Close under the name of solan goose. The reward for this initiative was the princely sum of 20 pence per bird. The economic success of this venture can be seen in the fact that, though 25 sheep still grazed on the island, its principal produce was the young gannet.

The bird was also apparently cooked in a very different way from the manner in which the bird is prepared in Hebridean households today: it was taken home, skinned and cooked like a beef-steak. Another traditional recipe, for cooking either gannet or goose, appears on the website of a London butcher, Cooksleys of Mill Hill. Those familiar with the former bird will note the instruction relating to excess fat and wonder how an old-fashioned oven was equipped to deal with the vast quantities that must have been produced by the bird:

Peel, quarter, boil potatoes until tender. Melt butter in skillet, cook onions until soft. Mash potatoes with enough cream to make a fluffy mixture. Add onions, salt, pepper to taste, stuff into goose cavity. Sew up or skewer cavity to close. Rub outside of goose with more salt and pepper. Prick skin all over to release fat as it melts during roasting. Preheat oven to 325°F (165°C). Place goose on rack in shallow roasting pan, roast 3–3 ½ hours. Pour off goose fat every 20 minutes, save. Simmer neck and gizzards with small carrot, onion in 4 cups water. Reduces to 1–1 ½ cups of stock after 1 ½–2 hours. Spoon 3–4 tbsps ice water over goose during last 15 minutes to crisp skin. Remove goose to platter, keep warm. Remove all but 1 tbsp fat from roasting pan. Set over burner, stir in flour, brown lightly. Slowly add chicken or goose broth, stir until thickened. Season with salt, pepper, strain, serve in jug with goose.

Perhaps due to the fact that Hebridean households were not equipped with ovens till recent times, this was not the way Lewis people cooked their guga. In fact, even during my childhood, the average Ness household set out its meals in a way that resembled Henry Ford's dictum about his Model T – 'You can have your food prepared in any way you like as long as it is boiled.' In the guga's case, the filleted fowl is washed carefully, making sure that not one grain of coarse salt remains. (From hard experience, I am aware how the grains grind against your fillings.) For this purpose, the bird is often boiled before cooking even begins, using a handful of washing soda crystals or, even more bizarrely, Fairy Liquid, to ensure the bird is clean. Sometimes the four portions (or *ceathramhan*) that the bird is cut into are scraped clean with the edge of a knife. After this, it is boiled for an hour with a water-change after 30 minutes. (Some people do this more than once through the process.) And accompanying the guga is a cup or two of milk or water and a serving of potatoes – boiled, of course.

Most of the time, too, the people of Ness are even specific about the type of potato that should accompany the dish. It has to be the Kerrs Pink; its red jacket bursting open as it lies invitingly beside the bird, oozing with melted butter. For some bachelors living in the area, this has a disturbing effect, the close proximity of that first guga the closest to an erotic experience they enjoy each year.

The smell produced by the food, however, as it cooks upon the stove has fewer admirers. Some have described it as the worst they have ever experienced, causing their throats to gag and choke. It has been likened to diesel fuel, putrid woollen socks, the equivalent of the fumes that steam out of the lower rings of Dante's Inferno, the salty counterpart to smoke emerging from the inner confines of Hell. A friend of mine tells me of the visit of an insurance agent to his parents' tenement flat in Partick in the West End of Glasgow. It was a place where Hebrideans used to congregate in exile, Gaelic heard almost as often as English in its streets.

'I don't know what you're cooking,' the insurance agent declared. 'But I think they're boiling another portion of that same fisherman in number 36.'

The meat and skin are two quite distinct experiences. The former has been described in a number of ways by those who come to praise it. In my view, its taste resembles salt mackerel-flavoured chicken. Others claim the meat has the texture of steak and the flavour of kipper. Some rhapsodize over it, claiming it is like salt goose – one with very little fat. Those who have eaten 'reistit mutton' while in Shetland argue that there are certain similarities between the two foods. Both are pickled in salt, though the northern equivalent is also smoked above the stove and has a different texture. From my personal experience, both also provoke an almighty and fearsome thirst – one which few main-landers are equipped to withstand.

Even its admirers, however, freely admit that in terms of its appearance, the skin has little to commend it. It has been said to resemble a dirty cloth employed only a short time before to clean up a grimy, dirt-engrained floor. Others have likened it to the stubbled chin of a centenarian, one on whose grizzled face Gillette and Wilkinson Sword have long given up an unequal challenge. There are more who believe that the original model was uncovered when archaeologists discovered the inner chambers of Tutankhamen's tomb. Some individuals have even been fooled into believing the folds of skin surrounding the bird resemble a deflated bagpipe, attempting to obtain a note from one of its drumsticks from time to time.

Yet there are many citizens of Ness and elsewhere who believe that the skin is the most exquisite part of their native delicacy. Some liken it to tripe, what was at one time the central culinary experience of Britain's industrial past. Others enjoy it as a titbit, storing it in the fridge and nibbling a small piece at a time like Americans are said do with beef jerky. In contrast, one man preferred the gannet's tail, taking a collection of them home to eat as he preferred this to the rest of the guga. They said that every time he spat into a fire, his phlegm would sizzle and burn. Some also fed their sheep with guga fat or *gìoban*, making sure their ewes were fit for market. There were those, too, who saw it as a type of relish or dessert, adding savour to their meal – clearly the most adaptable of foods.

And then, in contrast, there are the unfortunate souls who tell jokes about the bird. They speak about the parcels Nessmen and women used to send to those exiled among their diaspora in White Street or Gardner Street, Partick in Glasgow. They talk about how sometimes tiny claws used to poke through the brown paper packaging, alerting a dozy-eyed postman to the fact that something might be afoot. According to legend, a policeman might be called and a poor Nessman living in that area questioned about a strange plot by cruel, native tribesmen from the Isle of Harris to send shrunken human heads all around the country. There is even, too, a story about a postman who stole one of these parcels to give its contents to his young son. Believing the guga to be a deflated leather football, he spent hours trying to pump it up before finally discarding it in a bin. There are rumours that the boy later spent much of a brief sporting career playing for a side named 'Partick Thistle Nil'. There is the story, too, that it is to be marketed as a midge-repellent. 'Rub into the skin and it will keep the midges away. Unfortunately, too, it may also have the same effect on women. The sheer number of bachelors in Ness can testify to its effectiveness.'

Someone has even gone so far as to point out to me that the Hungarians have the word 'guga' in their dictionary. The English equivalent is 'wen' and it describes a 'sebaceous cyst, especially on the head'.

'Just about sums it up,' this boor declared to me.

There are jokes, too, told about how the bird should be cooked. One 'recipe' for guga reads as follows:

Ingredients
One guga & one stone.
Place both in a pan of water & boil. Once you can pierce the stone with a fork the guga is ready for eating.

There are inevitably, too, many jests about its taste. Some have described it as being similar to strong duck stewed in cod liver oil and salt. Others have claimed that it has all the consistency and flavour of oiled chamois leather with a frame of bone attached. Another – clearly with an interest in all things Egyptian – has compared it to the wrappings of a mummy uncovered in Tutankhamen's tomb, but possessing the savour of fishy beef. There are some who argue that it might be improved by being marinated in Madras sauce or engine oil, or being buried for a fortnight or so in peat, as those on Islay used to do; and that the entire voyage to Sulasgeir should be sponsored by Dynorod . . .

However, let these individuals mock. Those of us fortunate enough to come from Ness can only be grateful that the gannet came to Sulasgeir. It provided us with a new and powerful sustenance, one that – according to Murdo Angus Murray's poem in the Lionel school magazine – granted strength and health to those who enjoy the richness of its flavour. The day of its arrival is recorded in the following story, one that builds upon the legend of St Ronan and his departure from Ness to North Rona and also the myth of his sister, Brunhilda or Brianuil, who died on Sulasgeir. I can only apologise in advance to any pedants or purists for the liberties I am about to take with the tale.

HOW THE GANNET CAME TO BE . . . IN SULASGEIR

The longer the monk they called Ronan spent in the township of Eoropie, the more he became tired of the company of his own species – and especially the female section of its population. Just about everything about them confused and irritated him. This ranged from the way they swayed and swirled as they moved around the house, their slim, curvaceous forms distracting him from prayer, to the manner in which they whispered to each other, muttering about what this or that one might be wearing.

'Oh, Gormel's wearing a bone clasp in her hair.'

'It seems Tormod gave her that the other night.'

'But I thought it was Raonaid he kept looking at.'

He would close his eyes, contemplating the wonder of the Creator while refusing even to listen to the empty chatter of His creations. Even his sister Brianuil seemed to be infected by this kind of talk. He had overheard her talking about one of the village men the other night, her voice hushed and low.

'He's a strong man. With such powerful hands.'

'There's no doubting that. But listen . . .'

He refused to do so any more. Instead, he would go and seek solace among the animals, seeing more of the light of God in their presence than in his fellow man.

'How long do I have to remain here?'

The little black bull standing in front of him didn't answer, but one of God's angels did, whispering softly in his ear.

'As long as you choose . . .'

Ronan decided to remain a little longer. After all, there were souls to be saved, other members of mankind he had a duty to tend and care for. He did his best to proclaim and enlighten them about the mysteries of faith. Standing before worshippers, he would attempt to draw their attention to the brevity and fragility of human life, the permanence and power of God.

And then he would notice the women. There might be Ealasaid staring in the direction of some young man who stood near her in the congregation. Her mind was clearly as restless as a bird's, flitting from one thought to another, rarely remaining perched on any idea for long. There would be Mineag, too, twirling her long black hair as if she were twisting some dark rope designed to snare and entrap his soul.

Why was he troubling himself for these people?

Why was he wasting his time?

It was during one night in his cell that Ronan prayed harder than ever before. 'Let me go from here,' he pleaded with the Lord. 'I do not care where you take me, only that you release me from this place. Deliver me now from those who surround me here.'

And in the darkness, he heard the voice of the angel responding to his words.

'*Eirich! Eirich!* Wake! Wake! *Tha an t-each iomhairraichte air an laimrig!* There's a strange steed on the shoreline!'

He tried not to listen or obey, placing hands over ears in case the angel's words seeped through. It was the behaviour of these women, he decided, that had led to such distractions and imaginings. Yet for all his attempts to silence them, the words came through yet again.

'*Eirich! Eirich!*'

He ground his teeth, shut his eyes, but the angel's voice could not be dammed or stopped.

'*Eirich! Eirich!*'

Eventually, he rose from his knees and went to Cunndal, a small bay to the west of Eoropie. There was a great beast waiting in the water for him there. Vast, shining and black, it resembled the whales he had seen so often powering their way through the waves around the Butt, but it was so much larger than any of them. There was even a large white bird with great wings, a yellow head and a huge beak perched on its back. Never having seen one before, he watched in wonder as it flapped its wings and, flying around the creature's head, appeared to whisper a few words in its ear.

He knew exactly what the massive creature was – the *cionaran cro*, a legendary huge beast that was said to haunt the depths of the ocean. He had heard about its existence in a piece of verse men sometimes chanted as they tried to find some meaning in the circle of life in the sea.

> *Seachd sgadain,*
> *Sàth bradain;*
> *Seachd bradain,*
> *Sàth ròin;*
> *Seachd ròin,*
> *Sàth muc-mhara bheag;*
> *Seachd muca-mhara beag,*
> *Sàth muc-mhara mhòr;*
> *Seachd muca-mhara mòr,*
> *Sàth cionaran-crò,*
> *Seachd cionarain-crò*
> *Sàth mial mhòr a' chuain.*

> Seven herrings,
> Feast for a salmon;
> Seven salmon,
> Feast for a seal;
> Seven seals,
> Feast for a small whale;
> Seven small whales,
> Feast for a great whale;
> Seven great whales,
> Feast for a cionaran-crò;
> Seven cionaran-crò,
> Feast for the great beast of the oceans.

As the last line of that old verse echoed in his head, he heard the angel's voice speak once more.

'Climb on its back. It will take you away from all this.'

He was just about to do so when he heard another sound just behind him. He looked round to see his sister Brianuil racing towards the shoreline. Her hair was tangled and unkempt; her voice barely coherent.

'Wait! Wait for me!'

He paused, his foot perched in mid-air for an instant before stepping on that massive, sea-creature's back.

'Brianuil . . .'

'Ronan, take me with you. I know you are going away from here. All I ask is that you take me with you . . .'

He shook his head. 'No . . .' he said. 'I must go on my own, wherever the Lord sends me.'

'But . . . I will cook for you. I will sew for you. I will give you the opportunity to spend more and more of your time serving God.'

'Brianuil . . .'

'Please . . .'

Eventually, he gave in. He was fond of his sister, even if there were times when she irritated and angered him with her wilfulness. Besides, she shared the same flesh and blood as his and he felt he owed her some loyalty for this reason. Finally – and he admitted this only rarely to himself – there was the fear that he might be lonely somewhere else, that his annoyance at the ways of others only disguised a greater frustration with himself. The presence of birds, seals and the good Lord might not be enough to conceal this any more.

And with these thoughts jumbled together, both brother and sister voyaged together on the back of the *cionaran-crò* to the isle that came to be known as North Rona, some distance from Eoropie and around 12 miles away from the crags of Sulasgeir.

After the trouble Ronan and Brianuil suffered on their arrival, life soon became very peaceful on the island. The night they first arrived, there had been strange, wild creatures waiting for him at the place they called Sròn an Tintinn. They looked like fierce dogs with sharp claws and fangs like serpents. They barked and snarled when they stepped on shore, snapping particularly in Brianuil's direction, anxious, it seemed, to feast upon her flesh.

Yet all he had to do was raise a hand and they cowered from him. All he had to do was pray and they retreated, tails drooping between their legs. Making the sign of the cross, he whispered: 'O Lord that took the Children of Israel through the Red Sea and Jonah to land in the belly of the Great Whale . . .'

They backed away as he moved forward, powerless before the strength of his faith.

'What sorrow can befall us, while God the Father is with us?'

Whimpering as they raced away, their feet scrambled and slipped as they tried to cross a bare field.

'What sorrow can befall us, while God the Son is with us?'

Before long the creatures were on the rocks on the

southern end of the island, the waves that the *cionaran-crò* had carried Ronan and Brianuil across breaking against the stone, snapping at their tails. They whined and whimpered as Ronan moved forward. From the force of his goodness, there was no way of escape.

'What sorrow can befall us, while God the Spirit is with us?'

Moments later and they had toppled into the sea, having no option but to fall and stumble into its depths for all that they tried to remain ashore, clinging onto its crags. They yelped and moaned as they did so, unable to listen even to the final words of his prayer.

'No sorrow can befall us while He is at our side.'

Soon, it was only the marks of their claws that remained, the only evidence these beasts had ever been present on its shores. They scored and scratched rock, slashed their way through grey stone in their efforts to remain on land.

After that, there was peace . . .

Not that this really made Ronan any more content. Even the birds had started to irritate him. Each cry and scream disturbed his prayers. He would barely utter the words 'Look down upon Thy faithful servant' when an oyster-catcher might start to scold him, bringing his worship to an end. Or else it might be seals. They appeared to honk at him, mocking his litany of praise. Even flies troubled him; the way they droned round a rotting carcass on the shore seemed to drum and buzz like doubts within his own head, a chorus of questions and whispers he could never quite manage to still.

And then there were the memories of the women he had left behind in Eoropie. They would flit through his thoughts as he prayed, mentioning the names of Raonaid, Gormel, Mineag and Ealasaid as he stood at the altar before his congregation of one, urging them to leave behind the petty vanity of their lives.

It was Brianuil who brought this to his attention, talking of how often he mentioned their names while proclaiming the glory of God.

'You talk of them all the time and never pray for the men you left behind.'

'They trouble me more,' he said, defending himself.

'In their flesh?'

'No. Only in their souls.'

Brianuil raised an eyebrow – her doubts increasing a day or so later. She was leading the way as they climbed the slope from Fianuis, when she heard his footsteps halt. Turning round to speak, she noticed how his blue eyes gleamed in her direction, his tousled grey hair flapping in the wind.

'Why have you stopped walking?'

'I was just thinking what a handsome woman you are, Brianuil. What beautiful, white legs you have.'

She stared at him, her own blue eyes glinting for a different reason. 'It is time for me to leave here,' she declared.

'What?'

'It is time for me to leave,' she repeated, 'Don't worry. I will not go far. Only to Sulasgeir where I can always be sure that you're all right. I will be able to see the smoke from your peat fire from there.'

He tried to dissuade her, arguing her plans for the remainder of the day, but she refused to listen. Instead, she prayed to the angel that Ronan had called upon all those years before, pleading to be allowed to leave the island in order that her brother might find peace.

'Remove me from here in order that I will no longer be either a trial or tribulation to him. Remove me from here to allow him to be at peace.'

It was just as the sky began to lighten with the coming of another day that she finally obtained her answer; that voice speaking as it had to Ronan while he prayed in his cell at Eoropie.

'*Eirich! Eirich! Thig sìos gu Leac na Sgròb!* Wake up! Come down to Leac na Sgròb! '

When she walked down to the place the voice had named, where the claw-marks of the great beasts were still visible in the rock, she looked to see not the giant form of the *cionaran-crò*, but the white bird that had perched on its great back. She saw it flying above the shoreline and called out, summoning the bird to her side.

'Take me away from here and you can stay in Sulasgeir with me. Take me there and all the birds of your kind can gather round me.'

As if in answer, the bird flew down and perched on her shoulders. She could feel its beak clamping on the collar of her dress, lifting her up from the rock where she was standing. It took her away from the island we now call North Rona, across the sea to the bare rock we know these days as Sulasgeir. Within days she'd built her stone shelter there, facing the place where her brother spent his hours worshipping and praying, knowing that he was still alive and well from the sight of smoke rising from his fire, conscious that he was still mentioning the same words in his worship as he had done while she was still there.

'Gormel, Mineag, Ealasaid, Raonaid, Brianuil . . .'

She sat there and watched out for him as the white birds whirled around her in greater and greater numbers with every passing year. She sat there, too, until another angel visited her – this time a dark and chilling figure, casting a cold spell on her breath.

When the men of Ness found her, surrounded by the hordes of white birds they had come all that way to hunt, a cormorant had built its nest inside the bare bones of her chest.

6

Men in the Shadows

SULASGEIR – SEPTEMBER 1939

I'd had my fill of squabbling seabirds,
their squalls and squawks of anger over nests,
and grown impatient for some quieter world
where those around me did not puff their chests,
flail feathers, strut and stride in ritual displays
to show it could not let its neighbour be
if some line was crossed over, wing and beak not kept at bay.

And then came my arrival back, breakwater lashed with foam,
the message yelled while men clustered round the stern,
informing me it was time to pack and head from home,
that mankind's squalls and squabbles had returned,
and the hour had come around that we
would have to button uniforms, make a stern display
to stop another nation not letting neighbours be
by crossing over borders, keeping boot and fist at bay.

And I heard an old man mutter: 'So it's come to this
again within my lifetime, this puffing out of chests,
politicians' squalls and squabbles, each peck and bite and hiss.
armies setting from parade grounds to flock both east
    and west.'
Then I thought back to Sulasgeir, that barren territory,
and wished all land was like it: empty, stark and grey
with no men ever stepping there who could not let
    neighbours be;
no men ever needing uniforms to keep boot and fist at bay.

The truth is, perhaps, a little more prosaic – as it sometimes tends to be. The regular boat – named, ironically, the *Peaceful* – headed out to Sulasgeir in the middle of August, despite the uneasy situation in Europe at the time. The crew were still there when the call-up papers for war were being sent out, with one of them, a reservist, clearly not at home as he should have been when they arrived. The ignorance of the men about the conflict only came to an end when they arrived in Skigersta with that year's harvest of birds: an event which must have been around the time when war was finally declared. For all that he must have been exhausted after his time on the rock, the poor reservist, Donald Morrison, or Dòmhnall Alasdair Iain Ruaidh, had to head for Portsmouth the following morning. One can only imagine his Commanding Officer's sceptical eyebrow after he had listened to the reason for his delay.

'You were – where?'

It was eight long years after September 1939 that the men of Ness stepped onto Sulasgeir again. There had been an attempt to head out there by Alastair Gunn – known as 'An Ciobarach' – in 1946, but bad weather prevented him and his boat leaving the shores of Lewis. In 1947, they made up, to some degree, for their absence when three vessels sped past North Rona in the direction of the island. Two of these were the traditional *sgoth*, the last vessels to make the entire journey under sail. These were the *Jubilee* and the *Peaceful*. This was one of those occasions when only good seamanship and good fortune prevented a tragedy taking place. As they sailed into Skigersta, eye-witnesses can recall the precipitous waves that rocked both small vessels, the wind and rain that crashed against both bow and stern. It was only the experience and skill of the seamen involved that took her safely through the nightmare of those waters to shore.

Like the war before it, that storm heralded change. Even when the sea was calm and placid, the *Peaceful*, the boat that had taken men to Sulasgeir since 1930, had shown it was no longer fit for the task of taking men the 40 miles to Sulasgeir and back. Built in 1914, the vessel formerly known as the *Thelma* with its 19-foot keel had not been at sea for several years before, stranded and tied up ashore during the years of conflict. As a result, it leaked badly, its planking having dried out. From the instant that it was emptied of its cargo, it was obvious it was not going on that arduous voyage again.

The storm, too, had its effect on those who sailed in it. The skipper of the *Jubilee,* Murdo Mackenzie from Skigersta, was said to have never fully got over the experience. A man in his mid-60s at the time, his strength was sapped by the exhaustion and effort he expended that day. Yet his absence from the vessel was not the only transformation that year's turbulent weather caused the *Jubilee*. The next time it went to Sulasgeir, in 1948, it would do so fitted and equipped with an engine for the first time. While it was not the first boat to make the journey in that way, as another boat, the *Pride of Lionel*, had possessed one as early as 1931, there is little doubt it set the pattern for the future.

Murdo Mackenzie's age suggests another reason why change occurred after the war. By the last years of the 1930s, when the *Peaceful* was making its regular trips to Sulasgeir, the majority of the crews were either in their mid-60s or older. They were the ones who arrived at Geodha Phuill Bhàin after a voyage of anything between ten hours and two days, hauling their vessel to safety by the light of lanterns. During the six years of war, some of these had passed away; others were too infirm for the crossing. A new generation and a new approach were now needed if the long tradition of men going to Sulasgeir was to continue.

This came in the form of some of the men taking part in a video recorded in the Taigh-Cèilidh in the village of South Dell some years ago. They include Seonaidh Saidh (John

Macritchie) and Murchadh Ruadh (Murdo Smith), part of the crew of the *Commando*, who were the first Nessmen to step on Sulasgeir since 1939. While they were there, they adapted some of the techniques that might be associated with the name of their vessel – a 16-foot Orkney boat with a Giants Universal petrol engine. 'Raiding' the rock, they visited only briefly, with two of the five crewmen remaining on the boat. The other three gathered around 200 young birds before they made their way back to Lewis in the thick, blurring silence of a heavy fog. Of the five, only two had ever made the voyage on any previous occasion. No doubt buoyed by their experience, they managed to return once again that season, reaping a further harvest of around the same number of birds.

And there was need of it. The years after the Second World War were, to paraphrase Dickens, both the best and worst of times. Despite the bleak economic situation, Attlee's new Labour Government introduced greater change for the majority of the British people than any before or since. A National Health Service was being introduced. A new Welfare State was created, one that provided care for most of the population. There was the prospect of change in the country's educational system too, providing greater opportunity for people. There was a sense of hope that, unlike the one engendered by Lloyd George who had promised 'homes fit for heroes' after the First World War, had some prospect of being realised.

However, there was also still the same want and deprivation that had existed before the war. There was, too, the existence of the ration card that dictated the quantity of food that most people could have before them on their table. Its restrictions had its effect even in places like Lewis, despite the fact that the people there probably had, in culinary terms at least, a richer, better existence than their urban counterparts during this period. Fresh rabbit could be easily obtained; fish caught from the foreshore. There were also, as the Breve pointed out in this little piece of verse for the *Stornoway Gazette*, ways in which the crofter could deceive Lord Woolton, serving at that time as the Minister of Food, finding ways of making a 'wether' (or castrated male sheep) disappear:

> There's no wether
> On the tether
> Where the wether
> Used to be.
> There are joints
> Upon the rafters
> That Lord Woolton
> Mustn't see.
> We shall say
> It was the weather
> That the wether
> Couldn't stand.
> Though it died of influenza
> Yet the smell of it
> Is grand.

Yet there was little doubt that while no one was actually starving at this time, there was a tedium and blandness to people's diet. It was for this reason that the price people paid for the guga caught by the men of the *Commando* and others suddenly increased. In 1938, it was 1/- (or £2.34 today). In 1939, it was 2/- – the doubling of its cost probably one of the lesser known effects of the invasion of Poland that year. In 1947, the gugas gathered by men like Seonaidh Saidh and Murchadh Ruadh were exchanged for 5/- apiece. There were probably a number of reasons why people were prepared to pay this. An everyday item before the war had clearly been transformed by shortage into something of a luxury – one that would be particularly enjoyed by those exiled away from home. It gave a little savour to the dull and uninspiring round of food and drink people were faced with day after mundane day. Its taste, too, must have reminded them of times before Hitler and the ration book, when the likes of Lord Woolton did not hold sway.

And so it was that Seonaidh and Murchadh were joined by other men of similar ages in the following few years – like Eve (Alasdair Murray) and An Gaisean (Donald Murray) who, together with Dods (John Murdo MacFarlane) and Alastair Bàn (Alastair Campbell), took part in that interview recorded on video. Apart from the last two names, they are all men from the shadows now, having died since this amateur film was made, yet, listening to their laughter, one gains a sense of the many energetic conversations and discussions that must have taken place on that rock during the decades they sailed there. In the case of a number of these men, this stretched from the late 1940s to the early or even late 1980s, in the course of time these men being transformed from the young guns to the old guard.

They all look different, these men. Murchadh Ruadh is probably the quietest, his time-worn face falling silent each time he draws in another mouthful of smoke from his cigarette. Eve's cloth-cap is like a prop for his conversation. One moment, it flaps in his hand as he tries to make some point. The next, it's slipped back on his head again. Murchadh Mhurdaidh waits for a quiet moment to make his observations, probably the most thoughtful and considered of them all, before his words are engulfed by laughter again. Another, Seonaidh Saidh, with his glasses and thick, grey hair parted down the middle, resembles a university professor; his mild demeanour disguising an inner toughness. An Gaisean makes his points dramatically, the firmness of his jaw underlining the firmness of his opinions, his gaze almost unblinking behind his glasses.

They joke and jest with one another, rarely using a word of English in their talk; each man knowing the strengths and weaknesses of the other and determined to exploit them. One man is prone to exaggerate the number of gannets he is able to pluck within a given period. They tease him mercilessly about this, wondering aloud about how he ever succeeded in getting past the infants class in school. Another talks about a rare event – once when an adult gannet veered towards him on two occasions. Its yellow head struck his hip as it tried to force him from his position on the crag and into the waters below. A further conversation is about how a member of their company once took the wheel of the fishing boat while it made its way across calm seas from the island. Tired, he barely looked outside, taking his position instead from the compass before him. A little time later, he looked up from the compass to see Sulasgeir in front of him again, his destination well behind. Scratching his head, he wondered what had gone wrong. His puzzlement only came to an end when he noticed his tobacco tin lying beside the compass, swinging the tip of the needle away from its proper course.

Moments later, the same man begins to tell another story against himself.

'There was this night I was supposed to stay up and listen to the Shipping Forecast. But I was exhausted that night and long before the words "Dogger", "Malin", "Hebrides" were heard, my eyes had shut. When they opened, the forecast was over. Rather than admit to this, I told them it was going to be a fine day tomorrow. Little did I know the forecaster had predicted a good Storm Force Ten . . .'

They tell jokes about others too – the japes and jests they used to play on newcomers.

'We used to send them first into the bothys, especially the ones where we knew fulmars nested while we were away. They used to come out a few minutes later, all yellow and stinking of oil from their heads down to their feet. The fulmars used to spit that liquid they gather in their throats at them, to repel all invaders, you might say. We'd stand outside and laugh at them all.'

Or a variation of the same trick they played on others. Dods recalled handing over a candle and a biscuit tin to someone who was about to cross the threshold of one particular shelter.

'What's that for?'

'You'll see . . .'

The man is barely in the bothy for a minute before he's out again, fingers clawing at the earwigs that plague his clothes, hair and skin, raining down upon him as he steps within its walls. And all the time, he's still carrying the candle and biscuit box he was given a few moments before.

'You haven't used it, then?' Dods grins.

'Used it? How? What's it for?'

'Wait . . .'

Dods shows him then, stepping into the darkness with a lit candle and the biscuit box. Its flame touches the inside of the roof. A few earwigs fall from their perches, landing on the bottom of the tin below. He moves along, repeating the process. There's a ping each time one drops, like the tapping of a drum.

'There. That's it. A few gone.' he says. 'But you'll still have to sleep with cotton wool in your ears.'

'Why?'

'It'll stop them going in there . . .'

Or there was also the time they advised one of their latest recruits to arrive on the island with more than a few layers of clothes on his back.

'It's a really cold wind out there.'

And then they watched him as he struggled with each sack, his face reddening and sweating as he took every step. One minute he's taking off his jacket. The next a jersey is gone. The moment following this, another jersey is divested in an act that resembles some bizarre Gipsy Rose Lee impersonation, his discarded clothing strewn across the entire length of the island.

Yet it is not only the new arrivals who are subjected to their humour. They indulge in a great deal not only of self-mockery but also the gentle ridicule of some of the most long-standing members of their group. There is the tale of the man who always used to sleep with one eye open. ('That's because he didn't trust any of the rest of you,' someone declares.) There is talk about the tall individual who cracked his skull each time he entered the door. ('You could tell how many times he went in and out by the number of cuts on the top of his head.') There is, however, time and time again evidence of that peculiar male obsession with both the quantity and quality of food. There is a sense, too, that the poor man who is in charge of producing it does not quite meet the same standards of either culinary or hygienic excellence as the woman who waits at home. ('Well, I haven't got quite the same facilities here', one used to defend himself by declaring.) And they swoop down on the poor man who performs this role rather in the same way as a gannet might plunge upon on a fish.

'*Bheil cuimhne agad air an àm* . . .? Remember the time . . .?'

Their sport begins. They speak of some poor man who left the scrambled eggs so long on a flame that they turned a rather unsightly shade of green; the same individual who placed a basinful of jelly down to set for a few moments, only to see one of his fellow workers step up towards it and, reaching for some soap, dip his hands into its depths. There was also a cook's attempt to make Guga Soup.

'What's it like?' one of his fellow-workers kept asking. 'If it's good, it'll really fill our bellies.'

'Yes . . . And if you keep asking about it, the pot will fill it too.'

Such sparks of rage often blew, too, in the direction of the cook. One of the men recalls how he felt so angry after their dinner had been carbonised that he dived into the geo in order to cool his rage.

'It was the only way I could control myself . . . The only way.'

From their conversation, it is clear that much of the comradeship shared by these men is created by humour. Their eyes twinkle even before some of the stories are fully told. They laugh before the punchline is reached; grin almost as soon as the first words are spoken. However, there is more to their friendship than this. They share a similar history; a sense of themselves created by both their own and their island's past.

Part of this was engendered by the war-years most had in common. Dods told me of one story he heard time and time again while he was on the island. It was from the mouth of one of the men with whom he had been in the Merchant Navy, explaining how he had reacted when his vessel had been sunk.

'I jumped into the water even though I didn't have a clue how to swim. Three times I went down. Three times I hauled myself back up again. And then that third time when I felt I had at least half-mastered the water and was making my way to a life-boat, I heard another man yelling, screaming out for me to come back and give him help. But I just kept going. What else could I do, eh? What else could I do?'

He would look blankly forward, as if the young man who sat in front of him, untouched by any war, could provide him with answers.

'What else could I do?'

The wars of other men seemed largely a litany of the ports they had visited. 'Tangiers,' they would ask, 'Were you ever there?'

'What about New Zealand?'

'Australia?'

'Murmansk?'

Seonaidh Saidh was the one who nodded when that place-name was mentioned. He had been an officer in the Arctic convoys during the Second World War, bringing goods and arms to the Soviet forces fighting against Hitler in the east. There was little doubt that those years had a huge effect on him. A mild-mannered man normally, he would rage whenever the Royal Family – and especially the Duke of Windsor's behaviour in the war-years – were mentioned. The conflict also may have granted him the toughness for which he was celebrated in the district. There was the occasion when he took the pliers to a rotten tooth rather than make a journey to the dentist. Alastair Bàn found him wandering around the house with a towel against his cheek, attempting to staunch the copious flow of blood. However, it was not solely hardiness that made him act this way. As someone who spent much of his later life racing illegally around Ness on either his motorbike or tractor, he was also extremely reluctant to go to Stornoway and would risk anything – including pliers – to avoid a trip in the town's direction.

This desire to remain at home could also have been a reaction to his war-years. Like most of his fellow Merchant Navy men at this time, he must have feared the appearance of a Stuka above his ship, a U-boat surfacing from below during his voyages beyond the Arctic Circle. In this, he probably had much in common with An Gaisean, also in the Merchant Navy though largely journeying in a southerly direction, to Australia and New Zealand, during his war-service instead. The two also certainly shared an unconventional attitude towards any road safety legislation. Despite being an elder in the Church, An Gaisean could also be seen breaking the law during the peat-cutting and gathering season. Unlicensed, he would head along the Skigersta Road on his motorbike with his wife's arms circling his waist.

There were other moments when An Gaisean would behave like a teenager. One of these would be the moment he met his fellow guga hunter Eve, or Alasdair Murray, on the quay the day they were going out to Sulasgeir. The pair would stand toe to toe with one another, swapping fake blows while practising some strange Ness version of the Ali Shuffle; the two of them about to embark on their annual holiday on the rock.

Again, Eve was a man involved in the Second World War, joining the HMS *Bonaventure* on 1940 on its first operational trip, taking a precious cargo of gold bullion across the Atlantic to Halifax, Nova Scotia. Later, that same ship was torpedoed by an Italian submarine near Crete. Nearly 140 lives were lost. Eve only saved his life by clinging onto a piece of timber till he was rescued. Like many who lived near the sea at that time, he was unable to swim.

This was not his only moment of drama during the conflict. Another occurred while he was helping a naval unit in Tobruk. With the Germans only ten miles away, he and his fellow servicemen were under continual bombardment for days on end. Later on, while he was one of the crew of the *Harrow*, his vessel was sent to the aid of a hospital ship that was blazing at the time. Injured by a blow from one of the ropes that failed to prevent the rescued ship from listing, he was Mentioned in Dispatches for his part in the action.

It was perhaps as a reaction to all this that, like Seonaidh Saidh, Eve preferred the quieter pleasures of life on his return home. Together with his fondness for Sulasgeir, which he sailed towards for 30 years, he enjoyed, too, the Ness moor and the sheep that grazed on its empty, barren acres. He was familiar with all its lochs and hillocks, able to recite its place-names almost as well as the prayers and psalm-tunes that came to his lips in his early 60s when he came to a deep Christian faith. He was often to be heard singing the latter when he walked down the village road, alerting people to his presence long before they first saw him. There were, too, the joys of family – his wife, Dolina, whom he married at the tender age of 40; children Annie, Morag and Alex. They took him to places worlds away from the bloody, brutal times he had experienced in places like Crete and Tobruk; these days perhaps a distant memory to him by the time he died in November 1999 at the age of 87.

Dods's father, Murchadh Mhurdaidh, was also involved in the conflict. His life at sea, however, began many years before, when he was taken on as a member of a fishing boat crew on a local boat at the age of 14. Later, wider waters became familiar to him as he travelled to Curaçao in the Dutch Antilles, Panama and even Pitcairn Island, a place known to those familiar with the tale of Fletcher Christian and the Mutiny on the *Bounty*. The war began dramatically for him. Signing on as a bosun's mate on the ship, the *Akora*, on 31 August 1939, he encountered a very different vessel from the ones he had sailed on before. Every porthole was painted black; the crew's 200 passengers unable to glimpse daylight while they were on board. A day later, after they left Southampton, they heard the ominous news that war had been declared. As they took a southerly route across the Atlantic, a German U-boat followed in their wake. When they reached their destination's end in New Zealand, an antique 4' gun from the First World War was added to the ship. As one of the RNR men on the crew, he had to go through a gunnery course. It was not a success. In his own words, he declared: 'We were taken out for a firing run. We only did one round and all the windows in the after end of the ship were broken. We were lucky we did not have to fire again.'

Yet this did not mean he escaped hostilities. Murchadh Mhurdaidh's notes are incomplete. They do not tell, for instance, how he was involved in one of the low points of the war: when Norway fell, he was on one of the fleet of ships protecting King Haakon of Norway on the *Dorsetshire* when he fled from Tromsø in the conflict's early, dark days. When the struggle was about to be won, he was present, too, on one of the US landing craft when they faced the German guns in the D-day landings. The fortunes of war had swirled round in the opposite direction from the one which Murchadh had first known.

His notes are not the only ones left behind by his generation. Another interesting if sketchy document encountered in the writing of this book is an account of his life given by Murchadh Ruadh (Murdo Smith). In its few pages there is much to be valued. He showed the earliest inclination of all of them to head in the direction of Sulasgeir, telling, for instance, of the time he was a stowaway on a boat to the rock's nearest neighbour, North Rona. He helped the men work with the sheep there – a scrape he claims to have got away with because his face was so black on his return that his family didn't recognise him. Like several of the others, too, he was also at sea during 1939–45, his account of these years a litany of some of the more dramatic place-names of the war. For some time, he worked on what was called a boarding vessel, making sure there was nothing either belonging or going to Germany on any of the ships they halted. At the fall of Dunkirk, he was on board a ship sent out to pick up survivors, 'lifting them off the beaches as close in as possible'. From there, it was work guarding convoys through the Channel, which Murdo describes with masterly understatement as a 'bad place to be in'. From there on, it was Halifax, Newfoundland, the coast of Africa, the Northern Convoy, on a ship bombed in Scapa Flow. At some point during his years at war he received the Distinguished Service Medal for his actions. It says much for the man's modesty that he does not even mention this in his account, far less provide great detail on the incident. In this, he was fairly typical of the men of his time; their stiff upper lips barely shifting when called upon to speak about the conflict.

Yet if some talked about the war at all it was only, perhaps, to underline the faith in God that had brought them through it. An Gaisean, perhaps, would pray and read a chapter of the Bible, a reading, perhaps, from Job Chapter 12, verses 1 to 9, and sing one of the psalms – say Psalm 104 with its verses:

25 Mar sin an cuan tha farsaing mòr,
's gach ni a shnàigeas ann,
Na beathaichean tha beag is mòr,
gun orra cunntas cheann.

26 Tha longan siubhal ann gu tiugh;
's tha 'n Lebhiàtan mòr,
A chumadh is a dhealbhadh leat,
ri sùgradh ann le treòir.

27 Na slòigh ud uile tha, a Dhè,
a' feitheamh ort a-ghnàth,
A chum dhaibh biadh gun tugadh tu
gan cumail beò gach tràth.

28 Na bheir thu dhaibh ad thoirbheartas
ga thional siud tha iad:
Tràth dhfhosglas tu do làmh gu pailt,
le maith sàr-lìonar iad.

This ritual would occur at the beginning of each day and when someone placed three thick peats down on top of their fire every night, preserving its flame; the words of the Old and New Testament as important to bring with them to the island as any bedding or food. In this, Murdo was like many of the men who had made the same journey earlier in the century – keepers of an ancient tradition, preservers of the faith.

It is actions like these that, according to the writer and thinker Alastair McIntosh, make the guga hunt a morally justifiable act. In his view, killing can be defended if 'the attitude of mind that conducts it is Providentially grounded – replete with gratitude for the grace of God – as it will, of course, be the case in any true Niseach worthy of bearing the tradition of being a Guga hunter. For a Guga to meet its end in this way is a "natural" death, for we human beings, too, are a part of nature when we engage mindfully as distinct from meaninglessly with our environment.'

It is for this reason, he goes on to say, that 'the Hunt could never endanger the Guga as a species. If their numbers fell, the application of innate Hebridean traditions of veneration for the environment would cause the Niseachs to curb their practice accordingly, and they would be the first to recognise that the balance of nature was not right.'

Such an attitude of mind clearly goes back to the days of the Old Testament, and indeed, long before that – to the hunter-gatherers who sought their food on the cliffs and crags on the edge of Europe. In other ways, however, the lives of An Gaisean and their men contained more change than any of their ancestors. During their time, an end had come to the rivalries between the different communities laying claim to Sulasgeir. (These even occurred within villages. The *Commando* was the boat of one end of the community of Port, *The Star of Hope* the other. And the dividing line? This was the 'river' that ran through the village. Hardly the Forth or the Clyde, most communities on the mainland would not have glorified this rush of water

with such a title, calling it simply 'burn', 'stream' or even –
in the dry days of summer – 'trickle'.) Referring to an old
tradition that a deer coming to the villages of Ness was a
sign of an impending death, the old hunters speak about
how the arrival of a man from one township in another at a
particular time of year was not always appreciated.

'A deer appearing in Port was sometimes just about as
welcome as a man from Skigersta.'

There was no doubt, of course, why the man from
Skigersta was there. Under the pretence of visiting relations,
he would be trying to find out what plans were afoot in the
other village: was a raid planned, if so, when and how. He
would do this in order that those in his home township
might be able to make a swift guerrilla raid before the men
from Port, snatching a hasty harvest of birds from the rock.
Likewise, the Port men would behave in the same way, each
group scouting the nearby community like some strange
and secret intelligence agency intent on obtaining information about the movements of others. At one time, the road
through the entire district must have been a labyrinth of
intrigue and rumour, whispers and half-truths. These were
the days when communities from as far south as Cross sent
out their boats to Sulasgeir with each village being allocated
their own special place. This was a situation that finally
came to an end in 1951 when, in order to stop the rivalry
that had existed for so long, men from the communities of
Port and Skigersta mingled together on the two boats,
Catriona and *Jubilee*. It is not recorded how long it took
their former enmities to finally fade away.

Murchadh Ruadh has left behind evidence of a time when
the rivalry was even wider than this, writing of the end that
came to the raiders' visits to Sule Stack, some 40 miles
north-east off the coast of Sutherland, in the early 1950s, an
expedition that may have occurred for centuries before. Yet
throughout much of this period, boats from another part of

the north of Scotland may have gone there for sea-fowl. Like nearby Sule Skerry, a gannet-free zone until around 2000, it is part of the parish of Stromness in Orkney. Seabird eggs from the last-named location were still being sold in the shops of that town as late as 1890. This does not mean it was a regular event. Eggs may have been regarded as a treat rather than a regular part of the Orcadian diet, appearing in the kitchens not only of Stromness itself but also of nearby islands like Graemsay and Hoy. While it is impossible, at this date, to trace any records of the practice, it seems likely that the Orcadians stopped going to either island for seabirds near the end of the nineteenth century. For some reason, they no longer felt inclined to hunt gannets from these distant locations.

There might have been a number of explanations for this. Perhaps the people of Stromness lost their taste for guga. Some of the Orcadians could have sacrificed their lives on the crags of Skerry or Stack. It may have been the results of a few altercations with men from Ness over their right to hunt the seabirds on the rock, a difficult one for men to land upon or ascend. Maybe, and more mundanely, it was the greater prosperity of Orkney that determined the change – their close ties with the Hudson's Bay Company and the regular postal order sent from the Canadian Arctic being the main reason for the end of that practice. Whatever their motives, there is little doubt that the Orcadians ceased hunting for the guga at the far end of their parish and left the Nessmen to claim Sule Stack and its neighbour, Sule Skerry, for their own.*

For all that, 'the Sule' left its mark on the Orcadian imagination. According to Orkney writer and historian

---

* I have also heard but been unable to confirm in writing the tale that Nessmen also travelled to St Kilda in order to obtain a harvest of seabirds. Apparently, they were permitted to do this on one occasion, but were not exactly made welcome, told by the men from Hirta never to return to their cliffs again.

Sigurd Towrie, it was regarded as a fearful place where
bogies and ghosts held court, told about in childrens' stories
with the threat, perhaps, that if they were naughty, they
might be sent in its direction. Even in the case of the Skerry,
there appears to be good reason for their fears. It is home to
an 80-eight foot lighthouse, among the oldest in Scotland.
Automated in recent years, it stands on an island that
measures around three quarters of a mile long and a quarter
of a mile wide. According to former lighthouse keepers, the
seas there were so treacherous during the winter that spray
would literally rise over the island, soaking its peat-covered
surface with salt.

Naturalist Adrian Blackburn offers his own testimony of
these fears. He has sailed to Sule Skerry for the last 30 years,
ringing the puffins and other birds there. In an interview
with the *Orcadian* in 2002, he tells of how difficult it was in
the early 1970s to persuade a boatman from Stromness to
sail in the direction of either Sule Skerry or Sule Stack. He
said, 'Orcadians seemed almost fearful of the island. Some
presumably had ancestors who drowned in shipwrecks off
the skerry and they seemed frightened of it. When we tried
to get a boat to take us to the island, they would say "there's
no way we're going to that Sule" and "beware the Sule".'

Yet terrifying though Sule Skerry can be, there is little
doubt that the Stack provides a greater challenge for boatman and cragsman alike. In 2002, Adrian Blackburn
claimed that the year's 'twelve strong-group of naturalists
sailed for five hours to reach the Skerry on board the
Stromness dive boat *Halton*, succeeded, for what is believed
to have been the first time, in accessing the south hump of
the skerry's neighbouring stack'. He went on to note that
'Despite the near-perfect weather conditions, the journey
from the boat's inflatable onto the skerry and stack was a
precarious one. One false move and they risked being
engulfed within the large swell. Even the photographs

provided by Adrian and his party confirm the truth of his tale. They show large cliffs, a difficult landing place, the swirl of wind and wave. Nevertheless, there is little doubt that, contrary to his view, Adrian and his party were not the first to step on its surface. That honour belonged to the Nessmen, and perhaps even the Orcadians, many years before. It may even be the case – and there is no opportunity these days to question living men about the issue – that they climbed the north stack.

Adrian Blackburn's son, Jez, did that on some of the occasions he landed on Sule Stack, stepping from one to another. He pays great testimony to the difficulties of arriving there, noting how it needs 'a confident leap' from a vessel 'even on the calmest of days. Any swell greater than three to five feet is likely to cause difficulty for less nimble people and certainly getting back on board is harder than getting off.' While wearing a wet suit lessens the problems of getting on and off the rock and getting wet, 'there is still the risk of being slammed against the rocks'. Later, too, there is a ten-foot drop of rock and narrow ledges they have to step precariously along – a task made even more difficult by gannets taking off above them 'and potentially crash into us, with the risk of our being knocked off the cliff'.

Clearly, modern equipment has decreased the dangers of stepping on and off Sule Stack, yet they still remain. By contrast, in the 1950s there were times when a stumble into the sea when there was a heavy swell meant the possibility of drowning. One small step for man – especially when they were loading over 500 guga – could mean one great loss for a family.

Despite these difficulties, Sule Stack was undoubtedly a location that the men of Ness sailed towards until 1956, probably a year or two after the Protection of Birds Act legally required them to cease. By all accounts, it was a choppy and dangerous voyage. This can be testified by three

words – 'Stranded in Durness' – that appear in accounts of
the guga hunt during these years. These times are given
greater detail in the recollections left by Murchadh Ruadh
than any mention of his war years, perhaps a measure of
their importance to him. He goes so far as to declare of his
time marooned on the mainland: 'I never had a holiday so
good.'

Yet their arrival was dramatic. Murdo describes how the
people of Durness saw them from the land as they came
close to a house in that area owned by the Rootes family,
one-time owners of one of the largest car factories in Britain.
'They thought we were survivors from a shipwreck,' he
explained. 'There was a bad sea that morning and we saw
the top of the rocks full of cars and people with life-saving
gear. They were signalling to us to come to land but it was
too wild for us to go so close to the shore.'

A young Michael Mather, still resident today in that area,
was among the ones who saw the boat from the coastline of
north-west Sutherland. In fact, he claims to have been the
first to see the vessel off Sanyo Bay, raising the alarm. From
his vantage-point, he saw the entire drama unfold – how
the Durness fishing boats signalled them to go in another
direction rather than their home port. 'It was too tricky to
go to Durness that day,' he declared.

Eventually, the crew managed to take the *Star of Hope*
into Loch Eriboll, where they were met by a small gathering
of people, including members of the Rootes household, who
kept asking them their destination. Deafened by the wind
and cold they had experienced, Murdo went ashore with
another Nessman. They were greeted there by an Admiral of
the Navy who, thinking Murdo was the skipper of the boat,
presented him with a bottle of whisky. It was a gift he
accepted gratefully, just as the men, too, were delighted to
come ashore and stay in a place they called the Fish-room in
a lodge in Rispond, receiving the key courtesy of Angus

Campbell, a Nessman who was employed at its caretaker. The lodge stood in a sheltered location, one in which their boat could see out the winter if it were required. Some of the other men went elsewhere, staying at Hector Stewart's house in Sanyomhor. Yet despite the fact that he never had 'a holiday so good', Murdo still felt marooned on Sutherland's shore. He recalled how they spent a fortnight there, unable to move the *Star of Hope* out of the bay.

'Lady Rootes was very good to us,' he recalled. 'In the end, we started working at making new shingle paths and bringing home peats by car. We sent word home to tell them we were there, and they sent money over to us.'*

My late relative Roddy Murray had his own distinctive tale to tell about the events of that time. His widow, Peggy, spoke about them as she sat beside her kitchen fire one evening in her home in Port. At that time, Roddy was at university studying for the ministry – a vocation he followed for many years. He faced the prospect of being stranded in Durness, without either books or proper clothing, when term-time began. It was for this reason that Lady Rootes decided to test out one of the products, perhaps, of her husband's car factories by driving him along the twisting roads down the west coast of the Highlands to Kyle of Lochalsh – at that time the place where the steamer for Stornoway sailed from. Wearing a large blue coat, oversized dungarees and a pair of dirty sandshoes, the prospective minister was left behind in the small port of Kyle.

His form of dress caused him a few difficulties. The ladies of Kyle looked him up and down imperiously, believing he was a down-and-out deposited on the pavements of their town. Sniffing the air around him, undoubtedly full of the

---

* One man among the party whose grasp of the English language was clearly lacking a little distinguished himself by greeting Lady Rootes on that stormy September day with the following words: 'Merry Christmas, your Ladyship. Merry Christmas.'

aroma of uncooked guga, they refused to offer him either bed or breakfast within their homes. Fortunately, Roddy stumbled on the house of a woman from Skigersta who gave him a place for the night. Whether it was his face, accent or strong smell that alerted her to the fact that he came from her native district is unrecorded.

Roddy's misadventures did not end when he reached the island. As he travelled home on the Ness bus, both his strange clothing and his wedding ring were noted by a cluster of housewives on a seat behind him. Peggy chuckled as she recalled what one of them said.

'Wonder what kind of wife that man has. Letting him go out in a state like that.'

There were other problems, recalled by Michael Mather. After the storm, the Kelvin paraffin engine took a while to dry out and work once again. 'It took oil from a local tractor to get it going again,' he remembered.

In the end, breaking with their usual customs, they left on a Sunday morning before daylight had broken. It was a sign of their need to be home and anxiety to be back at their domestic firesides. When they reached Cape Wrath, they discovered that the sea was calm and it was as well to head for Ness.

For all their ordeal, the boat returned again to Sule Stack the following year, this time coming back with a full cargo of guga. Their good fortune did not, however, last too long. They were caught again in the same location the following year. On this occasion, the Nessmen hid from the Rootes family, embarrassed to receive their hospitality once again. Instead, the ordinary people of Durness welcomed them, offering them food and shelter and shaking their heads in mock-dismay.

'They thought we weren't wise,' Murdo admitted.

Given the outcome of many of these voyages, it was, perhaps, a conclusion that many could have come to. All in all, Murdo and the others went to Sule Stack on four occasions, overcoming the extreme difficulties of approaching and landing there. Even after this, their problems were not over. On a number of occasions, the weather was so fierce and the rock so whipped by spume it was hard to stay upright on its ledges. It was not, however, storm-force winds that made the Nessmen decide not to go there any longer. Instead, two pieces of legislation got the better of them. The first decided that the guga hunters could not go there till the 1st of September – too far back in the year for either their personal safety or comfort. Later a law was passed prohibiting them from going anywhere but Sulasgeir for the guga.

This was a change that had been coming for a number of years before the war. There had been occasional letters about the need for the hunt in the local and national press, especially from concerned naturalists who thought the entire practice was both barbaric and unnecessary. One of the more furious interventions came from the pen of J.A. Harvie-Brown, who, as far back as 1887, made known his horror at the entire activity. Describing Sulasgeir in the most ghoulish and melodramatic terms, as noted earlier, he remarked on, among other sights, the 'heads of defunct Gannets strewn all over (its) surface'.

The note would be repeated again, providing evidence of a major clash in attitudes between two radically different groups. In the 'blue' corner were members of the leisured, largely urban middle and upper class, who saw nature mainly in terms of its aesthetic beauty and worth. Opposing them in the 'red' corner were men like those from Ness. Coming from rural and coastal areas, the crofter saw birds like the gannet largely in terms of their utilitarian value, how they could provide a little extra cash for their households and more food for their plates – a necessity for their survival. In the resulting battle, there would be little sign of either mutual understanding or meeting of minds. The gap between them was wider than the span of any geo waves had battered into the coastline of Sulasgeir.

One example of this was Malcolm Stewart, who in 1938 contributed an article to *British Birds*, no. 6, vol. 32. In this, he outlined a recent visit to the 'Gannetry of Sulasgeir', where he notes a decline in the numbers nesting since some five years previously. In 1932, he counted 6,500 birds nesting there – in itself a reduction from the 7,000 in 1883. In 1937, there were, by his reckoning, only 4,500. 'This is evidenced,' he claims,'by the fact that the breeding ground has been reduced nearly fifty per cent in the last five years.'

He does not have to look far for the reasons for this decline – the fact that Sulasgeir is one of the few places from which nestlings are taken each year for their 'supposed food value', clearly qualifying any 'nutritional value' they may have. Abandoning all pretence at academic detachment, he fulminates at length at the way this gannetry is 'gradually becoming exterminated'. He notes that 'in the early days of September . . . a party of men from the district of Ness in the island of Lewis have nothing better to do than to undertake the unpleasant visit to Sulasgeir and stay there a few days, taking all the gugas, or nestling gannets, they can. These are taken back with them and eaten. Not even the most grumbling Lewisman can complain of a food shortage, and this annual venture is nothing short of an unnecessary destruction of bird-life.'

After this, he makes a brief attempt to draw breath, noting some vague statistics. This includes a point which might just about explain why it was about this time gannets began to settle in Shetland – for all that the first colony was found in Noss in 1911. Their emigration further north may not have been exclusively the responsibility of Nessmen but the fact that 'During the [Great] war, shell-fire practice by warships made a large number of gannets desert Sulasgeir.'

The evidence of the scoring done at that time remains on the rock till this day, marking and scarring its surface. There are also the remains of a shell, used by the men on occasion to test and demonstrate their strength. In addition, there was said to have been at one time a target painted on the neighbouring rock of Gralisgeir – left there to allow Admiral Jellicoe and his crews to prime and aim their guns, and terrify a passing gannet or two. More seriously, the naturalist fails even to consider the possibility that there may have been too many gannets in the colony and this was the reason there had been a decline in numbers. With Sulasgeir unable to support the large numbers he had observed before, some had flown off to seek nesting places new.

After this brief truce, however, it does not take Stewart too long to launch a few more shells in the direction of Ness. Mourning the fact that 'there seems little one can do to stop this destruction', he calls first of all upon the proprietor to intervene, before confessing 'that the only action that could really be relied on to put an end to the situation would be to speed up the passage through Parliament of the Wild Birds Protection (Scotland) Bill. Once this Bill is on the Statute Book it will be illegal to take wild birds at any time during the year.' He completes his diatribe with a final, waspish remark, noting that 'No doubt with a maximum fine of five pounds per bird the Lewismen will think gannet an extravagant luxury.'

It was an article that generated a fierce debate both in local and national newspapers, particularly *The Times*. During that year, the argument filled almost as many columns of its letter page as 'the first cuckoo' traditionally did or the little piece of paper Neville Chamberlain waved in his fingers might have produced at the time. Among the contributions came one from the pen of the Breve in the *Stornoway Gazette*. He makes the point that

A London naturalist alleges that the population (solon goosey speaking) of Sulasgeir has gone down from 7,000 pairs in 1883 to 4,500 pairs in 1939, and blames the Niseachs. But doth he realise that the human population of the Highlands has gone down even more drastically since 1883 and one can't blame the Niseachs – far from it.

The Breve is perhaps slipping on his customary jester's cap in the above paragraph; clearly there is little connection, logical or otherwise, that can be made between the human population of the Highlands and the number of gannets flocking around Sulasgeir. Interestingly, however, in a letter dated 1985, Alastair Bàn picks up on the issue of depopulation. Focusing solely on the population levels of Ness, he makes a similar and more precise point. Applying for a licence to kill gannets on Sulasgeir, he notes that

One important reason why the cull should continue is the need in this community to make use of all natural resources – always having due regard for conservation – and [it] should be encouraged by the State because the trend at the moment is a decrease in the human population while the birds are ever increasing.

Donald MacRitchie, a Maths teacher at Lionel school since the late 1970s, has some information that backs up, at least, part of Alastair Bàn's argument. As a statistical exercise among his pupils, he has been gathering information about the numbers living in the district that show that the decline Alastair complained about is still continuing. He asked them to go round the villages of Ness, making sure they establish the numbers living in each house in the parish. The figures he has established tell their own story, with a drop in the population of the district as a whole, from Port to South Dell, of over 300 from 1,561 in 1979 to 1,232 in 2004. This is a total of over 20 per cent.

These figures, however, conceal a great deal. In the north end of Ness, the furthest away from Stornoway, there has been a drop of some 40 per cent of the population during the period 1979 and 2004. This includes villages like Knockaird, Eorodale and once-thriving Port of Ness. In South Dell, at the district's other end, by contrast, there is only a decline of 5 per cent – a drop that is of little significance, though perhaps even the extent of the decrease in this part of the community is concealed by the presence of council houses in that part of Ness. The bare statistics might also hide other symptoms of decay. There are probably fewer children in the houses that remain; more old people, bachelors and single women . . .

In the context of Ness, however, these figures are neither the beginning nor end of the story. The decline in the number living in the outlying parishes of Lewis has been going on for many years, a pattern that has persisted since the beginning of last century, since the start of the Great War and the sinking of the *Iolaire* that brought death to so many households in the district. The people there have been waiting for a long time for the arrival of a phoenix to bring new life to the district.

7

The Rising of the Phoenix

Let us picture that day at the end of August 1912.

There are a number of the district's people gathering outside the schoolhouse that blustery afternoon. Not long in the area, the headmaster takes in their faces. They look wet, chilled and drawn, as if the blustery wind and rain of the last week or so have succeeded in seeping into both nerve and bone. Their clothes flap around them like tattered rags; the scarves of the women are either blown in the storm or are used to stifle the sobs that shake them almost as much as each passing gust. He scans their faces, too, for resemblances. The tall, angular woman sheltering by the wall is clearly with her son. His features are as sharp and angular as her own. He notes, too, other similarities. There are at least three other members of another family before him. The same shade of brown hair. A piercing blue that shines in all their eyes. He sighs deeply before he steps out of his home, aware that there is an air of desperation about these people, perhaps connected with the weather that has battered the island for the last few days.

'Can I help you?'

He asks the question with trepidation, expecting all their voices to gabble together, breaking into his senses like a relentless wave. Instead, it is a teenage girl who answers, her hair hidden under a checkered scarf, her eyes the chilly blue of the others in the group. She holds her mother's hand as she faces him, her younger brother by her side. For a moment, words falter on her tongue – as with so many in the district, her use of English is clumsy and limited.

'We're looking for your help, Headmaster . . .' she says.

'Yes. If I can . . . What do you want me to do?'

'My father and some of the men of the district are out on Sulasgeir. Hunting the gannet. They've been out there in that terrible storm a few nights back. And we haven't heard from them since.'

They headmaster looks at her gravely, considering her words with the long silence that always unnerves the children sitting before him. It occurs to him that he recognises the boy by her side from the hours he has spent at the school. Donald something or other. He is unable to remember the exact surname, one from the limited number they share in this part of the world.

'And how long have they been out hunting the gannet?'

'Three weeks now. Too long, sir. Much too long.'

He nods, acknowledging her distress. He can picture the horrors they must be imagining. The people of this place know only too well how much rent can be extracted from them by the sea.

'We were wondering if you could help us, sir.'

Her voice puts an end to his distraction. He is forced to take in once again her harassed, troubled look, hair blown wild and unkempt.

'Of course. Of course,' he declares. 'But tell me, how can I do that?'

The girl looks irritated by his answer – her eyes narrowing, a wrinkle creasing her nose. 'You could see if they can send a fishery cruiser out. Check if the men are safe.'

'Aye . . .' And he asks almost the same question again. 'How would I do that?'

The girl gives an exasperated sigh. 'Get in touch with Mr Anderson the councillor. You could send a telegram to him. He'll get things done.'

He looks at her, wondering at how much knowledge is contained in the head of one the world would deride as ignorant and ill-lettered. 'Aye,' he nods, 'I'll do that. I'll do that right away.'

A few hours later and Anderson's clerk, Prince, is standing on the quay, watching the fishery cruiser, the *Phoenix*, making its way out of Stornoway. In his hands there is a copy of the telegram the teacher over in Ness sent earlier to his employer, the broad and burly former Provost, a man of boundless energy and pace. Prince creases the message between his fingers till they are black with the possibility of death and loss.

'Well, that should do it,' he says as the boat's wake laps against the harbour walls. 'They can find out if these men are alive or not.'

Prince walks quickly from the quay, heading in the direction of the legal practice where he works. On his way there, he looks out over the houses of the small burgh where he has lived and worked for the last few years. It is still an alien place to him and he suspects it might always remain that way. He doesn't, for instance, much understand the people of Ness, whom his employer, Anderson, repre-sents in Council. The way they speak English is torturous to him – a man who has spoken only that language all his life. And as for their Gaelic, it is as incomprehensible as their liking for that strange bird they favour for their meals. He wouldn't be his employer for all the money that existed in the island. He doesn't have a fraction of the man's appetite for work, or his patience in dealing with such people.

It is rough sailing that day. Stormy waters well around the Minch, churning back and forth. It is even worse in the open Atlantic when they meet the ocean's full force rounding the Butt. Clouds seem etched in black on the skyline, promising more storms and rain on their way. Waves squall. There's times when the *Phoenix* is lifted over a crest only to be swallowed by a trough a moment later, protected for an instant from the gale.

One man – an experienced sailor – is sick on the deck. The captain eyes him coldly, knowing he has drunk too much the night before. It all adds to the sense of resentment he is feeling at this moment. Too much is going on this year, 1912, with all its attendant miseries – his French wife, Margot, causing him trouble with her feigned illnesses, her litany of mysterious headaches and dizzy spells; his youngest son apparently inheriting these traits. He knew what lay behind these problems. Politics. The constant talk of war. The Union Jack being brandished against the Tricolor. The German eagle flashing its talons before the Russian bear. And now these men stranded on a rock, unable to take their foul catch home because of a storm.

'There's Sulasgeir,' he hears someone say. 'We're not far away.'

He doesn't check the charts. All he does is lift his binoculars and stare outwards through the rain-blurred window in the direction of the island they have just seen. He looks out for signs of life upon its shores, larger than he imagined before he set sail. Bigger than some of the fishermen he had spoken to had led him to expect. Hardly any gannets either. None nesting on its shores, though he is sure he was told that was why they had gone there. He looks, too, for a safe harbour where the *Phoenix* can touch land. Shaking his head, he notes that there is none, in this weather. Nowhere he can go ashore without putting his own men at risk.

'Let's go round it one more time . . .'

They circle the island again, noting how nothing moves upon it apart from birds and seals. Despite the wind, a fulmar swirls. A cormorant flies out. Gulls soar and follow in their wake. But of men, there is no sign. No evidence of their movement. No mark of a boat being wrecked near the shore. Nothing. No one. Not even a broken piece of wood.

He turns to the telegraph officer, ordering him to tap a message back home.

'Arrived at Sulasgeir Stop No signs of life on shore or nearby waters Stop . . .'

Yet the men on Sulasgeir do not see the *Phoenix* either. They arrived late on the island, blown off course by a wind that veered to the north and unable to obtain a landing on the rock. Instead, they had sheltered for a few days in the lee of North Rona, landing and sheltering in one of the stone buildings that clustered there. Eventually, the waters were calm enough for them to make their way to Sulasgeir, making up for the days they had lost by going around the rocks, catching the birds, building up their bodies into dark cairns of flesh and salt. There is good profit to be gained from this exile, this absence from home: riches to be reaped in this blizzard of feather and down. It will mean that both their bellies and those of their families are full throughout the winter.

So much so that they forget themselves, unaware of how long they have been away. If any of them had seen the fishery cruiser circling North Rona in the distance through thick sheets of rain, they would have rubbed their eyes in disbelief, not daring to speak in case the sight might be an illusion and others think them mad. They would have thought the women back home had no good reason to be alarmed by their absence. There was no cause for concern.

If they think of boats at all, they consider the *Loch Naver*, a steam trawler from Aberdeen which landed at Sulasgeir a week or so before. Captain Palmer and his men had provided them with fish, a little water for them to drink. Their coming had added a little variety to their meals, provided them with sustenance to make their time stranded on that rock more bearable. They had spent a little while together, too: the Nessmen speaking faltering English, the men from the North East talking in an indecipherable version of the same tongue. The hunters had even shown some of them how to kill and pluck a guga, offering them a bird or two to eat.

But they are unaware of the other boat leaving nearby shores, the captain of the fishery cruiser heading back home to Stornoway. He says a short prayer for the men he believes have been lost in the vicinity of Sulasgeir.

'O Lord, grant mercy to the souls that are gone from our midst . . .'

Yet, if he were honest, he would admit to being distracted, thinking of ways of curing his wife of all the ills she seems to suffer, and preventing his son from imitating her. It is a hard task that lies ahead of him, a difficult road indeed.

They are gathering around the schoolhouse again. The headmaster sees them from the window, watching them outside as he holds the telegram the postmistress has just given him. They are much the same group as earlier. There is the tall, jagged-featured woman with her son. A round-faced, dull-witted looking man. And then there is the trio from the same household with their identical brown hair and blue eyes. Their clothes look even more torn and worn than before. He reflects on the fact that they will become more tattered still – when they have gone for a few years without husbands or sons to hand over a little money to help their households. The sea is harsh and cruel to men, but it is even more so for women. It makes them widows on too many mornings, too many days like these.

He tries to find the words that will tell them that their men have gone . . .

And when he does so, there is crying and moaning, the keening sound that he has heard once before from these

Hebridean women when a member of their family has died. A child that time. One who fell off the rocks and into the sea near Port of Ness. It was terrible that day, but it's even worse on this occasion. He tries his best not to react, turning to the words of Psalm 130, the verses that begin:

> Lord, from the depths to thee I cry'd.
> My voice, Lord, do thou hear . . .

It is not long before another telegram arrives. As she deciphers the words tapped out on the telegraph machine, the postmistress marvels at their strangeness. The message has come from Aberdeen. One of lads from the district is out sailing there. He tells of an encounter with the men from the *Loch Naver* in the harbour area of that city, where he was told that the men were still alive on Sulasgeir, waiting for wind and wave to take them home.

'Could it be . . .?' she stammers to someone standing at the counter. 'Could it be . . .?'

She does not take it to the headmaster for translation, not as she had done before. Instead, she takes it into the next door neighbour's home, interrupting their prayers by gabbling out her information. The men are fine, she tells them, just caught on the rock by the weather. It will not be long before they are home. And a moment later, a child is sent next door with the news.

'Go and tell them . . . Go and tell them . . . Hurry! Right away!'

From that house too, there is the sound of rejoicing. Their men are safe. The women can set aside the widows' black they have put on over the last few days. There is no need of it. The words of Psalm 130 are stifled and stilled. Instead, there is a new song on their lips. The praises found in Psalm 149. The thanks and gratitude of Psalm 105.

And there is further rejoicing a few days later when the

crew of men return from Sulasgeir. Money is exchanged on the quayside for the 2,000 birds they have brought home. Seventy crisp pound notes slipped into their hands.

'Well worth all the trouble we seem to have caused . . .' one man says.

'It'll take more than that to pay the price of our tears,' a mother sniffs.

They are greeted, too, by their wives and children. One, a young woman newly wed, even goes so far as to embrace her husband on the breakwater, giving him a full-blooded kiss on his lips. Some of the other wives shake their heads when they see this, dismayed at this display of affection. Another feels a quiet sting of jealousy. It has been a long time since her own man treated her like that. A long time indeed. Though perhaps tonight, in the silence of the box-bed they share in the darkness of their home, something might occur.

8

A Sheltered Life

Let us imagine too that we can freeze and frame a moment from Donald Murray's early life . . .

It occurred on a turbulent, tumultuous day when he was around eleven years old. Battered by the fierceness of the wind, he made his way to the local shop in Port – a little, grey, aluminium-framed building owned by Iain a' Chabair on the opposite side of the road from the village post office. With every step he took in its direction, he seemed to take another backward, reeled to and fro by the fury of the storm.

He was reeling in other ways too. Just about a year before, his mother had gone to hospital in Inverness. 'I'll be back soon,' she had told both him and his brother Angus when she left their doorway, bending down to give them both a hug. He remembered how he had felt embarrassed as she did so – too big to be receiving cuddles in public – yet how, too, he had clung onto her words. She would not be long away. She would return to their fireside. Soon.

But that hadn't happened. The word 'soon' had lost all meaning as he contemplated her empty chair in the evening when he came home from school. And now, there were the words he was forced to hear when the grown-ups who came to his house didn't think he was listening. 'It's longer than we expected. We never thought she wouldn't be back yet.' Again and again, they swirled within his mind, leaving him barely upright.

He tried to dash them all from his head as he stepped through the doorway of Iain a' Chabair's shop, clutching the money an aunt had squashed into his hand to get one of J & E's loaves. She had told him that he could use the change to buy a bottle of Portello, the local lemonade. His father was away on Sulasgeir at the moment, and when he came back, there might be a few more coins for him, rewards for being a good lad while Dad was away. Cash from the sale of those precious gugas that also provided so many of the family's meals. And so, he squeezed the door shut, listening to the storm shake and rattle the tiny building's outside walls.

The others in the shop barely heard him enter. Instead, the old men who gathered there most mornings and afternoon continued to take part in their usual conversation. The subject matter seemed to vary from day to day. Sometimes it was about local or national politics: their MP, Malcolm K. Macmillan, and the murky doings of Ross and Cromarty Council. At other times it might be about the wanderings of someone's sheepdog or flock of sheep, a wedding or funeral that might be taking place. The only thing that never changed for Donald was the sense of tedium he felt at their every word.

Yet this time was different. On this occasion, things had altered.

They were talking about his dad, also known as Donald Murray (An Gaisean), and the rest of the men on Sulasgeir.

'Something's happened . . .' one said.

'They'd have been in contact a while ago otherwise . . .'

Donald pictured his father as he heard them. There was the breadth of his shoulders; the firmness and defiance of his jaw; the certainty of his stride. He couldn't be gone. Nothing could go wrong with him.

'Aye. It looks black. No doubt about it . . . It'll have a huge effect on this place. A big loss.'

Tears stinging his eyes, Donald reached for the door handle. A moment later and he was out into the storm again. His legs and arms akimbo, he felt himself run in the direction of the harbour, his coat flapping at the back of his legs and boots. He would be safe when he reached there, far enough away from everyone to be allowed to cry.

He stopped when he reached Bàrr a' Iairrd. Standing there, he looked down at the waves thundering on the breakwater below. Each one spurted like white flames from a chilly volcano; its uproar trembling through rock and stone to reach his hearing; its water like a heavy opaque sheet covering concrete. He froze as he watched them, knowing only too well the damage that could be wrought by the ocean. Hadn't he heard his own father talk about it often enough, telling him how on one December day in 1862 no fewer than four of the boy's great-great-grandfathers had been taken? On his father's side, Donald Murray, drowned at 36, with two of the others also dead that day: John Thomson, lost at 44; Donald Macdonald likewise at 48. And on his mother's side, another Donald MacDonald, his life over at 47. Each one leaving a widow and children behind. His dad had recited the names like a litany – as if each one were evidence that the sea had already done enough damage to his family. Surely they had seen enough. Surely enough damage had been done.

Yet the names had the opposite effect on young Donald. Some of these men had probably been as hard and strong as his father was now, yet the sea had broken them with its power. It could crack his father's bones and boat too. Easily. Completely. Powerfully.

The word 'death' began to have a new meaning for him. He tested out all the ways he had heard people speaking about it, rolling the different expressions around his mouth.

'*Bhàsaich e.* He passed away, he died. *Chaochail e.* He met his end. *Dh'eug e.* He's no longer with us.'

The range of words all tasted just about the same.

Bitter on his lips.

Many years later, in his house on the edge of the village of Tarbert on the isle of Harris, Donald Murray recalled that day for me. It was clearly a dark and hurtful time for him, lightened only by his father's safe return on the boat, the *Mairi Dhonn*, on 17 September 1952. The seas had only delayed him, not prevented him coming back to the family home. This was not the case with his mother. Quite unexpectedly, the end of her life came a week later on 24 September 1952, with her being the victim, perhaps, of a reaction to the anaesthetic used in her operation. (The precise reason is unclear even to Donald today. Her death certificate reads unhelpfully – 'a supposed failure of the circulatory system'. He is not even aware why she went through an operation in the first place.) Like anyone whose early life has been touched with sadness, it is an event that he must have at times have struggled to get over. Yet clearly, he succeeded, becoming Headteacher of Sir E. Scott Secondary School in Tarbert in 1981 and remaining in that position for 20 years, until he retired in 2001.

Donald Murray's father, Donald Murray, featured in this Donald Murray's first moment of awareness that there was anything distinctive about the parish his own father came from. At that time, our family were part of the Hebridean diaspora settled in the new town of East Kilbride in Lanarkshire near Glasgow. In this, we were by no means unique. There was another family just up the road from me who came from my own village of South Dell; another boy of my own age whose parents hailed from the other end of the district, Cross Skigersta Road. Clearly my dad and these people must have spoken in Gaelic to one another but, strangely, this never impinged on my consciousness.

What did, however, was being allowed up one night till the unearthly hour of 7 p.m. to watch my first ever grown-up 'Adventure' programme. In flickering black-and-white, it featured the guga hunters from Ness and it was the first time their activities had ever appeared on screen. In pyjamas and dressing gown, I recall sitting at my father's feet with a cup of hot cocoa in my hand, wondering what might happen in this small diversion from my usual television fare of *Circus Boy, Champion the Wonder Horse, Blue Peter*. It was like being given a golden ticket allowing entrance into the secret world of the Grown-up.

I seem to remember a compass, a map of Scotland where the TV camera zoomed in on the northern tip of the Outer Hebrides, Finlay J. Macdonald's sonorous Hebridean accent coming across loud and clear – especially distinctive at a time when most people who appeared on the medium had either an American accent or sounded like Michael Aspel. In contrast, this man sounded not unlike my dad.

And then there was a man who shared my name.

I cannot recall how I first saw him. It may have been the shot of him building the walls of a house – a great sturdy man dressed in his dungarees, a trowel tight in his hand. At that time, he worked with 'Innseag' Gillies of Lionel, building houses throughout Ness. Though they were untrained, it was clear that the two men were skilled in fashioning wood or dressing stone, taking rocks from the quarry in Beirgh at the end of Port to construct walls that sheltered many families in the district.

Or perhaps it was the way he stood with other men, inching out one of John Macleod's boats from his yard in Port of Ness. Again, one can see the intense concentration in his features, the weight upon his shoulders, the care and strength of his fingers.

And always, too, that black beret fixed permanently in position. It perched upon the head of a man who looked every inch a leader, not only because of his strength and agility but also due to the firmness of his gaze. This was a man in whom people could trust. His fellow-hunters' faith in him came from a mixture of his knowledge both of the Bible and those rocks he voyaged out towards for 35 years of his life. His affection for the place came across in the video filmed in the Taigh-Cèilidh when he compared himself to a man called Iain Buidhe who felt the same kind of affection for North Rona. When told he could see the island from Beinn nan Caorach near Beann Dhail, Iain shook his head and declared: '*Cha sheasadh mo chridhe ris*. My heart couldn't take it.'

One sensed the same longing to return to Sulasgeir in the elderly man sitting in the chair. In his imagination, he would be scaling the same crags and cliffs as Dods and his men during the time they were away.*

It might even have been the setting of Ness in the BBC programme that helped keep An Gaisean in my mind. It was the first time I had ever seen the place where I went on holiday on a screen. There was the power of the waves on Eoropie beach; the stillness of the moorland; the bustle of Port. There were faces, too, that were familiar to me, or at least, to my dad. He probably pointed out Willie Macleod or Uilleam Iain Mhurdo, inventor of the Blondin, and his wife Maisie behind the Post Office counter in Cross, hamming it up a little for the camera; their pretty blonde daughter Kay dancing down a Ness road. He probably knew, too, James Morrison broadcasting to Sulasgeir from the Decca Station on Lionel machair, telling me his name before Finlay J. had the chance to frame the words on his lips. All half-familiar names and voices. Half-familiar locations.

At the centre of that film too, however, there was also a touch of the exotic that might have made my recollections

---

* It is tempting, too, to draw some parallels between the lives of the two Donalds, father and son, at this point: the older man born in 1914 at the beginning of the First World War representing the older harsher, crofting, sea-going life; the younger one born three years into the Second World War in 1942 a representative of the changes that came over the island in the latter half of the twentieth century, leaving croft and sea to go to university and obtain white-collar employment. It is even more tempting to do this when one considers that both men shared the same birthday: the first day of January.

of it even sharper. It was of men going to a distant island, scaling rocks while strange white birds swirled around them; living in stone shelters; cooking over open fires. There was much of the excitement of these Boys' Adventure Stories I might watch on children's TV or read about in storybooks both at home and in school about the exploits I was viewing that night. I felt thrilled about the fact that it was men from my dad's native district who were taking part in all this – the brave men of Ness.

There was one man responsible for much of that programme. It was someone one of the guga hunters had probably met for the first time when they were bringing sheep to and from the nearby isle of North Rona – like Sulasgeir, part of the more southerly parish of Barvas on Lewis, for all that it had always been traditionally associated with Ness. The part-time nature warden on North Rona, James McGeoch, possibly gave them a hand with their flock, impressing the Niseachs with his hard work and good humour, telling them perhaps about his other life, where he followed a trade similar to a number of Hebrideans in exile on city streets on the mainland, as a police inspector in Inverness.

His main job could have been one of the earliest reasons why he earned the islanders' faith and trust, but there were others. There was a nimbleness and litheness about him that made him safe enough to accompany them on the crags – always an important consideration for anyone to be permitted as part of their group. Although originally Glaswegian, he was married to a Lewiswoman, Catriona Graham from Flesherin in Point, and had a strong interest in all aspects of the Hebrides, especially the Gaelic tongue. His fondness for the culture made him long to build a house in Ness, one perhaps built from the red-veined stones quarried by Innesag and An Gaisean from Beirgh. His enthusiasm for this district's way of life was clearly infectious, perhaps simultaneously convincing and confusing individuals who had, for instance, been taught that their native tongue was worthless in this new world they were about to inherit for themselves.

There was also his sheer love of birds. He may have pointed them out as he strode energetically across the bogland of North Rona, identifying even the rarer ones blown in that direction by fierce and unpredictable storms. He could have shown them the photographs he had taken of the creatures, capturing their splendour and beauty with his lens. It all made a pleasant change from the images he captured sometimes in his line of work as a police photographer – a crime scene; a traffic accident; one of the victims.

It was this skill that must have persuaded the Nessmen to allow McGeoch to accompany them on their trip to Sulasgeir. They felt intrigued by the notion that their relatives would see them on cine-film scrambling over rocks to bring home a harvest of birds. They might be amused on a winter evening by the sight of themselves going about these activities: the cook allowing the 'guga soup' to boil dry; the new arrival surprised by a downpour of earwigs as he stepped into one of the bothys. They would make their own special midwinter return to Sulasgeir at a time when wind and weather prevented their voyage. It was all done, as his daughter informed me, in terms of a gentleman's agreement between the men and McGeoch; the secretive nature of their actions would be preserved.

How the film managed to be shown as part of a BBC programme remains a matter of conjecture. Most of those who were involved are now long gone and the only one remaining, Alastair Bàn, has a tact and reticence that would prevent him commenting on what might have been at that time a controversial affair. (He did, of course, reveal his fondness for McGeoch in my conversation with him, indicating how he had learned a great deal from him.) In certain ways, however, it does not matter. The arguments over the 'public face' of the guga hunt still resonate today. I heard them while I was putting together this book: the notion that the guga hunt could and should remain an entirely private concern, that the secrecy that once surrounded it should remain.

One recognises how that attitude came to be. It was born – from the realities of other times – in 1938 when the letter columns of local and national newspapers had been filled with arguments over the future of the gannet hunt. The row erupted again in the 1950s, when there were exaggerated accounts of the numbers of gannets killed and the effect this was having on the gannet population. (It was this rather hyperbolic and hysterical approach that enabled Ross and Cromarty County Council to mount a defence of the practice when it argued for the Nessmen to continue their trade.) There was also a defensiveness on the part of the men and women in the district; again quite understandably when articles like the following one in the *Stornoway Gazette* drew on writings, say, in the Canadian press. One can only wonder how many Lewismen and women were teased and tormented about the original report in the *Vancouver Sun* headlined with the words:

Hebridean Fishermen Can't Eat Own Goose – Vow To Eat MPs

Focusing largely on the debate on the Wild Birds in Parliament and anticipating – wrongly! – its outcome, it went on to declare:

Somebody's goose has been cooked in the Hebrides and there's the dickens to pay for the situation. After 500 years, the guga bird or solan goose has disappeared from the menu. One guga killed in violation of a ban imposed by Parliament in London is worth up to £5,000 in fines . . .

And so it goes on, piling one error on top of another, referring to an 'annual guga festival' and predicting that 'the feathers will really fly [at the General Election of 1955] as all other issues fade into insignificance'. (One can only wonder at the absence of any geese laying golden eggs.) Yet almost as enlightening, however, as the original report is the *Gazette*'s response. One can accept its factual accuracy. There was little if anything said about the guga hunt in the election campaign of 1955. (I have Kenny Macleod from South Dell to thank for checking this.) However, the tone of the article reveals a great deal about the attitude of the town of Stornoway to the hunt. In the *Gazette* of 25 February 1955, the writer refers to the visit to Sulasgeir as 'a centuries-old pastime', putting it on a par, perhaps, with the game of golf. He reassures his readership that, 'Believe it or not, but we have it on good authority that at the political meeting held last week at Stornoway, not one little question was popped about the fate of the gugas, so after all it doesn't seem likely to become an election issue.' He goes on to confess, 'It's with a certain feeling of relief that we watch the much-publicised but modest guga slip back – until next September.'

And with these words, I am transported back into the Stornoway of my youth: a place that was embarrassed by its hinterland and the Gaelic-speaking crofters who lived 'back there'; a community that should have had its proudest boast, 'You know . . . we have a Woolworths', engraved above the entrance to its town hall; a people that wanted to live somewhere else. On the mainland, perhaps. Somewhere near the Central Belt. Somewhere without all that backwardness and history. Cumbernauld, perhaps. East Kilbride.

Middle-England-By-The-Minch . . .

Yet for all the changes that have taken place, particularly over the last decade or two, in some ways that old debate and its accompanying attitudes still linger. The future of the guga hunt can be considered by no means secure. In the course of writing this book, I asked a number of people whether they thought it would survive or not. I obtained a variety of replies to this question – the most vainglorious of these was, beyond doubt, a young guga hunter's response.

'As long as a guga is in the sky,' he declared, swaggering down the village road, 'there will be a guga in the pot.'

More than a few among those I questioned did not share his confidence. They found a variety of reasons for having doubts about the hunt's long-term future. One pointed out solemnly that the taste for seabird had all but disappeared elsewhere. 'Young people don't even have the stomach for fresh fish any more,' he added contemptuously. 'Far less guga.' With the population now appreciating less salt on their food, it was unlikely that even natives of Ness would continue enjoying what Alastair McIntosh has described as 'a freshly killed hen that had been dried out in the rafters of the byre over winter and then marinated for a generation in cod liver oil' forever. Sooner or later, no doubt encouraged by women long grown tired of guga-smoke clouding their ultra-clean, ultra-perfume-scented kitchens, the people of Ness would learn to act like everyone else, spicing their meals with, say, coriander and ginger rather than coarse-grain salt.

The women living nowadays in Ness might have yet further reasons to want to put an end to their husbands' outings to Sulasgeir. At one time, while it was necessary for the table, it was also partly a holiday for the 'lads', escaping what was – in my youth – a female-dominated society for a few weeks every year. (The heavy toll taken of male life in both World Wars and events like the *Iolaire* disaster left the district's population heavily imbalanced for much of the twentieth century.) Such rejoicing in the comradeship of men might, however, be less acceptable for women these days. There are a variety of reasons for this. One is the understandable desire among many households in the district to enjoy a 'break abroad' as a family unit, rather than Dad and husband spending his few weeks of annual leave stranded with a group of other males on a rock before bringing home a harvest of the Hallowed Bird. Another objection could arise from the way in which more and more Nessmen are marrying 'out' – whether just 'outside' of the parish or the island or islands as a whole. A young woman bred outwith the tradition is likely to be far less understanding about her true love 'Donald', 'Iain' or 'Murdo''s overwhelming need to spend time among the feathered nests of Sulasgeir each year than her Niseach equivalent, especially when he is setting out to acquire a clutch of sea-fowl with a taste too foul for her to ever learn to savour. The bird's flavour is unlikely to be made any sweeter for her by the thought that her partner may actually be losing money by spending time out on the rock.

Another argument people might provide for fearing for the future of the hunt is actually the existence of Dods, the man who has done so much to ensure its existence for the last few decades. 'What happens when he goes?' people ask, shaking their heads sadly at the prospect of his absence. It is all too easy to see that there might be some justification for their woe. Not only has he been an excellent 'hunter', able to predict the ways and wiles of bird, wind and wave on Sulasgeir, he has also been a wonderful organiser, doing much of the unheralded organisation work behind the scenes that makes the expedition possible. There is one role, however, that he has received less praise for but which has been vital in this day and age – that of the hunt's Public Relations Officer. The day has long gone when such activities could go on in private – the experiences of groups such as the Masonic Order should have been enough to convince even the most secretive of guga hunters of that. It is to Dods' credit that he has realised this and taken the arguments in favour of the hunt to a public arena. Journalists from the *Herald* have visited the island and a book, *Sula*, by John Beatty, been written. Gordon Ramsay – with the assistance of Nesswoman Mary Ann Morrison – has cooked guga in a television studio. Each enterprise has opened up the private world of Sulasgeir a little, dispelling the myths that might have flourished otherwise.

Nevertheless, it is Dods's view that the hunt will not end when he grows either too old or infirm to accompany the men. Someone else will take his place. 'They used to say the same about Alastair Bàn when it was near his time to go,' he grins, 'And look what happened. I stepped in. No one is irreplaceable.' He is also quick to mention possible alternatives to his leadership: names like Bobby Ruadh and Angus Murdo Gunn coming to his tongue.

And then, too, there is the main reason people gave for expecting the demise of the guga hunt – the way in which the population of Ness is both changing and dwindling. The first alteration can even be seen in the native Niseachs themselves. A young lad brought up within the parish is more likely than his predecessors to be raised within a household where his parents do not discuss the day-to-day concerns of croft and village life in Gaelic. They come from a place, too, where Dad (or Mum) is less and less liable to work the land or tend their flock of sheep. The church-going tradition is no longer as strong; that tight net of tongue, work and faith doesn't bind men as firmly to the commonplace concerns and toil of their district. Far from resenting this change, many clearly feel exhilarated by it, experiencing a sense of freedom in it, unaware, perhaps, that they are surrendering their individuality and the more unique aspects of their lives to a larger, more anonymous whole.

The 'native Niseach' may be fading from the scene in other ways too. More and more children in the classrooms of Ness come from 'incoming' families who have little knowledge or awareness of the guga-hunting tradition. While there already have been some from 'outside' who have enthusiastically adopted the hunt as their own, these are likely to be a minority, especially when their parents' way-of-life is far away from the old realities of croft and shore. And, as Donald MacRitchie's statistics tabling the decline in Ness's population demonstrate all too vividly, there is the likelihood that there will be many fewer young people – of any background – to choose from. Among them, too, there will be more young men with middle-class, white-collared parents who are less willing to become involved in a fortnight's stay on Sulasgeir. It is even the case these days that fewer of the men involved in the expedition are passing on the rope and blow-torch to their offspring, with more of the guga hunters coming from the south end (my part) of the parish.

There may even be a problem in the way the guga hunt is perceived by some both within and outside the community itself. One young woman confessed shamefacedly to me that she couldn't stand the taste of guga. 'Yet I could never admit that to anyone when I was in my teens,' she said. 'Imagine the teasing I might have got at school for saying that. A Niseach who didn't like guga!' While such voices may be stifled and hushed at present, it is unlikely to remain that way forever. The same cohesion that was once an occasionally oppressive feature of community life is no longer present, weakened by the arrival of such developments as television and the internet. Outside voices are seeping in – and some may echo the opinions of groups like Advocates for Animals.

They make their annual headlines in August, when in an activity almost as seasonal these days as the guga hunt itself, members of the media pick up their phones and invite a number of so-called animal lovers to fill up a column inch

or two. And, of course, these ladies and gentlemen duly
oblige.

'Guga Hunt Belongs In The Dark Ages' booms a thick
dark headline in the *Stornoway Gazette*'s issue of 24 August
2006. And, just as predictably, a gentleman called Ross
Minett, spokesperson for Advocates for Animals, steps
forth to give voice to his opinions, expressing their 'grave
concerns about this mass slaughter and the suffering it
causes. We are convinced that the hunt will be ended in
the near future – it belongs back in the Dark Ages. We just
believe that such a barbaric and out-dated slaughter of wild
animals will increasingly be viewed, by people in Scotland
and beyond, as unacceptable in the twenty-first century.'

He then goes on to declare in the pages of the *Indepen-
dent* that he is 'sure that this killing would have ended a long
time ago if it were conducted in a more accessible location
on the mainland, where we would be able to show people
how these baby birds are treated.'

Before one can even suggest that the practice could
possibly be switched to a poultry farm in, say, Norfolk,
a politician sometimes comes in on the act. The candidate
on this occasion was Catherine Stihler, a Labour MEP for
Scotland, who said: 'Exceptions [to EU rules] should always
be reviewed. It's always a balance between cultural tradition
and animal welfare. But there shouldn't be an exemption
until the end of time.'

This is despite the fact that there is no evidence that the
guga hunt has affected Scotland's population of gannets
one iota. In fact, over the last 20 years or so, the number of
solan geese in this part of the world has been steadily
increasing. There have been new colonies in places as far
apart as Fair Isle and Sule Skerry, with a number of birds
having emigrated there from elsewhere, including other
parts of Shetland and Sule Stack. There were, however,
some notes of concern in 2005, when the Natural Environ-

ment Research Council Centre for Ecology, based in Banchory, Aberdeenshire, reported that 'there were signs that the seemingly relentless rise in numbers could be coming to an end'.

Enter on cue Ms Stihler, making noises from off-stage in distant Brussels about the need to 'review' current practices. This was despite the fact that the report went on to declare that 'at present, it is unclear how much [the fall in the gannet population] is due to the larger colonies being close to their carrying capacities, either because of a lack of breeding sites or because of competition for food during the breeding season.'

Hence, perhaps, the creation of new colonies in the locations mentioned. The report also went on to mention other possibilities, unnoticed by Ms Stihler in her office in distant Belgium. It noted the 'increasing concern that climate change is affecting the east Atlantic eco-system and causing major changes to the food-web, particularly in the North Sea'. It recorded, too, the possibility that the species could also be adversely affected by 'changes in discarding practices by fishing vessels'. It was also troubled by the way in which the death-rate of adult gannets was a trend that had increased over the last few years, though the reason for this is not clear at this point. For all that the MEP drew attention to the guga hunters, what was entirely absent from the document was any reference to the effect their activities were having on their numbers.

And the reason for the report's silence on this topic, Ms Stihler? There seemed to have been none. So much then, so familiar. A similar charge can be made about the representations coming from animal activists way back in 1955 when James Shaw Grant, writing in the *Stornoway Gazette*, declared that the argument that the gannet was being 'exterminated' by the guga hunters was 'untenable'. In those Cold War days, he noted that 'the future of the gannet seems a good deal more secure than the future of homo sapiens in the world of the atom and H-bombs.'

Yet there is a greater dishonesty even than this in the tone and tenor of much of these reports. It lies within the language that these campaigners use. As Michael Robson pointed out in a letter to the *Scotsman* back in 1984, phrases like 'senseless slaughter', 'barbaric ancient ritual', 'baby gannets' and 'clubbing' used in some reports are absurd and inappropriate to the argument. They only serve to stir emotions and to cloud clear thought.

So are the comparisons that are sometimes made to 'sports' such as fox-hunting – a practice which Linda Colley in her book, *Britons*, describes as 'patriotic, patrician machismo' that enables 'a gentleman to flaunt his leisure without seeming in the process to be idle or effete'. The guga hunt is not the callous destruction of a Noble Bird to provide a trophy that might hang within a baronial hall. Instead, to employ Michael Robson's words again, 'it [gannet-hunting] is a practice that observes good conservation', gaining the support of bodies such as the Nature Conservancy Council and 'puts to shame many an accepted farming and sporting practice in the rest of the country'. It is also done not by the idle rich but by a group of hardworking men who are largely an integral part of both their community and tradition.

However, the tragedy is that the day may come when our people, too, echo the strange notions of Ross and Catherine, claiming them for their own, especially now that so many crofts are bereft of sheep and cattle, becoming simply fences that enclose empty acres of unused grassland. As Alastair McIntosh so eloquently writes, 'The peril that faces us in today's world is not the killing of a sheep or a Guga by a crofter.' The former is an activity that – as noted before – I undertook on a few occasions in my teenage years after my father's early death, helping a neighbour butcher some of his (or our) flock. While an unpleasant task, it is one that is sometimes a necessity – and has been, as even Ross Minnett might admit, part of our existence 'since the Dark Ages'. It was done in these pre-EU directive days because we needed meat for our tables. One of the more unfortunate by-products of that piece of largely beneficial legislation may be the way it has helped us to forget how mankind is interdependent with other creatures on the planet.

Instead, to quote McIntosh again, 'the peril for people today is that modern people are so out of touch with the natural cycles of life, death and rebirth, and with the natural elements – fire, air, earth and water or the land, air, water and sun – that they become literally unhinged.' It is the absence of any true moral bearings and meaningful attachment to Creation that allow us to tolerate what men and women in the Dark Ages would never have accepted for a moment – industrial fishing and factory farming practices that are barbaric and cruel to the life-forms trapped within. Pick up a chicken from the supermarket for a moment and consider its existence. Dods and his crew do not inflict on the gannet chicks the horrors that modern man is capable of wreaking on other creatures. In fact, there is little doubt in my mind that if ever he and his men became aware of a sizable decrease in the number of gannets nesting on Sulasgeir, they would react in much the same way as the people of Fair Isle when they noticed a fall in the quantity of guillemot eggs found on its shores. They would very quickly stop.

It is for this reason that Alastair McIntosh declares that 'the hunt could never endanger the guga as a species. If their numbers fell, the application of innate Hebridean traditions of veneration for the environment would cause the Niseachs to curb their practice accordingly, and they would be the first to recognise that the balance of nature was not right'.

It is an argument that Professor Donald Macleod, a

native of Ness and Principal of the Free Church College in Edinburgh, takes up. An acclaimed writer who writes regularly on moral issues both for the *West Highland Free Press* and the *Observer*, he answers the question whether it is right to kill and eat the guga with his customary wit and aplomb – and more than a little forgivable local pride. Examining the issues of ecology and the environment, he declares:

> It's as right to kill the guga as it is to kill elephants in South Africa's Kruger Park, on the principle that if they're not culled, the ecological balance goes haywire.
>
> Besides, for every guga eaten, a chicken is spared, and the gugas have had a much happier life. Over and above which, vegetarians must remember that every time they eat an apple millions of beautiful little creatures are slaughtered, devoured by the grinding maws of humans desperate to achieve the right personal body-shape. And anyway, it's very hard for *homo* to live on nothing but greens. We may not, like lions, be pure carnivores, but we very nearly are, and we need meat to keep warm; and not only to keep warm, but to expose the sloppy thinking of *homo attenburgus,* who thinks the king of the jungle magnificent though he tears antelopes, buffalo and wildebeest to pieces, but thinks the noble Niseach a savage because he eats guga.
>
> And who wouldn't, once you've tasted it? Delicious, especially if not scrubbed, vacuum-packed, rubbed down with washing soda, desalinated, served with orange sauce or cooked by Gordon Ramsay. The best way to get one is through the post, anonymously; then an hour-and-twenty-minutes in the pot, served with tons of Kerr's Pinks and a pint of water (followed, at intervals, by gallons).
>
> But none of the above, or all of them together, constitute the real reason for eating gugas. The real reason is the environment, and the bearing of guga-eating on that most

fundamental of all ecological questions: whose environment is it, anyway? The men of the south who built Milton Keynes and Spaghetti Junction have no such jurisdiction over Sulasgeir. They've never seen it, never breathed its air and couldn't even land on it if they tried. Indeed, on one memorable occasion in 1912, their Royal Navy couldn't even find it. It is for this reason Sulasgeir belongs to Niseachs, and the bird owes all its celebrity to the stunning contribution it has made to our diet.

Their ignorance about life on the periphery does not, of course, prevent those who come from an urban environment from doing what their forbears in the 1930s did when reading about the guga hunters in the letter page of *The Times* – casting judgement on the practices of others. As James Shaw Grant argued in the *Gazette* way back in 1955, it is a practice that human beings are rather skilled at undertaking, with many of our species deriving 'pleasure in preventing other people from doing things which they have no wish to do themselves'. In short, the pronouncements of Minnet and Stihler should be seen for what they are: displays of self-righteous interference in the existence of others. In a curious way, the scolding of these urbanites has much in common with those whom they might affect to despise, such as the ones who used to chain the playground swings of Stornoway when I was growing up, preventing the enjoyments of others.

Yet there are other reasons why the guga hunt must and should continue. A further case put forward by Alastair Bàn's son, John Campbell, is based on the very nature of many young men today. In our modern world, a good number, perhaps even the majority, lead a sedentary existence. The greatest risk they face is from an early death from either excess eating or speeding in their cars. According to John, a fortnight on Sulasgeir is the equivalent of an

'Outward Bound Course' – one that has the additional bonus of making young men familiar with the glories of the natural world. Angus Murdo Gunn tells a wonderful story of the way one of their number reacted when he saw his first and – in Sulasgeir's terms – extremely rare puffin chick. Observing this beaked ball of fluff, he rushed away from the bothy with the fear and alarm of someone encountering one of Spielberg's 'Gremlins' for the very first time. However, the time spent on Sulasgeir does more even than this. It both tests mind, body and spirit and teaches the young men how to get on with men who are older and more experienced, learning about their own strengths and weaknesses and their own heritage and tradition from their time out on the rock.

Even the mere act of eating the guga may also do this. It is one of the few foods we are likely to consume today that binds us to both a place and the practices of our ancestors. When we consume it, we are no longer the 'unrooted', disconnected people into which we have been transformed by progress and our modern consumer society. We are at one with those who have gone before us, people who at one time scouted the cliffs and crags of the coastline for such or similar food. We are in contact too with a sense of community and place that has no part or shelf-space in our local Tesco or Co-op. It is an example of the 'slow-cooking' movement par excellence. Buy local. Eat local. Protect the environment.

As a Niseach, I am particularly conscious of why it is important both to me and the people of my district. It represents a food-source on which my community could depend, which was safe and nourishing to eat. This is unlike some of the other forms of nutrition the population of Ness used to sustain their lives. The potato and other crops could be blighted – not only by disease but also the sound and fury of unpredictable weather. Salt could destroy grain or blast the green leaves sprouting from seed we had sown in spring. Fish might stray from our coastline, where we laid out our lines or nets. There would be seasons when there would be no full harvest from the sea, when the spaces where we looked for ling and mackerel would be empty.

Or there would be times when the rent charged by the ocean would seem a trifle high, even extortionate. The history of Port of Ness, like many other sea-ports, has – as has been outlined in these pages – contained more than its share of tragedy, where the price of fish often seemed far too heavy for people to bear. In contrast to this, there was the raid on Sulasgeir in which not one man has been killed for centuries. It is quick and profitable, a short 40-mile race across tide and current in what is often in weather terms the most pleasant time of year – if any point in the calendar at all might be considered 'pleasant' in these parts. When weighed against the expense of fish in 'human' terms, there is little doubt why the bird became precious to the community. It represents safety and security, a shield against the hunger that so often afflicted the people in these parts. It could be depended upon. In consumer terms and in the context of the history of Ness, it was the ultimate low-risk, high-return food.

Yet there is more to it than this. Ness is an embattled community. Over the last few hundred years it has lost one tongue, Norn, and is in danger of losing another, Gaelic. It is losing, too, one of the chief reasons for its existence – the agricultural life that sustained its people for centuries. Its seas are empty too, swept clean by deep-sea trawlers emerging from safe harbours its own shores so sorely lack. Its young people have left many of the crofthouses that studded the district, leaving their lights to be either extinguished or – what is much better – switched on again by those who have no great knowledge of the community's way of life. It is seeing, too, the possibility of its way of worship coming to an end; the kirks that once thronged with people now empty apart from a few brave, ageing souls. It is, perhaps, this that is the source of the guga's appeal, much more than its taste and texture, the very things that outsiders sometimes joke and jest about. Perhaps it is a gesture of defiance – one made against those forces that over the last centuries have made life here more difficult than it ought to have been.

For I know that when I eat guga, I am a Niseach again. Whether this feeling is imagined or not, its taste restores to me a sense of my place in the life of both that district and the island as a whole. I believe I am not unique in having this reaction. Others share it – and for as long as they do, men will continue to sail out to Sulasgeir, finding in their time out on that rock a way in which they can reconnect with both themselves and their world. In terms of the history of Ness, it, to paraphrase Psalm 124, represents a way in which the people here were protected from the worst ravages of hunger; from the flood that would have engulfed us; the torrent that would have swept over us; the raging waters that would have swept us away. As a result of its proximity, we were released from the trap of hunger 'like a bird out of the fowler's snare; the snare has been broken and we have escaped'.

Endpiece

Ceyx and Alcyone

When Morpheus, the god of sleep, cannot rest these nights, he always thinks of Ceyx: the old gannet in flight above the sea, looking for somewhere he can feed himself, his mate and chick, all who are connected to him in his present life. But there's nowhere for him to plunge any more, no place where he can dive to capture and lift the silver gleam of fish within his beak. Oil glimmers on the surface of much of the ocean, its rainbow gleam stretching for miles. There're other sections of dirty water too, contaminated forever by the stinking corpses of birds and fish. Dead gulls and fulmars float upon a grimy tide breaking on the coastline. The blue, bloated bodies of coalfish, haddock and cod drift lifelessly on the sea's ebb and flow. And always below them, there are the loose open shrouds of redundant fishing nets, shifting back and forth as if breathing in and out in a seascape empty of life they have done so much to help destroy. There is other debris, too, in the ocean's depths: untreated sewage; plastic pollutants; rusting iron and steel lurking below.

And so Ceyx flies over all this for many days and nights, searching for food, looking perhaps, too, for the kingfisher that used to greet him on rare, still days, but there is no sign of her either, no flash of her blue wings dancing across waves to greet him.

As he does all this, a strange, vague thought occurs to him. Perhaps man has not only choked and destroyed life in these waters. Perhaps he has visited ruin upon land too. He thinks of her then – that ancient love he enjoyed centuries before, her name restored to him once more, and how she, if she still exists, must dart across rivers and streams that are tainted and soiled by those beings with whom they have the misfortune to share this planet.

'Alcyone . . .' he says.

Sulasgeir Crews

This remarkable document was constructed by the guga hunters themselves – primarily by Murdo Deedo Macdonald, with considerable assistance from Dods MacFarlane, James Murray (Seumas an Bhain), Murdo Campbell (Am Blondaidh), Angus Mackay (Angus a' Ghiomanaich) and John Murdo Macleod. Inevitably, given the expanse of time and the number of individuals it covers, there may be occasional errors contained within its pages. Despite this, it is worth including. Few communities honour the past enough to attempt such a record of those who have gone before them. It says much for both these individuals and the people of Ness as a whole that they try.

Year 2007: *Heather Isle*
 1. John Murdo Macfarlane: 'Dods Mhurchaidh Mhurdaidh'
 2. Angus Morrison: 'Aonghas Chaluim Bob – Bobby Ruadh'
 3. Alasdair Macleod: 'Alasdair Alex Dan'
 4. Murdo Morrison: 'Murchadh Chaluim Mhurchaidh 'Ain Bhig'
 5. Alex John Bell: 'Mac Carola Bell'
 6. Angus Murdo Gunn: 'Angus Murdo Dhòmhnaill Bhàin'
 7. Alex Dan Smith: 'Dan Dhannsain'
 8. Finlay Burns: 'Mac Etta Thormoid Sheonaidh'
 9. Murdo Ferguson: 'Murchadh Cat'na Mhurchaidh 'Ain Bhàin'
10. William Gunn: 'Mac Alasdair Robhair' (first trip)

Year 2006: *Heather Isle*
 1. John Murdo Macfarlane: 'Dods Mhurchaidh Mhurdaidh'
 2. Angus Morrison: 'Aonghas Chaluim Bob – Bobby Ruadh'
 3. Alasdair Macleod: 'Alasdair Alex Dan'
 4. Murdo Morrison: 'Murchadh Chaluim Mhurchaidh 'Ain Bhig'
 5. Alex John Bell: 'Mac Carola Bell'

6. Alasdair Buchanan: 'AB'
7. Angus Murdo Gunn: 'Angus Murdo Dhòmhnàill Bhàin'
8. Alex Dan Smith: 'Dan Dhannsain' (cook)
9. Finlay Burns: 'Mac Etta Thormoid Sheonaidh'
10. Scott Davidson: 'Mac Fiona Mhurchaidh Mhurdaidh'

Year 2005: *Heather Isle*

1. John Murdo Macfarlane: 'Dods Mhurchaidh Mhurdaidh'
2. Angus Morrison: 'Aonghas Chaluim Bob – Bobby Ruadh'
3. Alasdair Macleod: 'Alasdair Alex Dan'
4. Murdo Morrison: 'Murchadh Chalum Mhurchaidh 'Ain Bhig'
5. Alex John Bell: 'Mac Carola Bell'
6. Alasdair Buchanan: 'AB'
7. Angus Murdo Gunn: 'Angus Murdo Dhòmhnaill Bhàin'
8. Alex Dan Smith: 'Dan Dhannsain' (cook)
9. Finlay Burns 'Mac Etta Thormoid Sheonaidh'
10. Scott Davidson 'Mac Fiona Mhurchaidh Mhurdaidh' (first trip)

Year 2004: *Heather Isle*

1. John Murdo Macfarlane: 'Dods Mhurchaidh Mhurdaidh'
2. Angus Morrison: 'Aonghas Chaluim Bob – Bobby Ruadh'
3. Alasdair Macleod: 'Alasdair Alex Dan'
4. Murdo Morrison: 'Murchadh Chalum Mhurchaidh 'Ain Bhig'
5. Alex John Bell: 'Mac Carola Bell'
6. Alasdair Buchanan: 'AB'
7. Angus Murdo Gunn: 'Angus Murdo Dhòmhnaill Bhàin'
8. Alex Dan Smith: 'Dan Dhannsain' (cook)
9. Kenny Murray: 'Coinneach a' Chiolais'
10. Norman Murray: 'Tam, Mac Coinneach a' Chiolais' (first trip)

Year 2003: *Heather Isle* (previously *Carona*)

1. John Murdo Macfarlane: 'Dods Mhurchaidh Mhurdaidh'
2. Angus Morrison: 'Aonghas Chaluim Bob – Bobby Ruadh'
3. Murdo Campbell: 'Am Blondaidh' (cook) (last trip)
4. Alasdair Macleod: 'Alasdair Alex Dan'
5. Murdo Morrison: 'Murchadh Chalum Mhurchaidh 'Ain Bhig'
6. Iain Morrison: 'Buckie'
7. Alex John Bell: 'Mac Carola Bell'
8. Alasdair Buchanan: 'AB'
9. Donald Macfarlane: 'Dòmhnall Mhurchaidh Mhurdaidh'
10. Murdo Ferguson: 'Murchadh Cat' na Murchaidh Ain Bhàin'

Year 2002: *Carona*
1. John Murdo Macfarlane: 'Dods Mhurchaidh Mhurdaidh'
2. Angus Murdo Gunn: 'Angus Murdo Dhòmhnaill Bhain'
3. Angus Morrison: 'Aonghas Chaluim Bob – Bobby Ruadh'
4. Murdo Macdonald: 'Murchadh Deedo'
5. Murdo Campbell: 'Am Blondaidh' (cook)
6. Alasdair Macleod: 'Alasdair Alex Dan'
7. Murdo Morrison: 'Murchadh Chalum Mhurchaidh 'Ain Bhig'
8. Alex Dan Smith: 'Dan Dhannsain' (first trip)
9. Iain Morrison: 'Buckie' (first trip)
10. Alex John Bell: 'Mac Carola Bell' (first trip)

Year 2001: *Sheigra* outbound, *Calina* homebound
1. John Murdo Macfarlane: 'Dods Mhurchaidh Mhurdaidh'
2. Angus Murdo Gunn: 'Angus Murdo Dhòmhnaill Bhàin'
3. Angus Morrison: 'Aonghas Chaluim Bob – Bobby Ruadh'
4. Murdo Macdonald: 'Murchadh Deedo'
5. Murdo Campbell: 'Am Blondaidh' (cook)
6. Alasdair Buchanan: 'AB'
7. Alasdair Macleod: 'Alasdair Alex Dan'
8. Glen Maclean: 'Glen Chaluim Aonghais Ghlen'
9. Murdo Morrison: 'Murchadh Chalum Mhurchaidh 'Ain Bhig' (first trip)

Year 2000: *Calina*
1. John Murdo Macfarlane: 'Dods Mhurchaidh Mhurdaidh'
2. Angus Murdo Gunn: 'Angus Murdo Dhòmhnaill Bhàin'
3. Angus Morrison: 'Aonghas Chaluim Bob – Bobby Ruadh'
4. Norman Murray: 'Tormod Dhoilidh Chaluim – Tormod Carrots' (last trip)
5. Norman Macdonald: 'Tormod Angie' (last trip)
6. Murdo Macdonald: 'Murchadh Deedo'
7. Murdo Campbell: 'Am Blondaidh' (cook)
8. Alasdair Buchanan: 'AB'
9. Alasdair Macleod: 'Alasdair Alex Dan'
10. Glen Maclean: 'Glen Chaluim Aonghais Ghlen'
    (Visited on 18 and 20 August by Barbara Jones, George Brown, Alan Hardwick, Bruce Greig, Neil Macinnes and Janet Crummy, who were camping on Rona.)

Year 1999: *Calina*
 1. John Murdo Macfarlane: 'Dods Mhurchaidh Mhurdaidh'
 2. Angus Murdo Gunn: 'Angus Murdo Dhòmhnaill Bhàin'
 3. Angus Morrison: 'Aonghas Chaluim Bob – Bobby Ruadh'
 4. Norman Murray: 'Tormod Dhoilidh Chaluim – Tormod Carrots'
 5. Norman Macdonald: 'Tormod Angie'
 6. Murdo Macdonald: 'Murchadh Deedo'
 7. Murdo Campbell: 'Am Blondaidh' (cook)
 8. Alasdair Buchanan: 'AB'
 9. Alasdair Macleod: 'Alasdair Alex Dan'
10. Glen Maclean: 'Glen Chaluim Aonghais Ghlen' (first trip)

Year 1998: *Calina*
 1. John Murdo Macfarlane: 'Dods Mhurchaidh Mhurdaidh'
 2. Angus Murdo Gunn: 'Angus Murdo Dhòmhnaill Bhàin'
 3. Angus Morrison: 'Aonghas Chaluim Bob – Bobby Ruadh'
 4. Norman Murray: 'Tormod Dhoilidh Chaluim – Tormod Carrots'
 5. Norman Macdonald: 'Tormod Angie'
 6. Murdo Macdonald: 'Murchadh Deedo'
 7. Murdo Nicholson: 'Murdie Rhoda' (last trip)
 8. Murdo Campbell: 'Am Blondaidh' (cook)
 9. Alasdair Buchanan: 'AB' (first trip)
10. Alasdair Macleod: 'Alasdair Alex Dan' (first trip)

Year 1997: *Sweet Promise*
 1. John Murdo Macfarlane: 'Dods Mhurchaidh Mhurdaidh'
 2. Calum Mackay: 'Calum an Tàilleir' (cook; last trip)
 3. Angus Murdo Gunn: 'Angus Murdo Dhòmhnaill Bhàin'
 4. Angus Morrison: 'Aonghas Chaluim Bob – Bobby Ruadh'
 5. Norman Murray: 'Tormod Dhoilidh Chaluim – Tormod Carrots'
 6. Donald Macfarlane: 'Dòmhnall Mhurchaidh Mhurdaidh' (last trip)
 7. Norman Macdonald: 'Tormod Angie'
 8. Murdo Macdonald: 'Murchadh Deedo'
 9. Murdo Nicholson: 'Murdie Rhoda' (first trip)
10. Murdo Ferguson: 'Murchadh Cat' na Mhurchaidh 'Ain Bhàin' (first trip)

Year 1996: *Pescoso*
1. John Murdo Macfarlane: 'Dods Mhurchaidh Mhurdaidh'
2. Calum Mackay: 'Calum an Tàilleir' (cook)
3. Angus Murdo Gunn: 'Angus Murdo Dhòmhnaill Bhàin'
4. Murdo Campbell: 'Am Blondaidh'
5. Angus Morrison: 'Aonghas Chaluim Bob – Bobby Ruadh'
6. Norman Murray: 'Tormod Dhoilidh Chaluim – Tormod Carrots'
7. Donald Macfarlane: 'Dòmhnall Mhurchaidh Mhurdaidh'
8. Norman Macdonald: 'Tormod Angie'
9. Murdo Macdonald: 'Murchadh Deedo'
10. Innes Mackay: 'Stan, Aonghas a' Ghiomanaich' (last trip)

Year 1995: *Pescoso*
1. John Murdo Macfarlane: 'Dods Mhurchaidh Mhurdaidh'
2. Calum Mackay: 'Calum an Tàilleir' (cook)
3. Angus Murdo Gunn: 'Angus Murdo Dhòmhnaill Bhàin'
4. Murdo Campbell: 'Am Blondaidh'
5. Angus Morrison: 'Aonghas Chaluim Bob – Bobby Ruadh'
6. Norman Murray: 'Tormod Dhoilidh Chaluim – Tormod Carrots'
7. Donald Macfarlane: 'Dòmhnall Mhurchaidh Mhurdaidh'
8. Norman Macdonald: 'Tormod Angie'
9. Murdo Macdonald: 'Murchadh Deedo'
10. Innes Mackay: 'Stan, Aonghas a' Ghiomanaich' (first trip)

Year 1994: *Kingfisher*
1. John Murdo Macfarlane: 'Dods Mhurchaidh Mhurdaidh'
2. Calum Mackay: 'Calum an Tàilleir' (cook)
3. Finlay Morrison: 'Fionnlagh na h-Earraid' (last trip)
4. Angus Murdo Gunn: 'Angus Murdo Dhòmhnaill Bhàin'
5. Murdo Campbell: 'Am Blondaidh'
6. Angus Morrison: 'Aonghas Chaluim Bob – Bobby Ruadh'
7. Norman Murray: 'Tormod Dhoilidh Chaluim – Tormod Carrots'
8. Donald Macfarlane: 'Dòmhnall Mhurchaidh Mhurdaidh'
9. Kenny Murray: 'Coinneach a' Chiolais' (last trip)
10. Norman Macdonald: 'Tormod Angie'

Year 1993: *Golden Sheaf*
1. John Murdo Macfarlane: 'Dods Mhurchaidh Mhurdaidh'
2. Calum Mackay: 'Calum an Tàilleir' (cook)
3. Finlay Morrison: 'Fionnlagh na h-Earraid'

 4. Angus Murdo Gunn: 'Angus Murdo Dhòmhnaill Bhàin'
 5. Murdo Campbell: 'Am Blondaidh'
 6. Angus Morrison: 'Aonghas Chaluim Bob – Bobby Ruadh'
 7. Norman Murray: 'Tormod Dhoilidh Chaluim – Tormod Carrots'
 8. Donald Macfarlane: 'Domhnall Mhurchaidh Mhurdaidh'
 9. Kenny Murray: 'Coinneach a' Chiolais'
10. Norman Macdonald: 'Tormod Angie'

Year 1992: *Golden Sheaf*
 1. John Murdo Macfarlane: 'Dods Mhurchaidh Mhurdaidh'
 2. Calum Mackay: 'Calum an Tàilleir' (cook)
 3. Finlay Morrison: 'Fionnlagh na h-Earraid'
 4. Angus Murdo Gunn: 'Angus Murdo Dhòmhnaill Bhàin'
 5. Murdo Campbell: 'Am Blondaidh'
 6. Angus Morrison: 'Aonghas Chaluim Bob – Bobby Ruadh'
 7. Norman Murray: 'Tormod Dhoilidh Chaluim – Tormod Carrots'
 8. Donald Macfarlane: 'Domhnall Mhurchaidh Mhurdaidh'
 9. Kenny Murray: 'Coinneach a' Chiolais'
10. Norman Macdonald: 'Tormod Angie'

Year 1991: *Golden Sheaf*
 1. John Murdo Macfarlane: 'Dods Mhurchaidh Mhurdaidh'
 2. Calum Mackay: 'Calum an Tàilleir' (cook)
 3. Finlay Morrison: 'Fionnlagh na h-Earraid'
 4. Angus Murdo Gunn: 'Angus Murdo Dhòmhnaill Bhàin'
 5. Murdo Campbell: 'Am Blondaidh'
 6. Angus Morrison: 'Aonghas Chaluim Bob – Bobby Ruadh'
 7. Norman Murray: 'Tormod Dhoilidh Chaluim – Tormod Carrots'
 8. Donald Macfarlane: 'Dòmhnall Mhurchaidh Mhurdaidh'
 9. Kenny Murray: 'Coinneach a' Chiolais'
10. Norman Macdonald: 'Tormod Angie' (first trip)
    (Accompanied by John Beatty with photographer and assistant
    Stuart Dale. This resulted in the book *Sula*.)

Year 1990: *Golden Sheaf*
 1. John Murdo Macfarlane: 'Dods Mhurchaidh Mhurdaidh'
 2. Calum Mackay: 'Calum an Tàilleir'
 3. Finlay Morrison: 'Fionnlagh na h-Earraid' (cook)
 4. Angus Murray: ' "Amos" Ruairidh Doe' (last trip)
 5. Murdo Macdonald: 'Murchadh Deedo'

6. Angus Murdo Gunn: 'Angus Murdo Dhòmhnaill Bhàin'
7. Murdo Campbell: 'Am Blondaidh'
8. Angus Morrison: 'Aonghas Chaluim Bob – Bobby Ruadh'
9. Norman Murray: 'Tormod Dhoilidh Chaluim – Tormod Carrots' (first trip)
10. Donald Macfarlane: 'Dòmhnall Mhurchaidh Mhurdaidh' (first trip)

Year 1989: *Golden Sheaf*
1. Angus Mackay: 'Aonghas a' Ghiomanaich' (last trip)
2. John Murdo Macfarlane: 'Dods Mhurchaidh Mhurdaidh'
3. Calum Mackay: 'Calum an Tàilleir'
4. Finlay Morrison: 'Fionnlagh na h-Earraid' (cook)
5. Kenny Murray: 'Coinneach a' Chiolais'
6. Angus Murray: ' "Amos" Ruairidh Doe'
7. Murdo Macdonald: 'Murchadh Deedo'
8. Angus Murdo Gunn: 'Angus Murdo Dhòmhnaill Bhàin'
9. Murdo Campbell: 'Am Blondaidh'
10. Angus Morrison: 'Aonghas Chaluim Bob – known as Bobby Ruadh' (first trip)

Year 1988: *Golden Sheaf*
1. Alastair Campbell: 'Alasdair Bàn' (cook; last trip)
2. Angus Maclean: 'Aonghas Ghliocais' (last trip)
3. Angus Mackay: 'Aonghas a' Ghiomanaich'
4. John Murdo Macfarlane: 'Dods Mhurchaidh Mhurdaidh'
5. Calum Mackay: 'Calum an Tailleir'
6. Finlay Morrison: 'Fionnlagh na h-Earraid'
7. Kenny Murray: 'Coinneach a' Chiolais'
8. Angus Murray: ' "Amos" Ruairidh Doe'
9. Murdo Macdonald: 'Murchadh Deedo'
10. Angus Murdo Gunn: 'Angus Murdo Dhòmhnaill Bhàin' (first trip) (Visited on the 18 August by Barbara Jones and daughters Emma (15) and Helen (12), George Brown, John Weston, Alan Hardwick, Bobbie Massie, Frenchman George and son Robert, who were camping on Rona.)

Year 1987: *Golden Sheaf*
1. Alastair Campbell: 'Alastair Bàn' (cook)
2. Angus Maclean: 'Aonghas Ghliocais'
3. Angus Mackay: 'Aonghas a' Ghiomanaich'

   4. John Murdo Macfarlane: 'Dods Mhurchaidh Mhurdaidh'
   5. Calum Mackay: 'Calum an Tàilleir'
   6. Finlay Morrison: 'Fionnlagh na h-Earraid'
   7. Kenny Murray: 'Coinneach a' Chiolais'
   8. Angus Murray: '"Amos" Ruairidh Doe'
   9. Murdo Angus Murray: 'Murchadh Iain Doe' (last trip)
  10. Murdo Macdonald: 'Murchadh Deedo' (first trip)

Year 1986: *Golden Sheaf*
   1. Alastair Campbell: 'Alasdair Bàn' (cook)
   2. Angus Maclean: 'Aonghas Ghliocais'
   3. Angus Mackay: 'Aonghas a' Ghiomanaich'
   4. John Murdo Macfarlane: 'Dods Mhurchaidh Mhurdaidh'
   5. Calum Mackay: 'Calum an Tàilleir'
   6. Finlay Morrison: 'Fionnlagh na h-Earraid'
   7. Kenny Murray: 'Coinneach a' Chiolais'
   8. Angus Murray: '"Amos" Ruairidh Doe'
   9. Murdo Angus Murray: 'Murchadh Iain Doe' (first trip)
  10. Murdo Macdonald: 'Murchadh Deedo' (first trip)

Year 1985: *Golden Sheaf*
   1. Alasdair Murray: 'Eve' (cook; last trip)
   2. Alastair Campbell: 'Alasdair Bàn'
   3. John Morrison: 'Iain Dubh a' Ghladstoin' (last trip)
   4. Angus Maclean: 'Aonghas Ghliocais'
   5. Angus Mackay: 'Aonghas a' Ghiomanaich'
   6. John Murdo Macfarlane: 'Dods Mhurchaidh Mhurdaidh'
   7. Calum Mackay: 'Calum an Tàilleir'
   8. Finlay Morrison: 'Fionnlagh na h-Earraid'
   9. Kenny Murray: : 'Coinneach a' Chiolais'
  10. Angus Murray: '"Amos" Ruairidh Doe'

Year 1984: *Golden Sheaf* (*Sheaf* alongside outbound)
   1. Alasdair Murray: 'Eve' (cook)
   2. Alastair Campbell: 'Alasdair Bàn'
   3. John Morrison: 'Iain Dubh a' Ghladstoin'
   4. Angus Maclean: 'Aonghas Ghliocais'
   5. Angus Mackay: 'Aonghas a' Ghiomanaich'
   6. John Murdo Macfarlane: 'Dods Mhurchaidh Mhurdaidh'
   7. Calum Mackay: 'Calum an Tàilleir'

8. Finlay Morrison: 'Fionnlagh na h-Earraid'
9. Kenny Murray: 'Coinneach a' Chiolais'
10. Angus Murray: '"Amos" Ruairidh Doe'

Year 1983: *Golden Sheaf* (*Sheaf* alongside both ways)
1. Alastair Murray: 'Eve' (cook)
2. Alastair Campbell: 'Alastair Bàn'
3. John Morrison: 'Iain Dubh a' Ghladstoin'
4. Angus Maclean: 'Aonghas Ghliocais'
5. Angus Mackay: 'Aonghas a' Ghiomanaich'
6. John Murdo Macfarlane: 'Dods Mhurchaidh Mhurdaidh'
7. Calum Mackay: 'Calum an Tàilleir'
8. Finlay Morrison: 'Fionnlagh na h-Earraid'
9. Kenny Murray: 'Coinneach a' Chiolais' (first trip)
10. Angus Murray: '"Amos" Ruairidh Doe' (first trip)

Year 1982: *Astronaut*
1. Alastair Murray: 'Eve'
2. Donald Murdo Macfarlane: 'Murchadh Mhurdaidh' (cook; last trip)
3. Alastair Campbell: 'Alasdair Bàn'
4. John Morrison: 'Iain Dubh a' Ghladstoin'
5. Angus Maclean: 'Aonghas Ghliocais'
6. John Campbell: 'Iain Alasdair Bhàin' (last trip)
7. Angus Mackay: 'Aonghas a' Ghiomanaich'
8. John Murdo Macfarlane: 'Dods Mhurchaidh Mhurdaidh'
9. Calum Mackay: 'Calum an Tailleir'
10. Finlay Morrison: 'Fionnlagh na h-Earraid' (first trip)

Year 1981: *Ripple*
While it was on passage to the island, a *Ripple* crew member was lost overboard. The sea was flat calm. A search, about seven miles southwest of the island, conducted by the *Ripple* and Stornoway Lifeboat, found no sign of life.
1. Donald Murray: 'An Gaisean' (last trip)
2. Alastair Murray: 'Eve'
3. Donald Murdo Macfarlane: 'Murchadh Mhurdaidh' (cook)
4. Alastair Campbell: 'Alasdair Bàn'
5. John Morrison: 'Iain Dubh a' Ghladstoin'
6. Angus Maclean: 'Aonghas Ghliocais'

7. John Campbell: 'Iain Alasdair Bhàin'
8. Angus Mackay: 'Aonghas a' Ghiomanaich'
9. John Murdo Macfarlane: 'Dods Mhurchaidh Mhurdaidh'
10. Murdo Campbell: 'Am Blondaidh'

Year 1980: *Ripple*
1. Donald Murray: 'An Gaisean'
2. Alastair Murray: 'Eve'
3. Donald Murdo Macfarlane: 'Murchadh Mhurdaidh' (cook)
4. Alastair Campbell: 'Alasdair Bàn'
5. John Morrison: 'Iain Dubh a' Ghladstoin'
6. Angus Maclean: 'Aonghas Ghliocais'
7. John Campbell: 'Iain Alasdair Bhàin'
8. John Macdonald: 'Iain Dho'll Alasdair Ghoilligein' (last trip)
9. Angus Mackay: 'Aonghas a' Ghiomanaich'
10. Donald Murray: 'Dòmhnall Mhurchaidh 'Ain Bhàin' (only trip)

Year 1979: *Ripple*
1. Donald Murray: 'An Gaisean'
2. Alastair Murray: 'Eve'
3. Donald Murdo Macfarlane: 'Murchadh Mhurdaidh' (cook)
4. Alastair Campbell: 'Alasdair Bàn'
5. John Morrison: 'Iain Dubh a' Ghladstoin'
6. Angus Maclean: 'Aonghas Ghliocais'
7. John Murdo Macfarlane: 'Dods Mhurchaidh Mhurdaidh'
8. Donald Gunn: 'Dòmhnall Bàn Aonghais Ghuinne' (last trip)
9. John Campbell: 'Iain Alasdair Bhàin' (first trip)
10. Norman Smith: 'Tormod Aonghais Ruaidh' – South Dell (only trip)

Year 1978: *Ripple*
1. Donald Murray: 'An Gaisean'
2. Alastair Murray: 'Eve'
3. Donald Murdo Macfarlane: 'Murchadh Mhurdaidh' (cook)
4. Alastair Campbell: 'Alasdair Bàn'
5. John Morrison: 'Iain Dubh a' Ghladstoin'
6. Donald Macleod: 'Dòmhnall Taraidh' (last trip)
7. Angus Mackay: 'Aonghas a' Ghiomanaich'
8. Angus Gunn: 'Aonghas Tola' (last trip)
9. Angus Mackenzie: 'Aonghas Ban Dhoilidh Fhionnlaidh' (last trip)
10. Angus Maclean: 'Aonghas Ghliocais'

Year 1977: *Ripple*
1. Donald Murray: 'An Gaisean'
2. Alastair Murray: 'Eve'
3. Donald Murdo Macfarlane: 'Murchadh Mhurdaidh' (cook)
4. Alastair Campbell: 'Alasdair Bàn'
5. John Murdo Macfarlane: 'Dods Mhurchaidh Mhurdaidh'
6. John Morrison: 'Iain Dubh a' Ghladstoin'
7. Donald Macleod: 'Dòmhnall Taraidh'
8. Angus Mackay: 'Aonghas a' Ghiomanaich'
9. Angus Gunn: 'Aonghas Tola'
10. Angus Mackenzie: 'Aonghas Bàn Dhoilidh Fhionnlaigh'

Year 1976: *Ripple*
1. Donald Murray: 'An Gaisean'
2. Alastair Murray: 'Eve'
3. Donald Murdo Macfarlane: 'Murchadh Mhurdaidh' (cook)
4. Alastair Campbell: 'Alasdair Bàn'
5. John Murdo Macfarlane: 'Dods Mhurchaidh Mhurdaidh'
6. John Morrison: 'Iain Dubh a' Ghladstoin'
7. Donald Macleod: 'Dòmhnall Taraidh'
8. Angus Mackay: 'Aonghas a' Ghiomanaich'
9. Finlay Thompson: 'Fionnlagh Aonghais Ruaidh' (last trip)
10. Angus Gunn: 'Aonghas Tola'

Year 1975: *Ripple*
1. Donald Murray: 'An Gaisean'
2. Alastair Murray: 'Eve'
3. Donald Murdo Macfarlane: 'Murchadh Mhurdaidh' (cook)
4. Alastair Campbell: 'Alasdair Bàn'
5. John Murdo Macfarlane: 'Dods Mhurchaidh Mhurdaidh'
6. John Morrison: 'Iain Dubh a' Ghladstoin'
7. Donald Macleod: 'Dòmhnall Taraidh'
8. Angus Mackenzie: 'Aonghas Ban Dhoilidh Fhionnlaigh'
9. John Macdonald: 'Iain Dho'll Alasdair Ghoilligein'
10. Angus Mackay: 'Aonghas a' Ghiomanaich'

Year 1974: *Rona*
1. Donald Murray: 'An Gaisean'
2. Alastair Murray: 'Eve'
3. Finlay Thompson: 'Fionnlagh Aonghais Ruaidh'

4. Callum Mackay: 'Calum an Tàilleir'
5. Donald Murdo Macfarlane: 'Murchadh Mhurdaidh' (cook)
6. Alastair Campbell 'Alasdair Bàn'
7. John Murdo Macfarlane: 'Dods Mhurchaidh Mhurdaidh' (first trip)
8. John Morrison: 'Iain Dubh a' Ghladstoin' (first trip)
9. Donald Macleod: 'Dòmhnall Taraidh' (first trip)

Year 1973: *Rona*

Last year with 12 men.
1. Donald Murray: 'An Gaisean'
2. Alastair Murray: 'Eve'
3. Donald Morrison: 'Dòmhnall nan Twins' (cook; last trip)
4. Finlay Thompson: 'Fionnlagh Aonghais Ruaidh'
5. Callum Mackay: 'Calum an Tàilleir'
6. Donald Murdo Macfarlane: 'Murchadh Mhurdaidh'
7. Alastair Campbell: 'Alasdair Bàn'
8. Donald Mackenzie: 'Dòmhnall Beag Dhoilidh Fhionnlaigh' (last trip)
9. William Campbell: 'Uilleam Alasdair Eorodail' (only trip)
10. Angus Macdonald: 'Aonghas a' Chabair' (last trip)
11. Angus Macleod: 'Aonghas Chalaips' (last trip)
12. John Macdonald: 'Iain Dho'll Alasdair Ghoilligein'

Year 1972: *Rona*

1. Donald Murray: 'An Gaisean'
2. Alastair Murray: 'Eve'
3. Donald Morrison: 'Dòmhnall nan Twins' (cook)
4. Norman Gunn: 'Tormod Aonghais Ghuinne' (last trip)
5. Angus Mackay: 'Aonghas a' Ghiomanaich'
6. Murdo Campbell: 'Am Blondaidh'
7. Finlay Thompson: 'Fionnlagh Aonghais Ruaidh'
8. Angus Mackenzie: 'Aonghas Bàn Dhoilidh Fhionnlaigh'
9. Callum Mackay: 'Calum an Tàilleir'
10. Donald Murdo Macfarlane: 'Murchadh Mhurdaidh'
11. Alastair Campbell: 'Alasdair Bàn'
12. Donald Mackenzie: 'Domhnall Beag Dhoilidh Fhionnlaigh'

Year 1971: *Rona*

1. Donald Murray: 'An Gaisean'
2. Alastair Murray: 'Eve'

3. Donald Morrison: 'Dòmhnall nan Twins' (cook)
4. Norman Gunn: 'Tormod Aonghais Ghuinne'
5. Angus Mackay: : 'Aonghas a' Ghiomanaich'
6. Murdo Campbell: 'Am Blondaidh'
7. Finlay Thompson: 'Fionnlagh Aonghais Ruaidh'
8. Angus Mackenzie: 'Aonghas Bàn Dhoilidh Fhionnlaigh'
9. Callum Mackay: 'Calum an Tàilleir'
10. Donald Murdo Macfarlane: 'Murchadh Mhurdaidh'
11. Donald Gunn: 'Dòmhnall Bàn Aonghais Ghuinne'
12. Angus Macleod: 'Aonghas Chalaips'

Year 1970: *Rona*

1. Donald Murray: 'An Gaisean'
2. Alastair Murray: 'Eve'
3. Donald Morrison: 'Dòmhnall nan Twins' (cook)
4. Norman Gunn: 'Tormod Aonghais Ghuinne'
5. Angus Mackay: 'Aonghas a' Ghiomanaich'
6. Murdo Campbell: 'Am Blondaidh'
7. Finlay Thompson: 'Fionnlagh Aonghais Ruaidh'
8. Angus Mackenzie: 'Aonghas Bàn Dhoilidh Fhionnlaigh'
9. Callum Mackay: 'Calum an Tàilleir'
10. Donald Murdo Macfarlane: 'Murchadh Mhurdaidh'
11. Donald Morrison: 'Biagaidh' (last trip)
12. Donald Gunn: 'Dòmhnall Bàn Aonghais Ghuinne'

Year 1969: *Fiery Cross*

1. Donald Murray: 'An Gaisean'
2. Alastair Murray: 'Eve'
3. Donald Morrison: 'Dòmhnall nan Twins' (cook)
4. Norman Gunn: 'Tormod Aonghais Ghuinne'
5. Angus Macleod: 'Aonghas Chalaips'
6. Donald Mackenzie: 'Dòmhnall Beag Dhoilidh Fhionnlaigh'
7. Angus Mackay: 'Aonghas a' Ghiomanaich'
8. Murdo Campbell: 'Am Blondaidh'
9. Finlay Thompson: 'Fionnlagh Aonghais Ruaidh'
10. Angus Mackenzie: 'Aonghas Bàn Dhoilidh Fhionnlaigh'
11. Angus Macdonald: 'Aonghas a' Chabair'
12. Callum Mackay: 'Calum an Tailleir' (first trip)

Year 1968: *Fiery Cross*
1. Donald Murray: 'An Gaisean'
2. Alastair Murray: 'Eve'
3. Donald Morrison: 'Dòmhnall nan Twins' (cook)
4. Norman Gunn: 'Tormod Aonghais Ghuinne'
5. Donald Morrison: 'Biagaidh'
6. Angus Macleod: 'Aonghas Chalaips'
7. Donald Mackenzie: 'Dòmhnall Beag Dhoilidh Fhionnlaigh'
8. Angus Mackay: 'Aonghas a' Ghiomanaich'
9. Murdo Campbell: 'Am Blondaidh' (first trip)
10. Finlay Thompson: 'Fionnlagh Aonghais Ruaidh' (first trip)
11. Donald Gunn: 'Dòmhnall Bàn Aonghais Ghuinne'
12. Angus Mackenzie: 'Aonghas Bàn Dhoilidh Fhionnlaigh' (first trip)

Year 1967: *Fiery Cross*
1. Donald Murray: 'An Gaisean'
2. Alastair Murray: 'Eve'
3. Donald Morrison: 'Dòmhnall nan Twins' (cook)
4. Murdo Morrison: 'Jellicoe' (last trip)
5. Norman Gunn: 'Tormod Aonghais Ghuinne'
6. Kenneth Morrison: 'Am Brounaidh' (last trip)
7. Donald Morrison: 'Biagaidh'
8. Angus Macdonald: 'Aonghas a' Chabair'
9. Angus Macleod: 'Aonghas Chalaips'
10. Donald Mackenzie: 'Dòmhnall Beag Dhoilidh Fhionnlaigh'
11. Angus Mackay: 'Aonghas a' Ghiomanaich' (first trip)
12. John Gillies: 'Seonaidh Gillies' (only trip)

Year 1966: *Queen of the Isles*
Unable to land in Port, men dropped off in Skigersta; gugas landed in Stornoway and taken to Port by road.
1. Donald Murray: 'An Gaisean'
2. Alastair Murray: 'Eve'
3. Donald Murdo Macfarlane: 'Murchadh Mhurdaidh'
4. Donald Morrison: 'Dòmhnall nan Twins' (cook)
5. Murdo Morrison: 'Jellicoe'
6. Norman Gunn: 'Tormod Aonghais Ghuinne'
7. Kenneth Morrison: 'Am Brounaidh'
8. Angus Macdonald: 'Aonghas a' Chabair'

9. Donald Morrison: 'Biagaidh'
10. Alastair Campbell: 'Alasdair Bàn'
11. Angus Macleod: 'Aonghas Chalaips'
12. Donald Mackenzie: 'Dòmhnall Beag Dhoilidh Fhionnlaigh' (first trip)

Year 1965: *Queen of the Isles*
1. Donald Murray: 'An Gaisean'
2. Alastair Murray: 'Eve'
3. Donald Murdo Macfarlane: 'Murchadh Mhurdaidh'
4. Donald Morrison: 'Dòmhnall nan Twins' (cook)
5. Murdo Morrison: 'Jellicoe'
6. Malcolm Maclean: 'Calum a' Bhodaich' (last trip)
7. Norman Gunn: 'Tormod Aonghais Ghuinne'
8. Kenneth Morrison: 'Am Brounaidh'
9. Angus Macdonald: 'Aonghas a' Chabair'
10. Donald Morrison: 'Biagaidh'
11. Alastair Campbell: 'Alasdair Bàn'
12. Angus Macleod: 'Aonghas Chalaips'

Year 1964: *Fiery Cross*
No further details.

Year 1963: *Fiery Cross*
No further details.

Year 1962: *Queen of the Isles*
First year with one crew of twelve men: no further details.

Year 1961: *Fiery Cross*
Both crews. No further details.

Year 1960: *Lilaac*
Both crews. No further details.

Year 1959: *Viking*
Both crews. No further details.

Year 1958: *Star of Hope* and *Ebenezer*

The *Star of Hope*, unable to land due to bad weather, returned to Port of Ness and chartered the *Ebenezer* along with the second crew. This was the last trip made by an open boat to the island: the *Ebenezer* went alongside the rock on both occasions. Skipper was John 'Jackie' Morrison.

Star of Hope crew

1. Donald Mackay: 'Dòmhnall Mòr Mhurchaidh' (joint skipper)
2. John Macritchie: 'Seonaidh Saidh' (joint skipper)
3. Norman Mackenzie: 'Tohan'
4. Murdo Smith: 'Murchadh Ruadh'
5. Murdo Morrison: 'Jellicoe'
6. Angus Gunn: 'Aonghas Tola'
7. Alastair Campbell: 'Alastair Bàn'
8. Angus Maclean: 'Aonghas Ghliocais'
9. Angus Morrison: 'Aonghas Bàn Chiorstaidh Fhionnlaigh'

Ebenezer

No record found. (Accompanied by Mr James McGeoch.)

Year 1957: *Star of Hope* and *Viking*

The *Star of Hope* was reported overdue and the Fishery Cruiser was sent to Sulasgeir to look for her but found nothing, as she was halfway home by this time.

Star of Hope: 1300 birds

1. Donald Mackay: 'Dòmhnall Mòr Mhurchaidh' (joint skipper)
2. John Macritchie: 'Seonaidh Saidh' (joint skipper)
3. Norman Mackenzie: 'Tohan'
4. Murdo Smith: 'Murchadh Ruadh'
5. Murdo Morrison: 'Jellicoe'
6. Angus Gunn: 'Aonghas Tola'
7. Alastair Campbell: 'Alastair Bàn'
8. Angus Maclean: 'Aonghas Ghliocais'
9. Angus Morrison: 'Aonghas Ban Chiorstaidh Fhionnlaigh'

Viking
Accompanied by Mr James McGeoch.
1. Donald Murdo Macfarlane: 'Murchadh Mhurdaidh'
2. Angus Smith: 'Liathan'
3. Murdo Campbell: 'An Duke'
4. Norman Morrison: 'Tormod Sheonaidh'
5. Donald Murray: 'An Gaisean'
6. Angus Macdonald 'Aonghas a' Chabair'
7. William Macleod: 'Uilleam Iain Mhurdo'
8. Kenneth Morrison: 'Am Brounaidh'

Year 1956: *Star of Hope* and *Frigate Bird*
Star of Hope: 1200 birds – catch at Sule Stack
1. Donald Mackay: 'Dòmhnall Mòr Mhurchaidh' (joint skipper)
2. John Macritchie: 'Seonaidh Saidh' (joint skipper)
3. Norman Mackenzie: 'Tohan'
4. Murdo Smith: 'Murchadh Ruadh'
5. Donald Morrison: 'Biagaidh'
6. Norman Morrison: 'Tormod Sheonaidh'
7. Murdo Morrison: 'Jellicoe'
8. Donald Mackenzie: 'Dòmhnall Aonghais Dhòmhnall Tàilleir'
9. Angus Gunn: 'Aonghas Tola'
The *Star of Hope* made an unsuccessful trip to Sule Stack and was stranded in Durness for some time due to bad weather.

Frigate Bird
No further details found.

Year 1955: *Frigate Bird* and *Star of Hope*
Frigate Bird
1. Donald Murdo Macfarlane: 'Murchadh Mhurdaidh'
2. Angus Macdonald 'Aonghas a' Chabair'
3. Donald Murray: 'An Gaisean'
4. Malcolm Maclean: 'Calum a' Bhodaich'
5. Donald F: Macleod: 'Dòmhnall Iain Mhurdo'
No record of the other crew members.

Star of Hope
Raid to Sulasgeir, then a successful trip to Sule Stack: no further details.

Year 1954: *Kilda* and *Star of Hope*

James McGeoch, a Glasgow police officer and keen photographer, was married to a woman from Point. He accompanied the crew to Sulasgeir on three occasions, taking numerous fine photographs and slides, many of which can be seen in Comunn Eachdraidh Nis. During this trip he took with him an ex-army two-way radio. He established John Murdo Macleod as his Ness contact, and the radio proved a success, and because of this the crew acquired a radio of their own some time later.

The *Kilda* was a motorised Fifie of over 40 feet and was skippered by Angus Mackay, 'Broman'.

Kilda

Accompanied by Mr James McGeoch.
1. Murdo Campbell: 'An Duke'
2. William Macleod: 'Uilleam Iain Mhurdo'
3. Donald Murdo Macfarlane: 'Murchadh Mhurdaidh'
4. Donald Murray: 'An Gaisean'
5. Angus Smith: 'Liathan'
6. Angus Macdonald: 'Aonghas a' Chabair'
7. Kenneth Morrison: 'Am Brounaidh'
8. Malcolm Maclean: 'Calum a' Bhodaich'

The *Star of Hope* carried out a raid and returned with 500 birds. She then made an unsuccessful trip to Sule Stack and was stranded in Durness for two weeks due to bad weather. Among the crew were the following.
1. Alexander Morrison: 'Santy' (skipper)
2. Murdo Smith: 'Murchadh Ruadh'
3. Donald Mackay: 'Dòmhnall Mòr Mhurchaidh'
4. Norman Mackenzie: 'Tohan'
5. Norman Morrison: 'Tormod Sheonaidh'
6. Murdo Morrison: 'Jellicoe'
7. Roderick Murray 'Ruairidh Doh'

Year 1953: *Scotch Lass*

1. Murdo Campbell: 'An Duke'
2. John Macleod: 'Sheonaidh Chaluim'
3. Donald Murdo Macfarlane: 'Murchadh Mhurdaidh'
4. Donald Murray: 'An Gaisean'

5. Angus Smith: 'Liathan'
6. Angus Macdonald: 'Aonghas a' Chabair'
7. Kenneth Morrison: 'Am Brounaidh'
8. William Macleod: 'Uilleam Iain Mhurdo'

The *Scotch Lass* was a new cruiser stern 40-foot fishing boat fitted with a Kelvin diesel engine, and was owned and skippered by George Clark of the 'Clarks Shoes' family. It was based in Bernera.

Year 1952.
Mairi Dhonn and *Mayflower*

The *Mairi Dhonn* was the first charter vessel used to go to Sulasgeir. She was a decked Loch Fyne-type boat, about 32 feet overall length, with a Kelvin diesel engine. The owner and skipper was George Clark of the 'Clarks Shoes' family. The other crew members of the *Mairi Dhonn* for this trip were Rev. Donald Macaulay and Murdo Maclennan ('Murchadh Stogaidh'), both Bernera.

Mairi Dhonn
1. John Murdo Macleod: 'John Murdo Iain Mhurdo'
2. William Macleod: 'Uilleam Iain Mhurdo'
3. Donald F: Macleod: 'Domhnall Iain Mhurdo'
4. John Macleod: 'Seonaidh Chaluim'
5. Angus Smith 'Liathan'
6. Murdo Campbell: 'An Duke'
7. Kenneth Morrison: 'Am Brounaidh'
8. Donald Murray: 'An Gaisean'
9. Angus Macdonald: 'Aonghas a' Chabair'

The *Mairi Dhonn* experienced some exceptionally heavy weather on the return trip and landed in Stornoway three days overdue: The gugas were then taken to Ness on one of Mitchell's buses.

Mayflower
1. Murdo Morrison: 'Jellicoe'
2. Donald Morrison: 'Dòmhnall nan Twins'
3. Angus Morrison: 'Aonghas Ban Chiorstaidh Fhionnlaigh'
4. Hector Morrison: 'Eachainn Chaluim Eachainn'

Due to bad weather the *Mayflower* broke her moorings and was lost. The *Mairi Dhonn* had left shortly beforehand with the weather rapidly deteriorating. After spending some time on the island with a meagre supply of fuel and food, the crew was rescued by the

Stornoway Lifeboat, abandoning their catch. As the lifeboat could not get close to the island due to the weather conditions, the crew were dragged through the surf to safety.

Year 1951: *Catriona* and *Jubilee*
Again, the *Jubilee* later made a 'successful' trip to Sule Stack.

In order to put an end to the rivalry that had arisen between the communities of Port and Skigersta, it was decided to use the two larger boats with a mixed crew from the three boats that went to the island in 1950. After this trip, the *Catriona* broke her moorings at Port and was wrecked. Some of her crew then had the *Star of Hope* built in Uist.

Jubilee
1. Donald Mackay: 'Dòmhnall Mòr Mhurchaidh' (skipper)
2. Donald Morrison: 'Dòmhnall Alasdair Iain Ruaidh'
3. Alasdair Murray: 'Alasdair Beag 'Ain Bhain'
4. Alastair Murray: 'Eve'
5. Kenneth Morrison: 'Am Brounaidh' (engineer)
6. Murdo Morrison: 'Jellicoe'
7. Donald Morrison: 'Dòmhnall nan Twins'

Year 1950: *Catriona*, *Jubilee* and *Mayflower*
The *Jubilee* later made a 'successful' trip to the Stack.

Jubilee, Part Crew.
1. Donald Mackay: 'Dòmhnall Mòr Mhurchaidh' (skipper)
2. Donald Morrison: 'Domhnall Alasdair Iain Ruaidh'
3. Alasdair Murray: 'Alasdair Beag 'Ain Bhàin'
4. Alastair Murray: 'Eve'
5. Kenneth Morrison: 'Am Brounaidh' (engineer)

Year 1949: *Catriona*, *Jubilee* and *Mayflower*
Catriona was launched on 9 February 1949 and lost November 1951 in Port of Ness harbour. She made a trip to Sulasgeir on 22 August and then Sule Stack on the 24th, sustaining a broken stern on her voyage.

The *Jubilee* and the *Mayflower* also sailed this year but had to turn back due to bad weather, succeeding on the second attempt. The

Jubilee then went to Sule Stack; the *Mayflower* returned to Sulasgeir a second time and, being overdue, was reported missing. Suffering engine breakdown, she was towed part of the way home by a Norwegian tanker and the *Catriona* completed the tow. The lifeboat, which had been alerted, returned to Carloway.

Catriona

1. John Macritchie: 'Seonaidh Saidh' (skipper)
2. Alexander Morrison: 'Santy'
3. Donald Murdo Macfarlane: 'Murchadh Mhurdaidh'
4. Norman Mackenzie: 'Tohan'
5. Murdo Smith: 'Murchadh Ruadh'
6. John Murray: 'Iain Doh'
7. Donald F. Macleod: 'Dòmhnall Iain Mhurdo'
8. Norman Morrison: 'Tormod Sheonaidh'
9. Donald Murray: 'An Gaisean'

Mayflower
2nd Trip

1. Murdo Morrison: 'Jellicoe'
2. Norman Macdonald: 'Am Bearlan'
3. Malcolm Maclean: 'Calum a' Bhodaich'
4. Angus Morrison: 'Aonghas Ban Chiorstaidh Fhionnlaigh'
5. Kenneth Morrison: 'Am Brounaidh'

Jubilee, Part Crew

1. Donald Mackay: 'Dòmhnall Mòr Mhurchaidh' (skipper)
2. Donald Morrison: 'Dòmhnall Alasdair Iain Ruaidh'
3. Alasdair Murray: 'Alasdair Beag 'Ain Bhàin'
4. Alastair Murray: 'Eve'
5. Donald Morrison: 'Dòmhnall nan Twins'

Year 1948
No records found.

There were no boats considered suitable for the trip available. The *Peaceful* had only just made it back in 1947 and was unseaworthy. The *Catriona* was being built at this time. There is, however, a suggestion that the *Jubilee* carried out a raid, but no further details of this have been traced.

Year 1947: *Commando, Jubilee* and *Peaceful*
The *Commando*, a 16-foot Orkney boat with a 'Gains Universal' petrol engine, travelled to Sulasgeir for two 'raids', the first to the island since the war. Severe fog affected the first trip.

Commando
1st Trip
1. John Macritchie: 'Seonaidh Saidh'
2. Murdo Campbell: 'An Duke'
3. Alasdair Gunn: 'An Caobarach'
4. Murdo Smith: 'Murchadh Ruadh'
5. Donald F: Macleod: 'Dòmhnall Iain Mhurdo'

On the second trip, John Murdo Macleod, 'John Murdo Iain Mhurdo', replaced his brother Donald, and Norman Morrison, 'Tormod Sheonaidh', replaced Alasdair Gunn

Jubilee
1. Murdo Mackenzie: 'Murchadh Dhòmhnall Tàilleir', 19, Skigersta (skipper)
2. Angus Mackenzie: 'Aonghas Dhòmhnaill Tàilleir', 12, Skigersta
3. Donald Morrison: 'Dòmhnall Alasdair Iain Ruaidh', 15, Skigersta
4. Alasdair Murray: 'Alasdair Beag 'Ain Bhàin', 14, Skigersta
5. Murdo Maclean: 'Murchadh na Rabaid', 9, High Street, Skigersta
6. Angus Thompson: 'Aonghas Ruadh', 2, Skigersta

The *Jubilee* had arrived in Skigersta from Borve in 1946 and had an engine fitted after this trip. It is worth noting that this was the last trip for boats wholly under sail. This was the last trip of the *Peaceful* to the island.

Peaceful
1. Donald Mackay: 'Dòmhnall Mòr Mhurchaidh', 21, Skigersta: (skipper)
2. Donald Morrison: 'Dòmhnall nan Twins', 12, Adabrock
3. Alasdair Campbell: 'Alasdair Eorodail', 11, High Street, Skigersta
4. Donald Maclean: 'Dòmhnall na Rabaid', 27, High Street, Skigersta
5. Norman Campbell: 'An Tunnag', 113, Cross Skigersta Road
6. Angus Mackenzie: 'Aonghas Thormoid Phìobair', 15, High Street Skigersta

These two boats experienced some extreme weather conditions on their return journey. It took some outstanding seamanship from both crews and especially the skippers to secure a safe return to Skigersta. Eyewitnesses can recall seeing these relatively small, open boats battling through some enormous seas. Less able and experienced seamen would not have avoided loss of life.

Year 1946: no trip.
Alisdair Gunn, 'An Caobarach', owned a 28-foot decked Fifie with a Kelvin engine called *Rossie*. A crew had been organised for a trip to Sulasgeir but the weather conditions were not suitable and the trip was cancelled.

No trips attempted during the Second World War.

Year 1939: *Peaceful*
A member of the *Peaceful* crew had been called up while in Sulasgeir. He set off for Portsmouth the morning after their return. This was Donald Morrison or 'Dòmhnall Alastair Iain Ruaidh', 15, Skigersta.

Year 1938: *Peaceful*
Limited information: Norman Maclean, 'An Rabaid', from 9, High Street, Skigersta, was skipper on this trip, having taken over from Murdo Mackay of 21, Skigersta

Year 1937: No records found.

Year 1936: *Peaceful*
1. Murdo Mackay: 'Murchadh Dhòmhnaill Ruaidh', 21, Skigersta: (skipper)
2. Alexander Murray: 'Alasdair Ruadh', 3, High Street, Skigersta
3. Norman Maclean: 'An Rabaid', 9, High Street, Skigersta
4. Angus Gillies: 'Dìlidh', 23, Outer Adabrock
5. John Mackenzie: 'Somailidh', 4, Fivepenny
6. Alasdair Morrison: 'Alasdair Chaluim', 2, Habost (cook)
7. Murdo Mackenzie: 'Murchadh Dhòmhnaill Tàilleir', 19, Skigersta
8. Angus Mackenzie: 'Aonghas Dhòmhnall Tàilleir', 12, Skigersta.
9. Murdo Macdonald: 'Murchadh Eòghainn', 16, Skigersta

During the 1930s the first four men listed above were regular members of the *Peaceful* crew going to Sulasgeir, whereas the other five varied. Others known to have been crew-members during the 1930s are:

Donald Campbell: 'Dòmhnall 'Ain Ghabhsainn', 30b, Lionel
Donald Mackay: 'Danaidh', 72/3, Cross Skigersta Road
Donald Morrison: 'Dòmhnall nan Twins', 12, Adabrock
Donald Morrison: 'Dòmhnall Alasdair Iain Ruaidh', 15, Skigersta
Alexander Murray: 'Alasdair Beag 'Ain Bhàin', 14, Skigersta
Malcolm Mackay: 'Calum Mòr', 7, Fivepenny
Donald Mackay: 'Dòmhnall Mòr Mhurchaidh', 21, Skigersta

Year 1935: *Peaceful*

1. Murdo Mackay: 'Murchadh Dhòmhnaill Ruaidh', 21, Skigersta: (skipper)
2. Alexander Murray: 'Alasdair Ruadh', 3, High Street Skigersta
3. Norman Maclean: 'An Rabaid', 9, High Street Skigersta
4. Angus Gillies: 'Dìlidh', 23, Outer Adabrock
5. John Mackenzie: 'Somailidh', 4, Fivepenny
6. Alasdair Morrison: 'Alasdair Chaluim', 2, Habost (cook)
7. Murdo Mackenzie: 'Murchadh Dhòmhnaill Tàilleir', 19, Skigersta
8. Angus Mackenzie: 'Aonghas Dhòmhnaill Tàilleir', 12, Skigersta
9. Murdo Macdonald: 'Murchadh Eòghainn', 16, Skigersta

Year 1934: *Peaceful*

Returned early due to the illness of Donald Mackay, 'Danaidh', 26, High Street, Skigersta. He later lived at 72/73, Cross Skigersta Road.

Year 1933: *Peaceful*

No further details.

Year 1932: *Peaceful* (26 days)

No further details.

The *Pride of Lionel* made a successful trip to Sule Stack and took 800+ birds. No further details.

Year 1931: *Peaceful*

No further details.

The *Pride of Lionel* made an unsuccessful trip to Sule Stack (engine now fitted).

Pride of Lionel
1. Murdo Macfarlane: 'Murdaidh', 21, Port of Ness (skipper)
2. Alasdair Gunn: 'An Caobarach', 11, Port of Ness.
3. Alasdair Macleod: 'Alasdair Slingem', Blairmoor Cottage, Lionel
4. Angus Macdonald: 'Sir Angus', 19, Port of Ness
5. Angus Macdonald: 'An Leamhnaid', 3, Lionel
6. Donald Mackenzie: 'Dòmhnall Spuirean', 16, Port of Ness
7. John Macdonald: 'Cowes', 8, Cross (engineer)

Year 1930 *Peaceful*
The *Pride of Lionel* (ex-*Dell*) also made a successful trip to the Stack. The *Peaceful* (ex-*Thelma*) came to Skigersta in 1930 and was the replacement for the *Ladysmith*. She continued to be the Skigersta–Sulasgeir boat throughout the 1930s. The shareholders were as follows:
1. Murdo Mackay: 'Murchadh Dhòmhnaill Ruaidh', 21, Skigersta (skipper)
2. Finlay Mackay: 'Fionnlagh Mòr', 17, Skigersta
3. John Murray: 'Ain Bàn', 1, Skigersta
4. Alexander Murray: 'Alasdair Ruadh', 3, High Street Skigersta
5. Norman Maclean: 'An Rabaid', 9, High Street Skigersta
6. Donald Thompson: 'Dòmhnall Mòr', 2, High Street Skigersta
7. Angus Gillies: 'Dìlidh', 23, Outer Adabrock
No record found of those who actually went to Sulasgeir as crew of the *Peaceful* this year.

Pride of Lionel
1. Donald Campbell: 'Dòmhnall Beag Aonghais Chaluim', 18, Lionel (skipper)
2. Alasdair Gunn: 'An Caobarach', 11, Port of Ness
3. John Morrison: 'Seonaidh Dho'll 'ic Ruairidh', 15, Port of Ness/ 107, Cross Skigersta Rd
4. Allan Maciver: 'Allan Iain Mhaol', 32, Lionel
5. Murdo Campbell: 'Murchadh Aonghais Chaluim', 8, Port of Ness
6. Donald Campbell: 'Geog Louden', 33, Lionel
7. Angus Macdonald: 'An Leamhnaid', 3, Lionel

Pride of Lionel
2nd Trip (Stack)
1. Murdo Macfarlane: 'Murdaidh', 21, Port of Ness (skipper)
2. Alasdair Gunn: 'An Caobarach', 11, Port of Ness
3. Alasdair Macleod: 'Alasdair Slingem', Blairmoor Cottage, Lionel
4. Angus Macdonald: 'Sir Angus', 19, Port of Ness
5. Angus Macdonald: 'An Leamhnaid', 3, Lionel
6. John Mackenzie: 'Spog', 16, Port of Ness
No record of other crew-members found.

Year 1927: *Dell*
The *Tolsta Head* (SY 306), a 20-foot keel *sgoth*, owned and skippered by Donald Campbell, 'Geadaidh', made an unsuccessful trip to Sulasgeir this year. The *Dell* (SY 455) was built for Alexander Macfarquhar, Dell Mill, in 1918. Ownership was taken over by John F. Macleod, 'Iain Mhurdo', Port of Ness, around this time and the *Dell* was renamed the *Pride of Lionel* shortly afterwards: This trip is notable for the biggest haul of birds taken on one *sgoth*. The crew was a mixture of men from Port and Skigersta.

1. Murdo Mackay: 'Murchadh Dhòmhnaill Ruaidh', 21, Skigersta (skipper)
2. Norman Morrison: 'Tormod Sheonaidh', 12, Port of Ness
3. John Macleod: 'Seonaidh Chaluim', 19, Port of Ness
4. Murdo Mackenzie: 'Murchadh Dhòmhnaill Tàilleir', 19, Skigersta
5. Alexander Murray: 'Alasdair Ruadh', 3, High Street, Skigersta
6. Norman Maclean: 'An Rabaid', 9, High Street, Skigersta
7. Donald Mackay 'Dòmhnall Allan Bhàin', High Street, Skigersta
8. Angus Macleod: 'Iceil Bhrodaidh', 128, Cross Skigersta Road
The boat was rowed all the way to Sulasgeir due to lack of wind.

Year 1924: *Ladysmith*
The *Ladysmith* (SY 209), a 21-foot-keel *sgoth*, was built in 1901 by John a' Mhurchaidh. She was owned by John Murray or 'Ain Bàn', 1, Skigersta. John Murdo Macleod recalls hearing that his father carried out extensive repairs to the keel of the *Ladysmith* before this trip to Sulasgeir. When John Murdo mentioned this to his father, he replied, ''*S e an ath rud a chuala mi gu robh i air a tarraing an-àirde ann an Sulaisgeir*. The next thing I heard she was being pulled up at

Sulasgeir.' One cannot be certain, but she may have been along with the much smaller *Kingfisher*, which belonged to Murdo Mackay, 'Murchadh Dhòmhnaill Ruaidh', 21, Skigersta.

The *Ladysmith* ended her days as a sail store at Skigersta quay, having been turned upside-down, with her port quarter cut away to allow access.

Year 1920: *Guide Me* (SY 26)

Limited details. However, there is a strong suggestion that the same crew went this year as in 1919.

Year 1919: *Guide Me* (SY 26)

The *Guide Me*, a 16p-foot-keel *sgoth*, was built in 1906 for Donald Smith, North Tolsta. Ownership passed to John Morrison, Merchant, Fivepenny, in 1910. Registration cancelled in 1923. The following were among the crew members.

1. Donald Morrison: 'An Duidean', 15, Habost
2. Malcolm Mackay: 'Calum Mòr', Fivepenny
3. Murdo Macfarlane: 'Murdaidh', 21, Port of Ness
4. Murdo Campbell: 'An Duke', 7, Knockaird
5. Donald Campbell: 'Poilidh', 11, Adabrock
6. Norman Campbell: 'Am Beadan', Shore View, Port of Ness

It is worth noting that Murdo, Donald and Norman Campbell were brothers.

During the return trip in 1919, the crew experienced some exceptionally bad weather and were very nearly swamped, when 'a broken sea passed over the tarpaulin that covered the birds'. They baled out with the water barrels and the mast thwart was slackened and lashed with the chain. The workers on the Ness to Tolsta road watched on as the boat battled against the weather. When the *Guide Me* was finally broken up, it was found that her keel was broken, probably on this trip.

Year 1916.

Thelma and *Good Luck*

Murdo Macleod, 'John Murdo Iain Mhurdo's' grandfather, built two boats of similar size, 19-foot-keel, in 1913. One was for a crew from Tolsta; the other for a Ness crew. Due to the war starting in 1914, the boats were not taken up as the crews were either in the Militia or the RNR and were called to active service. The boats then lay idle outside the workshop for two years. Eventually the Tolsta boat, *Thelma*, was bought by Iain Maciver, 'Iain Iain 'ic Iomhair', 'merchant' of Swainbost and Skigersta, and started fishing with Alastair Morrison, 'Biagaidh', from Fivepenny, as skipper.

The other boat, *Good Luck*, was bought by John Campbell, 'Poilis Mhurchaidh Dhùghaill', 4, Eorodale, and started fishing with his brother, Donald Campbell, 'Geadaidh', as skipper.

In 1916 these two boats went to Sulasgeir together. The *Thelma* arrived first but by the time the *Good Luck* arrived, the tide was too low for hauling out. With the weather deteriorating fast, both boats made for shelter in the lee of Rona, where they stayed for about a week. They finally made a safe landing on Sulasgeir and returned home with the catch in due course. Some of the crew members were as follows.

Thelma (later renamed *Peaceful*)
1. Alasdair Morrison: 'Biagaidh', Fivepenny (skipper)
2. Kenneth Mackenzie: 'Coinneach mhic Alasdair'
3. John Morrison: 'Iain Buachaille'
4. Donald Macdonald: 'Siurra', 16, Eoropie
5. John Mackenzie: 'Tharty', 11, Eoropie

Good Luck
1. Donald Campbell: 'Geadaidh', 4, Eorodale (skipper)
2. John Smith: 'Iain Allan', 9, Port of Ness

Some more of the 1912 crew could have made the trip this year. However, this is uncertain.

Year 1912: *Defender*
In 1912, ten men, many, if not all of them, experienced seamen, set off on 13 August in a boat laden with provisions and fuel. The day after they left, there was a severe storm. The men took shelter at Rona before continuing to Sulasgeir in better weather. When nothing was seen of them for over two weeks, a navy vessel, HMS *Phoenix* from Stornoway, went to look for them. Having 'circled the island', she returned to Stornoway and reported that no one was on Sulasgeir, though the men were there, getting on with their work. Once they had finished the crew had to wait 11 days before the weather was suitable for launching the boat to return home. The men regarded this as part of the normal hazard of the hunt, but their safe return on 12

September was an occasion of great joy in a community that had given them up for dead. It seems apparent that the naval vessel did not go anywhere near Sulasgeir during her reconnaissance mission, as they would have at least seen the boat.

Defender
1. Norman Campbell: 'An Einnsean', 4, Eorodale / 35, Swainbost
2. Donald Macleod: 'Dòmhnall Thormoid', 47, Swainbost
3. Murdo Macritchie: 'Murchadh Thòrmoid Mhòir', 37, Swainbost
4. John Morrison: 'Jockan', 1, Habost
5. Donald Morrison: 'An Duidean', 15, Habost
6. Donald Campbell: 'Geadaidh', 4, Eorodale
7. John Maclean: 'Iain Riabhach', Knockaird
8. Murdo Gunn: 'Am Brogach', 5, Knockaird
9. Donald Mackenzie: 'Croic', 21, Eoropie
10. Donald Morrison: 'Knox', 16, Swainbost

Year 1904: Forget Me Not
The *Forget Me Not* (SY 213), a 21-foot keel *sgoth*, was owned and skippered by John Murray, Port of Ness. This was also the year that Alastair 'Bàn' Morrison, North Dell, died on the island. This caused some controversy, as the rest of the crew returned with the catch and left the remains behind. The remains were later recovered by another boat.

Thanks and Acknowledgments

In many ways, *The Guga Hunters* is not simply the work of a single individual. Instead, it is the creation of a community, past and present, far and wide, and I have only been blessed with both the responsibility and good fortune to become its voice. This is especially true of the men who go to Sulasgeir year in, year out. I have tried my best to speak for them, reporting their experiences truly and fairly – not just now but throughout the centuries.

It is in this light that I ask for mercy when some of the book's readers – especially those from Ness – notice errors within its pages. Grant me the forgiveness you might seek for yourselves and your own mistakes. This extends to the following list of people and books that have helped me. Given the numbers who have given me assistance, I am bound to leave some names out. I can only hope – for my sake! – it isn't you.

To begin, in entirely random disorder, I would like to thank members of the following families and organisations either connected with or living in the district of Ness for the great deal of help I have been given in the creation of this work:

Bell, Campbell, Gillies, Macritchie, Macaulay, Marvin, Macleod, Gunn, Morrison, Macfarlane, Barrowman, Macinnes, Mackay, MacSween, Maclean, Macdonald, Hawkins, Graham, Mackenzie, Smith, Robson, the Guga Hunters named elsewhere, all connected with Comunn Eachdraidh Nis, Taigh Dhonnchaidh, Iomart Nis who provided me with much needed support – and especially the Murray family, Donald (who gave me so much assistance from his exile in distant Tarbert, Isle of Harris), Allan (who puts up with me), Angus, Eileen, Anna, Rebecca . . .

An exceptional debt of gratitude is owed to Dods MacFarlane, Murdo 'Deedo' Macdonald, James Murray, Murdo Campbell, Angus Mackay and John Murdo Macleod for their hard work in putting together the lists of Sulasgeir crewmen over the years and to those who allowed me to interview them and take up their valuable time – especially Norman Smith, who provided me with a great deal of material for this book

Thanks, too to these individuals also from Lewis and the other islands of the Outer Hebrides who have laboured for many years under the misfortune of coming outside the parish boundaries:

Angus, Macmillan, Crawford, Buchanan, Matheson, McIntosh (for encouraging me to think), Ferguson, Macleod, Smith, Murray (again!), Macinnes, Huckbody, Macritchie, Whiteford, Matheson, Morrison, Stephen, MacNeil, Thompson, Silver, Maciver, Morrison, Grant, the staff of the *Stornoway Gazette*, Western Isles Library Service, Comhairle nan Eilean Siar, Angus B. Macneil and Alasdair Allan's constituency office (especially Kenny), and also a certain member of the Wilson clan who suggested to Birlinn that I would be the ideal person to write this book.

From Shetland, members of the following families and organisations helped provide this book with an additional dimension:

Angus, Turner, Dyer, Lawson, Morton, Halcrow, Adamson, Williamson, Cluness, Wishart, Sinclair, Anderson, MacLennan, Morrison, Hadfield, Robertson, Finlayson, all the staff of the following: Shetland Library Service; Shetland Amenity Trust; Shetland Museum and Archives; Shetland Arts; Sandwick J.H. School; the constituency office of Alistair Carmichael and Tavish Scott – and also a certain 'Turbulent Priest' who brings much calm and peace to my – otherwise! – frenzied existence.

From Orkney:
Sigurd Towrie of the *Orcadian*, Peebles, Aberdein, Wright, the staff of Orkney Library and Archive Service.

From the mainland of Scotland, England – including, these days, Skye:
Andrew Simmons at Birlinn, Jamie, Robertson, Gilori (for her recipes), Macinnes, Hutchinson, Mather, the History teacher at Ullapool High School, the headteacher at Durness Primary School, Cleare, McGeoch, Harrington, Smith, Dale, Daltrey, Davies, Bonington, Calder, the Blackburn family – Jez and Adrian. A special debt of gratitude is owed to the following: Helen Bleck for giving sense and shape to all my ramblings; Ian MacDonald of the Gaelic Books Council for doing much the same to my Gaelic grammar and spellings; and Murdo Deedo MacDonald again for all his knowledge and enthusiasm about Sulasgeir.

From farther ashore:
Mikines, Asberg, Eliason, Blak, the Faroe Art Museum, Klein.

I would also like to thank John Angus Macleod for letting me reproduce 'Air Mo Chiad Bhlasad air a' Ghuga' and Cooksley of Mill Hill, butchers, for their permission to use a recipe for gannet from their website. A special note of gratitude goes too to Peggy and Margaret Murray for allowing me to use their late brother and my second cousin Murdo Angus Murray's poem about the guga. In addition, I wish to thank Robert Rendall for permission to use his uncle's poem, 'The Cragman's Widow'. I would like especially to acknowledge the following works for their assistance in the writing of this book. It would not exist without them.

Anderson Smith – *Lewisiana* (London, 1875)

Annandale – 'Notes on the Folklore of the Vestmanneyjar', *Man* 3 (1903), 137–39

Beatty – *Sula: The Seabird Hunters of Lewis* (Michael Joseph, London 1992)

Caimbeul – *Bàrdachd a' Bhocsair* (C. Macdhòmhnaill, 1978)

Cluness – *The Shetland Isles* (Robert Hale, 1951)

Colley, *Britons: Forging the Nation, 1707–1837* (Pimlico, 1994)

Davidson – *Penguin Companion To Food* (Penguin 2002)

Diamond – *Collapse* (Viking, 2005)

Duncan – *Scotland: The Making of the Kingdom* (Oliver and Boyd, 1975)

Fowler – *Countryman's Cooking* (Addington Press, 1965)

Grant – *A Shilling for Your Scowl* (Acair, 1998)

Grant – *Stornoway and the Lews* (J.S.Grant, 1985)

Harvie-Brown – *Further notes on North Rona* (Proceedings of the Royal Physical Society, 1886)

Haswell-Smith – *The Scottish Islands* (Canongate, 2001)

Islands Book Trust – *Traditions of Sea-Bird Fowling in the North Atlantic Region* (Islands Book Trust, Port of Ness, Isle of Lewis, 2005) (I owe a huge debt to this book and particularly to John Baldwin, a man I've never met. His research on the above topic forms an essential part of my work. A special thanks goes to all those involved in preparation of this volume.)

Jack – *GRANTA 52, Food: The Vital Stuff* (Penguin 1995)

Macdonald – *The Old Statistical Account of Scotland 1797*

MacGregor – *The Western Isles* (Robert Hale, 1949)

MacLeòid – *Bàrdachd a Leòdhas* (Gairm, 1969)

Monro – *Descriptions of the Western Isles of Scotland* (Morison, 1884)

Morrison – *One Man's Lewis* (Stornoway Gazette, 1970)

Muir – *Ecclesiological Notes on Some of the Islands of Scotland* (David Douglas, 1885)

O'Crohan – *The Islandman* (Oxford University Press, 1951)

Oliver – *Wild Geese: Selected Poems* (Bloodaxe Books, 2004)

Orcadian, The

Orkney Book of the Twentieth Century, The (Orcadian, 2000)

Robinson – *Conemarra* (Penguin Ireland, 2006) – for help with the description of potato blight.

Robson – *Rona: The Distant Island* (Acair, 1990). I've embellished Robson's tale of St Ronan in my work. I hope no one minds my minor deviations from the 'truth'.

Scott-Moncrieff – *The Scottish Islands* (Oliver and Boyd, 1961)

Stewart – in *British Birds Magazine*, no. 6, vol. 32, 1938

Stiùbhart – *The Early History of Ness – An Interpretation* (Comunn Eachdraidh Nis, pamphlet no 1)

Stornoway Gazette: '*Back in the Day*' – especially Norma Macritchie

Stout – *Cookery For Northern Wives* (Publisher unknown, 1925)

Thompson – *St Kilda and Other Hebridean Outliers* (David Charles PLC, 1970)

Works of Nelson Annandale – various sources

Other books and sources are mentioned in the text and noted accordingly, with one book – in the form both of my father's Gaelic Bible and the King James version of the same – being a particular source of inspiration and strength.

Thank you all.

Old Cemetery – Ness

When these graves open and dead souls walk,
will those who are left be able to comprehend
the words of those who died before their time,
their ancestors, their dead kin and their friends?
And will these ghosts turn their backs on those
who no longer held in safe-keeping their tongue,
allowing tales to slip out from the telling,
and punish our forgetting by fading till they've gone?

And on the day they step out from that twilight,
will they search for fields their taxing labours made
and find that bog has choked both drain and furrow,
shaking their heads like parents long dismayed
by weak and feckless offspring who let slip
rich legacies once granted by these shades?